The Employer's Survival Guide

The Business Guide to Employment Law, Policy and Practice

Terence J. Brimson

McGRAW-HILL BOOK COMPANY

London · New York · St Louis · San Francisco · Auckland · Bogotá
Caracas · Hamburg · Lisbon · Madrid · Mexico · Milan · Montreal
New Delhi · Panama · Paris · San Juan · São Paulo · Singapore
Sydney · Tokyo · Toronto

Published by
McGRAW-HILL Book Company Europe
Shoppenhangers Road, Maidenhead, Berkshire, SL6 2QL, England
Telephone 0628 23432
Fax 0628 770224

British Library Cataloguing in Publication Data
Brimson, Terence J.
  Employer's Survival Guide: Business Guide
  to Employment Law, Practice and Policy
  I Title
  344.1041
  ISBN 0-07-707595-1

Library of Congress Cataloging-in-Publication Data
Brimson, Terry, 1939–
    The employer's survival guide : the business guide to employment
  law, policy, and practice / Terence J. Brimson.
      p.   cm.
    Includes bibliographical references and index.
    ISBN 0 077075951
    1. Labor laws and legislation—Great Britain.   I. Title.
  KD3009.B74   1992
344.41'01—dc20
    [344.1041]   92-8774
                                                                            CIP

Copyright © 1992 McGraw-Hill International (UK) Limited.
All rights reserved. No part of this publication may be reproduced,
stored in a retrieval system, or transmitted, in any form or by any
means, electronic, mechanical, photocopying, recording, or otherwise,
without the prior permission of McGraw-Hill International (UK)
Limited.

1234 CUP 9432

Typeset by Cambridge Composing (UK) Limited
and printed and bound in Great Britain at
the University Press, Cambridge

Contents

Foreword		v
Acknowledgements		vi
Introduction		vii
Chapters	1 Before you employ	1
	2 Recruiting your employee	19
	3 Employing	35
	3.1 Legal requirements	35
	3.2 Contracts, terms and conditions of employment	35
	3.3 Restrictions on conditions of a contract	42
	3.4 Maternity leave and returning to work	44
	3.5 Non-permanent staff	46
	3.6 Data protection	53
	4 Payments and deductions	57
	4.1 Payment for working	57
	4.2 Deductions from gross pay	62
	4.3 Statutory Sick Pay (SSP)	79
	4.4 Statutory Maternity Pay (SMP)	92
	4.5 Pension contributions	98
	5 Health and safety	108
	5.1 Introduction	108
	5.2 Why health and safety?	108
	5.3 The costs of health and safety	110
	5.4 The Health and Safety at Work, etc., Act 1974	112
	5.5 Duties of employers	114
	5.6 Duties of employees	122
	6 Training and development	127
	6.1 Why train?	127
	6.2 Benefits of training and development	132
	6.3 Determining your training needs	134
	6.4 Designing your training programme	137

		6.5 Types of training	139
		6.6 How do people learn?	149
		6.7 Management development	152
		6.8 Organizational development	157
		6.9 Cost–benefit evaluation	159
	7	Motivation	162
	8	Discipline and grievance	173
	9	Redundancy	185
	10	Retirement	195
	11	Dismissals	203
	12	Industrial relations	210
	13	Industrial tribunals	223

Appendices	A	Application form	233
	B	Interview checklist	237
	C	Contracts of employment	238
	D	Terms and conditions of employment	242
	E	Special contract of employment	247
	F	Apprenticeship agreement	251
	G	Health and safety policy	254
	H	Induction training checklist	264
	I	Job description	266

List of abbreviations	268
Bibliography and recommended reading	271
Index	273

Dedication

To John, who convinced me of the necessity for this book.

Foreword

Employment legislation can be a headache for even the most experienced of employers. For the first time employer, the lack of legislative knowledge and procedure can very quickly lead to untold problems.

In this book the author takes us on a step-by-step journey through what he rightly refers to as the 'minefield' of employment legislation.

Every chapter has been thoroughly researched and is brimming with facts, figures and sound advice on how to avoid the fatal steps that could turn your business adventure into a business disaster.

Whether your business is a multinational corporation or a one person operation, this book will help you to stay on the right side of the law and at the same time assist you in safeguarding your most valuable asset: your employees.

The author's knowledge of the subject-matter and his easy flowing style of writing makes light work of the mass of rules and regulations which every employer is required to follow.

As an ex local government officer who was responsible for the recruitment, supervision and training of staff, I would have found this book invaluable as an easy, quick, reference tool. I could have avoided those frequent headaches!

Hugh Toomey
Advertisement Manager, ITD Journals

Acknowledgements

This book is not the work of just one person. Without the invaluable help and support of the following specialists in their fields who have checked my scripts and given constructive comments, and other 'checkers' who have contributed to quality, this work would not have been complete or authoritative. My most grateful thanks go to them all for their help and encouragement during the two years this work has been in preparation. They are:

Hugh Toomey, *Training and Development Journal*, ITD; Jim Davenport, JP, MIOSH, Group Safety Coordinator, MB-Caradon plc; Lorraine Gregory, DSS (SSP and SMP), The Adelphi, London; Hilary Morgan, DSS Deregulation Unit and NIC, Ray House, London; Stephen Alambritis, BA, MA, MSc, Press and Parliamentary Officer, FSB; Christine Smyth, Inland Revenue, London; Ian Handford, JP, Chairman, Employment Law Committee, FSB; Roger Bird, FCA, R.H. Bird & Co., Chartered Accountants, Stourbridge; Edwina Turner, LIB, Solicitor, Handsworth, Birmingham; Brian F. Cockbill, MIOSH, Safety Officer (Retired), Kalamazoo plc; Michael Mitchell, Research and Projects Director, ITD; Antonia Carr, Stress Management Counsellor, London; Anthony Fielder, MD, Stress and Motivation (UK) Ltd, London; Linda Rhodes, Music Teacher, Dudley; Department of Social Security (DSS—SSALE), Glasgow; Health and Safety Executive, London; and not least, Margaret who has spent many hours checking scripts.

Introduction

The old feudal days of 'servant and master' relationships, with the bowler hatted foreman-owner, have long since gone. We live in days of ever increasing and ever changing industrial legislation including the continual flow of laws on employment, taxation, social security, finance, training and development and health and safety. In recent years employees' expectations concerning conditions and 'what's in it for me?' have risen considerably.

Society places its expectations upon the owners and managers of industry and commerce, demanding that they conform, integrate and become more responsible and possess a 'social conscience'. It now takes a *professional* to cope with the modern-day demands, not only of business management but of 'people management'.

But who can truly put their hand on their heart and say 'I am truly knowledgeable in *every* aspect of running a business—including full knowledge of *all* the implications of employing people'?

Whatever your situation or level of experience, this book will be your handbook to suggest what to do before taking someone on, how to go about recruiting your employees, what is required of you when you take them on, what you (and they) *should* and *must* do while they are in your employ, how to get the best from your employees, and finally, how to go about terminating their employment (whether through dismissal or retirement) while keeping within the law.

- *Larger businesses:* with your own professional personnel services, the necessity of keeping up to date with all that is going on in the employment field and keeping pace with laws affecting people is formidable. There is also the need to give training and guidance to those recently appointed or in training for a professional qualification. This book can prove a valuable guide.
- *Managers in high-tech growth companies:* professionals in your particular technologies and specialisms, charged with recruiting and managing your employees as well as your departments. But as your companies expand and take on staff to meet new challenges, you realize that those specialisms may not include the skills of managing people. And it *is* a skill, which is why many larger businesses employ their own specialist personnel staff including training, health and safety, payroll and company law specialists who may sometimes be separate departments.

- *Owner-managers of small businesses and self-employed:* the entrepreneurs with specialist skills such as electronics, nursing, finance, selling, construction, joinery or engineering. You have, perhaps for reasons of redundancy or the desire to be your own boss, decided to use your skills for your own fulfilment—with perhaps little thought or intention of employing people when you started out. Yet sooner or later there comes the wish to expand or your workload demands some assistance. Immediately you take on just *one* employee, you are suddenly deemed to be 'expert' in every aspect of people management, whether it be the psychological and motivational aspects or the mass of law which regulates every facet of employment.
- *Head teachers*, particularly those of you struggling with Local Management of Schools (LMS), accountable for your own recruitment, employment conditions, training, total budget control and marketing. You need to be aware of the whole of employment law.

Private sector and state residential schools also have the same degree of accountability for employees (teaching staff).
- *Private sector nursing homes:* businesses in your own right which share the same accountabilities for employment, especially health and safety and fire precautions.
- *Students of personnel management*, already in training in a company or studying for a qualification to enter the employment field: there are many aspects of your intended profession for which this book will remove the aparent 'gobbledegook' and help you through those examinations.

The small business owner-manager or departmental manager says: 'I cannot be expected to understand every bit of legislation that affects my business'. But you discover that ignorance is no excuse when confronted by an industrial tribunal, a factory inspector (or environmental health officer) or worse still a magistrate or judge and the prospect of unlimited fines!

Employment laws are not neatly packaged under one heading but strewn through a hotchpot of laws and regulations scattered across the employment field. Legislation on employment has rightly been described as a veritable 'minefield' through which business managers and personnel specialists have to tread very warily because the way is strewn with hazardous devices, some of which you either did not know about or had forgotten were there! The 'mines' are many and varied, they can be pieces of industrial legislation covering employment, wages, payments and deductions, dismissals, pensions, health and safety and perhaps some aspects of human and interpersonal relationships.

Many changes are constantly rolling off the press so that one has difficulty sometimes in knowing whether a particular piece of legislation is still current, has been changed or has been repealed by another law. (Has that 'mine' you knew about been defused, changed in appearance or shifted somewhere else?) *One difficulty encountered in writing this book has been the many changes in legislation. We have endeavoured to be as up-to-date as possible at the time of going to press, including advance warnings of some future changes.*

So how can *you* avoid these potentially hazardous devices and come through unscathed? One way is by knowing what those 'mines' are, *where* they are, how you can *identify* them, *how* you can avoid them and *why* you need to know and avoid them.

That is where this book comes in, with step-by-step explanations to pre-empt problems and help you to avoid those otherwise inevitable 'explosions'. We shall approach our subject as if we were your employment consultant sitting in your office, giving advice and explaining the law. As you read we will be *your* professional adviser, hopefully relieving you of some anxious fears as we take you on a guided tour through this 'minefield' of people laws and every other aspect of employment.

We shall go into considerable detail on many matters, presented in clearly defined chapters and easy to find subsections with signposts to help you find what you need to know in more detail. In this way you will have *all* the available information at your fingertips—but in a very readable fashion.

You will find the subject-matter clearly indexed so that you will be able to find what you need when you need it. To ease things further for you, there will be a checklist at the end of each chapter for you to assess 'have I done what I need to do or *should* have done?'

In the appendices, we shall also give you some useful samples or ideas for the policies, contracts, forms or documents that are either suggested or required. Thus you will be armed with your protective gear as you negotiate your way through this minefield, led by one who has been through, has survived, and now leads others safely through.

1 Before you employ

Every business (large, small or sole trader) already has at least its first employee such as the director, owner or sole trader. In a private limited liability company (Ltd) with a minimum of one director, or a public limited company (PLC or plc) with a minimum of two directors, the directors are by law the company's first employees. If you are the sole trader or are a partnership, you are employing yourself (self-employment). This is very important because we shall see that where a requirement (in law) is based upon the 'number of employees', the head of the organization is the first part of that number.

As a manager of industry, especially if an entrepreneur, you have certain expectations—whether financial, social, or psychological. Your business will have a business plan, a sales forecast, a cash-flow forecast, and terms and conditions of business (we hope!). Employees are no different, they have expectations also. So what can you do to fulfil those expectations? A good way is to ask (on their behalf) the same questions that you asked for yourself when you started in business, or as a larger business manager, i.e. what your company's, or your own, requirements were.

Why do you want to employ someone?

It is important that there is a specific *need* for that person. Taking someone on just to help him or her off the dole queue may satisfy a social conscience but it will not return a company any dividends and (remembering the importance of cash flow) may create financial difficulties for any business and may even result in bankruptcy for the small business that is not truly geared up for employing people. It is important to consider the following points:

1 Is the job one which *must* be done?
2 Is it justified by an increasing workload, which the department manager or business owner cannot do personally but which (if it is done properly) will pay for itself *and* bring extra profit?
3 If the answer to points 1 and 2 is 'Yes', then ask: precisely *what* is it that you want this person to do? Just being a general factotum is not going to bring job satisfaction to any employee or be profitable to a firm's balance sheet. The employee may end up

'just pottering around' doing unnecessary things (the employee's idea of the job) and not doing what you really need to be done, or else not doing it properly. There could be cited many instances of employees spending much of their time doing things which their employer doesn't know they are doing (and doesn't need them to do), or else unbeknown to the boss, doing things in a different and 'long-winded' way to that which is required.

Suppose there is not really enough work to justify a full-time employee, would the services of a part-time worker help with the workload?

4 Finally can you *afford* an additional employee? Sometimes the workload may be there, but perhaps was not budgeted for or the cash flow is not good and the reserves in the bank are just not large enough or the benefits of employing an (additional) employee may not be cost effective. In these situations, it may be financially better to share the extra work around or, if you are a sole trader, to continue to employ yourself in that task—even *with* those extra hours—until you can afford to take on that needed additional employee.

Remember also that it costs more than just the salary/wages to employ someone (see 'Costs of employing' later in this chapter). If you *cannot* afford a full-time employee, would you find it affordable and still feasible work-wise to employ someone on a part-time basis or perhaps a 'casual' temporary worker? (Remember that 'temps' have rights also; see later sections.)

Let us look at points 1 to 4 another way. When you started out in your business or managerial post, you thought out what *you* intended to do (albeit that it did not work out that way). You formulated an action plan for your business or job, with every aspect of your business or job planned in some detail. You compiled a sales plan (or your company gave you one) to give you a sense of knowing how to make your business idea or job objectives achievable. A cash flow forecast of income and expenditure was also produced so that profitability could be assessed and borrowing requirements (if any) could be determined.

These are your management tools and their effectiveness is assessed through reviews or appraisals and ultimately quarterly and/or annual profit and loss accounts and balance sheets. In other words, these form your management *job description*, with objectives, key results checklists and periodic appraisals of your business peformance.

Your employee(s) will be no different and will need similar tools to help them in their jobs. They will want to know what their job is, that they have a set of tasks to perform, and that they have a set of objectives or goals to achieve (that is the same as your business plan for you or your company). Let us draw up a checklist of what is required *before* you can take on your new employees. You will need all or some of the following:

1 *Job title*: so obvious but would you believe that some employees today do not even have a job title? ('I just work here!')

   A job title should indicate, reasonably well, the nature of the job, and perhaps the status (status can sometimes be important to an employee).

   It should not be so brief as to hide the true nature of the job, e.g. 'clerk' or 'operator (what kind of clerk or operator?) although some one-word titles are readily understood, e.g. secretary. It should not be so verbose as to sound grandiose and confusing e.g. 'deputy assistant administrative under-manager' (i.e. a clerk) or 'assistant deputy hygiene consultant' (i.e. a cleaner).

2 *Job description*: this should 'describe' the job in a straightforward manner and should include the job title and the department. The main purpose of the job in a brief summary; also the position in the organization, i.e. to whom responsible, whom the employee supervises, links to others and the main duties and responsibilities.

   A word or two about these items. 'Department' only applies if you have more than just one section in your company. The 'main purpose' should answer an enquirer's question 'tell me about the job' and should be the summary description you would use in advertising the job—full but concise. 'Position', 'to whom responsible' and 'whom he or she supervises or is linked with' will become important as the organization grows. The 'main duties and responsibilities' should be just that—*main*, ideally no more than eight in a list, avoiding trivia (such as tea-making) and specific, not general factotum catch-all tasks (such as 'anything else I ask them to do').

   Included in the job description should be:

   (a) *Objectives*: the objectives of the job should be checked to correspond to the main duties and responsibilities in the job description (above) and they should be important, measurable achievements. This is often overlooked or avoided and yet without knowing what the objectives are, how will you or the job holder know what is expected? (In the same way, without a business plan, in which are stated *your* business's objectives, you would lose sight of your business aims.)

   (b) *Key results areas*: finally, the areas of achievement—the results by which you will measure performance (just like your business or action plan, in which you stated *your* key results areas). These may be qualitative (e.g. standards), quantitative (volumes/weights/numbers), ethical/professional (codes of practice) or personal (behaviour/attitudes).

(You will find a suggestion for a job description outlined in Appendix A. It is spread over four pages but you may amend it or abbreviate it, combining several sections into one if the job does not need such extensive detail.)

3 *Personnel specification*: what kind of person do you need in this job?

You will need to know the person/personnel specification in order to recruit the *right* employee for the job. First, however, there are some basic ground rules to protect you in your decision, as we want to protect you from making potentially damaging choices.

Remember the analogy of the minefield? You are just entering—so beware! There are certain things which, by law, you may *not* specify. They are:

(a) *Gender*: male or female?—explosive device No. 1!

When advertising for a new employee, you are *not* permitted to specify sex preference for any employee (male or female), as this is to discriminate against one or the other.

The only exception to this rule will be jobs where sex is a genuine occupational qualification (GOQ), in which there must be obvious preferences as in nursing where only a female nurse would be acceptable to some female patients, a male model to model male clothes, or where a part in a film specifically calls for a male or female actor. An employer may restrict a job to male or female *only* in this type of circumstance.

This is a most important point, as job applicants who are rejected on the grounds of sex (male or female) have the right to take the matter to an industrial tribunal for compensation. So, for example, if a male typist is better than the female applicants, *he* gets the job and if a female engineer is better than the male applicants, *she* gets the job.

(b) *Race*: colour preference?—explosive device No. 2!

You are similarly *not* permitted to specify *any* racial preference of any kind when advertising, as this is to discriminate between one racial group and another, whether ethnic or indigenous (except for certain GOQs—see also Chapter 2 on recruitment).

There is no legislation forbidding discrimination on the grounds of religion but beware—such discrimination can lead to prosecution on grounds of race, as some religions are of ethnic origin and such rejection may be construed as racial, e.g. Sikhs who, by a House of Lords Ruling, constitute a race. The safe course is not to specify or discriminate in any way.

While considering discrimination do remember that it is an offence also to differentiate between sexes or racial origins when determining salary or wage levels. The amount paid to an employee for working *must* be related solely to the nature of the work (its skill level, responsibility, accountability, complexity, etc.) and not to the sex or racial origin of the incumbent. So remember—equal pay for equal work.

(c) *Disabled*: you may not discriminate against a disabled person, *unless* that disablement would genuinely be a hazard to that person or to others, or would prevent him or her from carrying out the work competently. The Disabled Persons (Employment) Acts of 1944 and 1958 require companies with 20 or more employees to have a minimum quota of 3 per cent disabled persons. Thus, if a disabled person is competent, he or she gets the job.

Having determined what cannot be specified, what *should* the specification contain? It should include qualities necessary to enable your employee(s) to fulfil the job requirements competently, e.g.:

(d) *Qualifications*: what qualifications would you need for the job? Does the job really *need* any qualifications?

It is important to pitch the qualifications required at the correct level. For example, employing a PhD to do a filing clerk's job is ridiculous and will swiftly bring job dissatisfaction (although a well-qualified person can bring quality performance to the job), while employing a semi-skilled capstan-lathe operator to program and operate a computerized machining centre is just asking for trouble. Therefore, assess carefully what qualifications you need. National vocational qualifications (NVQs) may make this easier in future years (see Chapter 6—Training and development).

(e) *Experience*: is experience necessary for the position, or will the right person benefit from the experience you can give? What 'kind' of experience is needed to fulfil the job requirements competently?

Often, by specifying 'experienced', you may preclude someone from being considered who (with the right qualifications or aptitude) may be suited for you to *train* for the job. You may also consider experience as a 'qualification'.

(f) *Age*: do you *need* to specify 'age'? What is it about the job which makes age specification necessary?

A younger person, such as a school-leaver, may be more

teachable, could be trained to *your* methods, may be more adaptable than an older person and not be so 'set in their ways'. A younger person will provide your company with potential for future long-term development within the company, whereas an older person may not have so many years left before retiring.

On the other hand, consider the maturity and willingness which an older person may bring. The older person, having 'roots' and responsibilities, is less likely to leave after a short time for a 'career move', will provide stability and may make up what he or she lacks in qualifications with a wealth of wider and more valuable experience. Such a person may also be very *loyal* if given this opportunity to work. However, beware of knowledge and experience which are outdated, as companies need up-to-date knowledge and skill in today's fast-moving age of technological revolution. Smaller businesses also must endeavour to keep up-to-date with developments.

Another consideration is that for the remaining years of this century a slump in the numbers of 16–18-year-olds available for employment, added to the tendency to remain at school longer (53 per cent more staying in the 6th form, in 1991/92 than in 1990), will exacerbate this problem. Thus, do not dismiss the valuable service which an *older person* may render your organization in this period. With longer life-spans and better standards of fitness and health, *senior citizens* will have much to offer an employer in years to come, may not demand excessive above-the-rate payment, and could be a great asset to large and small businesses alike.

Recent changes in law regarding pensions also make it more attractive for able-bodied pensioners to work, as national insurance contributions (NIC) limits on earnings for pensioners have been lifted.

Either–or questions

Now that we have specified what kind of person we wish to employ, there are a few other matters to be determined. There are some 'either–or' questions to ask.

Do you want *full-time, part-time* or an *agency worker*? How many hours will this person work for you (per day/week/month)?

This will be determined by two things:

1 The volume of work needed to be done. Is it a steady flow, periodic, or at specified times?

2 How much can you *afford* to pay them? (A more serious consideration for a straight 'overhead' like a secretary, but perhaps less straightforward in the case of a producer whose volume of output directly affects income and profits.)

Often, part-time vacancies are easier to fill than full-time, as they suit the domestic situations of many parents, pensioners and students. They can also save you money in not taking on too great a financial burden in the early stages of a small business. Part-time workers can be useful in a social context, e.g. two part-timers can be given half-jobs (as in job-sharing innovations of the eighties).

Many firms employ two part-timers in one job—one occupying the desk/bench in the morning and the other in the afternoon. There is not always a benefit in PAYE or NIC terms in taking on part-time workers, as both are directly proportional to the rates of pay, except in the case of very low paid workers (see Chapter 4—Payments and deductions).

(For advice on taking agency workers see Chapter 3—Employing.)

Do you want *permanent* or *temporary*? For how long will this person be required? Is the job truly permanent or is it only temporary?

This will be a very important question, for several reasons:

1 If you offer someone a 'permanent' job when truly it is to be of only a short-term duration, you will cause much disappointment and ill-will as well as a poor reputation (bad news travels fast!).
2 If, on the other hand, you employ a person on a 'temporary' basis (when really the job is permanent), as a means of getting rid of him or her when eventualities arise, you could find yourself with problems with the law after two years (see Chapters 11 and 13 on Dismissals and Industrial Tribunals, respectively). There are, however, purely seasonal jobs which are temporary by their nature such as seaside café waiters or building site labourers.
3 There is also an important point concerning successive short-term contracts for temporary staff in Chapter 3—Employing, which you may like to consider.

We mentioned 'discrimination' earlier in relation to pay, you will not find the concept of paying less (per hour/week/month) just because staff are temporary or part-time very amenable either.

It is fairer to have a rate for the job, divisible *pro rata* according to the hours or days actually worked. After all, the same volume and quality of work is being done. So again, the advice is 'equal pay for equal work', though some companies may still like to reward 'permanency' with increments in pay, or some form of bonus structure.

Do you want *employed* or *self-employed*? You may think a self-employed person would be better in your company but let us look at the pros and cons.

Pros: A self-employed person will not have the same rights and protection in law against unfair dismissal or redundancy as an employed person, so you have no worries about ending the relationship if this becomes necessary. You do not have to concern yourself with PAYE or NIC, as self-employed persons are responsible for paying their own and for declaring their earnings. You also have no concerns about pensions, holidays, or any of the usual fringe benefits associated with an employed person.

Cons: While you have no legal obligations under employment law (outside of any contractual obligations you may have to negotiate), remember that the self-employed will have no obligation or commitment to you either, other than those afforded by goodwill. You may find it hard to apply 'discipline' to one who is not your employee (except perhaps the sanction of terminating an arrangement). Self-employed persons are just that—they are entitled to market their services or become sub-contractors to whomsoever they wish in addition to those services sold to you. You may contract for a minimum amount of their time (but not 100 per cent).

To satisfy the Inland Revenue requirements, a self-employed person must also be able to determine his or her own hours of work (though you may contract a minimum number of hours per week/month), must not use *your* equipment or tools only, or even exclusively your premises.

Beware also of another factor: the Inland Revenue (IR) does not look favourably on the conditions of a self-employed person who works permanently, exclusively, 100 per cent of the time, for one employer and, following an on-site visit, is likely to reclassify the person as 'employed'—rendering the *employer* (whether sole trader, owner-manager or director) subject to PAYE and NIC rules and with claims for any back-payment the IR may determine as being your (or your company's) responsibility.

There is no 'right' to automatic self-employed status, you must ensure that the authorities have granted the facility.

Do you want *out-workers* (sometimes called home workers)? Will your operation be well served by out-workers?

These are staff employed by a company to undertake work in their own homes (be it in a dining room, garage, or wherever). Typical examples of work done by out-workers would be packaging products, preparing mail-circulation brochures or doing helpful jobs such as typing or bookkeeping. (Some employers think that they have no liability for the health and safety of out-workers, which is not so. You will have a *duty* to them as outlined in Chapter 5—Health and safety.) Let us look at the pros and cons of this category of employee also.

Pros: The benefits of employing them are that they are not on your premises, do not have to conform to hours and days and they can fulfil a valuable function for you in a way which is useful to them. They may be parents with young children at home, disabled persons, or carers, who would all find 'going out to work' difficult or impossible for valid domestic reasons but who would nevertheless like to work.

A further advantage of this system is that you pay them only for the work actually undertaken, usually by volume. You save on costs of working space, heating, lighting, furniture, welfare facilities, etc., and on fringe benefits, such as holidays and various 'perks'. You also gain on 'leakage'—being able to count each item out and count each item back.

Cons: there are disadvantages in employing out-workers also. The obvious one is 'control'. You are unable to supervise them closely and thus very careful selection standards are needed, together with agreement to a firm set of 'rules', to assure quality of work and reliability. What happens when the dog chews your product or the cats do something worse with those accounts sheets or some other disaster occurs? Accessibility of your goods or work, delivery and collection can also be a problem. You may find your only control is setting targets and standards and your only sanction is termination.

Having considered all these factors and prepared the job description with objectives clearly defined and having drawn up the personnel specification of the kind of person you need for the job, you are ready to take on your employee. But, are you? Well, not quite yet. There are still some matters that need to be sorted out *before* you can recruit your employee.

There are four areas outside of the person which need to be considered. One is the question 'how much will I pay?', another is the matter of 'costs of employing', yet another is 'fringe benefits' over which in most cases you have little or no real control, and the fourth concerns 'transfer of undertakings' if you are considering taking over an existing business from someone else. So let us look at them.

How much will we pay?

Perhaps one should ask, first of all, 'How much can we *afford* to pay?' (The point needs to be pressed because it is important.) It will be a matter of comparing what the new employee will cost against the benefits and what can reasonably be afforded. There are three ways of assessing how much should be paid.

1 *Market value*: this is not an easy method of assessing a salary or wage level, as the market view of the worth of a particular type of employee will depend on the time-honoured test of supply and demand, i.e. how many are available and how many are demanded? Where jobs are in short supply and labour is plentiful, rates of pay will be lower whereas (as in many instances in the eighties and nineties) when jobs are plentiful but labour is in short supply, then rates of pay will be high.

Typical examples are technologists with a 'scarcity' value in expanding and technologically advancing organizations. Others are personnel specialists, marketing specialists, top-flight secretaries, accountants, production engineers, graphic numerical control (GNC) designers, sales professionals, or certain engineering technology skills.

2 *Job evaluation*: with the assistance of various guides you can assess the worth of a job in terms of merit, where each facet (responsibility/objective) of the job is given a numerical value. The total of the values is then translated into a scale—A, B, C, D, E, F—which can then be related to a pay band within which to pay your employee.

Another job evaluation method is the allocation of comparative values, i.e. the worth of each task in workload, responsibility and authority. In the case of management or supervisory positions, for example, the total score of the values corresponds to a salary level. Organizations such as the Institute of Personnel Management (IPM) or the Institution of Industrial Managers (IIM) will be pleased to assist and will usually lend evaluation guidebooks on request.*

Alternatively, you may wish to call upon the assistance of a specialist personnel adviser to undertake the evaluation but do bear in mind the cost.

3 *National wage rates*: you may, in the case of manual workers, need to consult with those bodies which fix wage levels nationally, particularly in the case of those who are not covered by Trade Union or Wages Council agreements. One such group of bodies is the National Joint Industrial Councils (NJICs), of which there is one for each trade or industrial category (e.g. NJIC for the Rubber Industry, or Agricultural Wages Board for the Farming Industry). If you pay at least the rates laid down in their respective agree-

* Telephone numbers: IPM: 081–046 9100, IIM: 081–579 9411.

ments, you will not go far wrong and can avoid much unnecessary disagreement. Some companies pride themselves in paying 'n per cent above NJIC rates' but that is a matter to be determined within your affordable budget.

Costs of employing

Obviously, one cannot just bring someone in and say 'there's your job, get on with it'. Your new employee will need certain things that will enable him or her to do the job.

- Where is he or she going to sit? In a workshop the employee will need a chair and a work bench, somewhere to put tools. Oh, and what about those tools—which ones will you provide or does the employee provide them? What about machinery and equipment for that extra worker?

    In an office they will need a desk and a chair—plus all the 'extras' which will go on the desk like filing trays, pen-pots, pens and pencils, paper, a stapler and the many helps which go to make office work that bit easier, including somewhere to put personal belongings. What about that typewriter for your first office assistant whom you need to take on for your department/company—perhaps even a word processor? It all depends on what you expect them to accomplish for you.
- **Be ready** for the employee: acting after the start-date suggests inefficiency and may result in higher costs for you.
- Perhaps you need a salesperson to boost sales: what about a car? what kind of car?—a 1.2 saloon, or a 1.6 estate, or a 4-litre executive, or a 'pick-up'? Or will you pay the employee mileage allowances for using his or her own vehicle and (if so) how much? What is the going rate? (The AA or RAC will advise the rate per mile.) Will your new salesperson be willing to run his or her own car into the ground on company business?
- What about health and safety? Also a cost. Protective clothing: helmet, gogles/glasses, ear defenders (plugs/muffs), gloves, face masks and filters, overalls, boots/shoes? Protective equipment—portable or static: extraction, ventilation, personal ventilators, VDU-screen filters, guards/fences? Temperature control—minimum/maximum? You will need to determine your situation and its requirements.

    Then add to health and safety the welfare requirements such as toilets, washbasins, cloakrooms, an area with eating facilities, minimum working areas and minimum working space (see Chapter 5).
- Employers' liability insurance cover is further required by law,

must be obtained by the time the first employee starts, and is a cost which will need to be considered (see Chapter 5).
- Another consideration is stock: we hope your new employee will generate additional sales for which you will need room for that extra stock to fulfil orders. Also, do not forget the stocks of consumables which the employee will use (stationery, forms, etc.). These are all a cost on sales. Increased stock levels will need added finance and may add pressure on cash flow.
- Finally, new employees need *training*. This is also a cost but is vital to quality, efficiency and profitability (see Chapter 6).

Fringe benefits

When you take someone on, there come with them certain obligations and expectations, which all add to the costs of employing. Some are compulsory and some are optional ones which you may like to consider in order to make the job you are offering more attractive (but only if they are affordable). First the *compulsory* ones—there are two:

- NIC: once the salary level has been decided upon, the employer will be obliged to pay the employer's portion of national insurance contributions (NIC) in addition to collecting the employee's contribution. Also do bear in mind that you personally or your company will be accountable to the Inland Revenue for passing both these NIC payments and PAYE across to them. (It is not exactly straightforward, but we'll tell you more about this in Chapter 4—Payments and deductions.)

  You may be saying 'surely, this is a cost and not a fringe benefit?' Yes, NIC is a cost but we include it here because it is also a benefit by law to the employee which many do not realize is earned by, and directly related to, payments of contributions. NIC payments equate to entitlement to pension or social security benefits; no NIC payments—no benefits. And remember that, for this reason, NIC rules are very strict with no flexibility or discretion unlike income tax rules.
- *Public holidays*: every employee is *entitled* to eight days' public (or statutory) holidays in each year January to December. If they are employed by you *at the time* of the scheduled holiday, you *must* give them the day or days off. The eight days in England currently are: New Year, Good Friday, Easter Monday, May Day, Spring Bank Holiday (some call it Whitsun), Late Summer, Christmas Day and Boxing Day. Holidays in Scotland and Ireland may be different. There is *no* stipulation as to when you give each day (on the date of the holiday or some other time). Also, when a bank holiday is worked, time off in lieu and/or extra pay is optional,

these are matters for mutual agreement. Oddly, there is no stipulation in law that you must pay employees for these days but you would find the idea of not paying them very unpalatable.

And the optional ones. There are several but even though the label 'optional' may apply to them you will need to remember the 'market rate' principle also. Prospective employees will always compare *your* fringe benefits with those of other prospective employers.

In today's highly competitive employment market with skills and shortages in many areas (despite high unemployment), it is not only job applicants who have to compete with each other to win jobs. Employers also have to compete with each other to win the services of employees. Job hunters will sell their skills to, and accept the conditions of, the buyer who pays the best price (pay, incentives, sick pay, perks) and gives the best future prospects.

This is not so in every case but depends on whether you are seeking a skill in short supply and high demand, or one in super abundance and low demand. An engineering design technologist may be an example of the former, while a capstan-lathe operator may be an example of the latter. So check the market.

What are the optional fringe benefits?

- *Holidays*: how many days of annual holidays will you give your employee? This, again, will depend upon the going 'market rate' (believe it or not) and there is no set number of days which must be given (there being, as yet, no 'Social Charter'—though a draft European Community (EC) charter is under discussion). Annual holidays vary widely across all industries, ranging from 10 to 30 days p.a., and are sometimes related to length of service.

    You will need to find out whether your industry, occupation or skill is governed by a trade union agreement (as in the engineering industry which gives 25 days p.a.) or an NJIC Agreement (which may give 20 or more days p.a.), or is not covered by any.

    Next, having discovered what the 'going rate' is, can you afford to release your employees for X days per year with full pay?

Employees often view the value of a job in terms of salary and benefits. Thus you may have to look at the following.

- *Pension*: will you give your employee the benefit of a pension? Can you even afford to? This is not compulsory and there are many jobs that do not offer a pension.

    There are three approaches to pensions:

    – The employer may arrange a pension through his own 'group' scheme, paying contributions to the pension fund on behalf of the employee and, of course, the employee may also pay a comparative contribution. There is no set rate (though insurance/pensions companies will suggest a rate), but it is usually expressed as a percentage of gross earnings in an employer : employee ratio of about 5 per cent : 7 per cent. Since April 1988, employees are also able to pay additional voluntary contributions (AVCs) into their fund, if they so wish.

- The employer can pass the employer contributions to the employee (at an agreed percentage rate) for *the employee* to invest in a personal pension policy of his or her own choice. This is becoming very popular with employees as by this method they are able to select the particular scheme which affords them the kinds of benefit they desire for themselves, including being 'portable'. It is an option which employees now have as a right under recent legislation.

- The employer may not offer any pension contribution, in which case employees may make their own arrangements with their own fund (as above) but without the benefit of any employer's contribution. Many employees have, in recent years, made their own arrangements in the absence of in-house 'occupational' pension schemes.

'The employer' in the above situations may be a large/medium company, owner-manager, sole proprietor, or self-employed.

There is more to pensions than just these three points. We have mentioned them briefly here as your 'options' and shall go into greater depth about 'technicalities' and variations in Chapter 4—Payments and deductions.

- *Sick pay*: security of income in times of illness can be important to employees. Will you pay any wage or salary to your employees when they are absent due to sickness or injury? If so, how much can you afford? Will it be full pay, or part pay only? There are no set rules. Sick pay schemes vary widely, from zero through 12 days per year (sometimes cumulative and in some cases with minimum qualifying service) to six months' full pay plus six months' half pay for longer-serving employees. You will need to assess local or sector rates. There is a statutory requirement to pay Statutory Sick Pay (SSP), also to pay Statutory Maternity Pay (SMP) after qualification, both of which we shall deal with in Chapter 4—Payments and deductions.
- *Life assurance*: what benefit will your employee's dependants receive in the event of your employee's premature death while in service? Can you afford to give life assurance cover as an added

fringe benefit? (Life assurance cover can be integral to the pension policy or separate.) This may become very important to someone who travels considerably for you.
- *Disability*: similarly, will your employees receive any benefit should they become no longer able to work due to illness or accident? This may be important to them also.
- *General benefits*: there are other 'benefits' which employees often (not always) look for as a part of their employment package. These can be difficult for very small companies, may be out of the question for businesses employing fewer than 20 people, but may be an expectation in larger firms. They surround the 'social and welfare' aspects of employment:

  – Do you have a canteen/restaurant? Is there a social club? What social activities do you arrange? What 'perks' are there (such as free products, discounts, luncheon vouchers, vehicles or travelling expenses, shares, bonus or profit schemes)?

  These benefits can be beyond the reaches of small businesses, but the question will crop up from time to time and the best policy (bearing in mind the costs of such benefits) is to explain that they are not within your grasp until you expand considerably.

  Larger firms may wish to consider their 'competitive edge' in providing these fringe benefits.

Transfer of undertakings

It may be that you or your company are taking over the operations of another business. Remember that in law, whenever a business changes ownership (through sale, acquisition or merger) the existing employees of that business will be entitled to retain all their existing rights, including reckonable or continuous service for the purpose of dismissal and/or redundancy. Their contracts of employment may be varied *only* by mutual agreement. If the interests of a company are purchased post-closure, the employees having been made redundant, then by re-employing some workers on fresh contracts of employment this rule does not apply.

This concludes our discussion of all that must or should be done *before you employ*. Have you been put off? How does your business shape up? Remember that there is no 'hard and fast rule' in deciding which of these principles you will apply in *your* business, nor how they should be applied, but however you decide to play the employment game, you must keep within the rules. As you progress through the remaining chapters, it will become apparent that it is 'not what you do, but how you do it' which is paramount in keeping the letter and spirit of the law.

You are now ready to move on to Chapter 2—Recruiting your employee. But before you do, to assist you in your 'action plan', we have drawn up a health checklist to help you assess *your* situation and plan *your* next moves.

Health checklist, pre-employment

1 *Why* do you want that new employee?
2 Can you *afford* him or her?
3 What is the (title) *job*?
4 Have you written a *job description* with duties and responsibilities, objectives; key results areas (as necessary)?
5 Have you decided on the *person* specification? Qualifications? Experience? Age? Full-/part-time? Permanent or temporary? Employed or self-employed? Out-worker?
   Remember, you cannot discriminate on grounds of sex, race, or disability. Have you fulfilled your three per cent disabled quota?
6 How much will you pay?
7 What are your *costs of employing* (apart from pay)?
8 Have you arranged employers' liability insurance?
9 What fringe benefits will you give? Holidays? Pension? Sick pay? Life insurance? Disability pension? Vehicle or travel expenses? Luncheon vouchers? Bonus? Shares/profit schemes? Plus the compulsory: NIC, public holidays.
10 Are you in a transfer of undertakings situation?

2 Recruiting your employee

Before commencing recruitment, there is an important consideration (if you already have one or more employees): can you fill your vacancy by internal promotion or transfer? If so, you should consider this option first, especially in the interests of good employee relations. Existing employees (even a sole worker) will view the prospect of someone coming in 'over their head' with some dissatisfaction—and may even cause poor relations with the new employee. You may either place an internal vacancy advertisement similar to the one suggested below or just offer the job.

If appointing internally, simply apply the process below to the vacancy. If you have no existing employee or there is no one available who is suitable and interested, you will then need to begin the process of RECRUITING YOUR EMPLOYEE.

The purpose of recruitment and selection can be said to be to appoint 'the person most likely to succeed' but there are no guarantees. Successful or otherwise, the law starts to impinge not just while your employees are with you but right from the very beginning, at the planning and advertising stages.

The process has several stages, and those stages are:

- Advertising
- Screening
- Interviewing
- Selecting
- The job offer.

We will deal with things in that order.

Advertising

There are five important considerations to remember when you advertise job vacancies:

1 Is your advertisement legal, decent, honest and truthful?
2 Does it discriminate?
3 Will it 'misrepresent' the job?
4 What about presentation and effectiveness?
5 Cost, including where should you advertise?

Recruiting your employee

Legal, decent, honest and truthful

The rules on advertising in Britain are quite strict, and rightly so. Your advertisement *must* conform to the requirements laid down by the Advertising Standards Authority. Are you offering a product or service which is legal?

A 'job' in this context is a product, something you are offering. Is the job legal? You cannot advertise for burglars, con-men, or an 'occupation' which, if practised, would produce illegal acts. This legality includes 'discrimination' which we deal with below.

Will the nature of the advertisement give offence to the average 'man on the Clapham omnibus'? Will it offend particular sectors of society (e.g., ethnic minorities), or will it offend public morals?

Is your advertisement honest? Are you really making the job which is advertised available to both prospective and successful applicants? In this respect, the job description or specification, of which we spoke in Chapter 1, will prove to be invaluable to you as employer and reassuring to the prospective job holder.

Discrimination

The two main grounds of discrimination concerned in advertising are sex and race.

Sex discrimination The Sex Discrimination (SD) Act 1975, forbids the (implied or expressed) description of a job being advertised as specifically 'male' or 'female'.

Thus, salesman, dairyman or man Friday are illegal as also are saleswoman, office girl or girl Friday. Even some jobs recognized as either sex yet technically implying one sex by their title (e.g. foreman, chairman) are illegal, *unless* you make a clear statement that the job is open to both male and female applicants. Manager and manageress have now become manager—male/female, and there are many female managers. The many sections of the SD Act apply in various ways, but their content can be summarized as follows:

1 You must not publish an advertisement which expresses or implies sex discrimination, either way, unless that discrimination would not be unlawful as in *genuine* occupational qualifications (GOQs) (e.g. a female nurse to care for certain female patients, or a male model for male clothes) (s.38). But see 'Exceptions to the Acts', below.

2 You must not treat one sex less favourably than the other, including laying down conditions which by their very nature mean that one sex could not reasonably be expected to fulfil them (e.g. 'Open to male or female, must be 6 ft tall, weigh 16 stone, be able to lift 250 lb weights and wield a full-size sledge hammer', or

'male or female, must be blonde, petite, attractive, wear high-heeled shoes and be able to type proficently') (s.1).
3 The SD Act also makes it clear that the use of marital status to deny employment is discriminatory.
4 Where one sex receives favourable treatment on the ground of sex, the motive for this discrimination is irrelevant and in no way diminishes the offence (House of Lords ruling).

Race discrimination The Race Relations (RR) Act 1976, also lays down prohibitions with regard to discrimination on the grounds of race in very similar ways to the SD Act and covers discrimination by colour, race, ethnic origin or national origin. Again, the many sections in the RR Act could be summarized as follows:

1 You must not publish an advertisement which expresses of implies any racial preference, except where discrimination would not be unlawful as with particular racial groups, or when being of a particular racial origin is a genuine occupational qualification (an Asian actor to play an Asian character, an Asian person to give personal counselling to an Asian), or where you intend to employ that person outside the United Kingdom, plus 'other general exceptions' summarized below (s.29).

Note: The Court of Appeal ruled (1990) that an employee in a managerial position could not provide a 'personal' service and being of a particular racial origin was not therefore a GOQ.
2 You must not treat a person of one race less favourably than another, nor apply conditions to one race which could not apply to others (again, the same 'general exceptions', below, apply) (s.1).
3 You must not treat a person of one race differently from another either in selection or in the terms and the conditions of employment offered (either by refusal or omission) (s.4(I)).

Exceptions to the Acts Both SD and RR Acts allow certain *general exceptions* and these are broadly:

- *SD Act*: charities (s.43), sport (s.44), insurance (s.45), communal sleeping accommodation (s.46), training for particular work (ss.47 and 48), and national security (s.52), plus those mentioned in Chapter 1.
  Discrimination imposed by other Acts (s.51) as an exception and GOQs regulated by legislation have both been overriden by the Employment Act 1989. Also, an Appeals Tribunal ruling (1984) states that it is *not* sex discrimination to refuse part-time work to a previously full-time female employee who returns from maternity leave to reclaim her employment.

- *RR Act*: charities (s.34), special racial group needs (s.35), non-residents of the United Kingdom (s.36), special 'positive' discrimination training, e.g. underprivileged groups (s.37 and 38), representative sport (s.39), Sikhs from the requirement to wear safety helmets (employers protected from claims of indirect discrimination) (Employment Act 1989), discrimination imposed by other Acts (s.41), and national security (s.42).

Most of the above general exceptions probably will not apply to you. But the best advice would be not to try to 'manoeuvre' into any of them, as you may give yourself problems in proving validity.

Note: The limits on compensation for both sex and race discrimination were raised to £10,000 from 1 April 1991.

Misrepresentation

This is akin to 'legal, decent and honest' but relates to *your* description of the job, either by title or content, as advertised and/or discussed and which the person has accepted. When the employee starts work the job is discovered to be something completely different, (e.g. advertising for a 'maintenance engineer' when the job is that of 'cleaner and handy-person' or advertising for a 'senior field training adviser' when the job is that of 'YT supervisor'.

Presentation and effectiveness

Walk around any town centre shopping area and you will see many shop windows 'dressed' in order to attract customers. What you see is their presentation. Their effectiveness is measured by how the customers are motivated to purchase. Your advertisement is *your* 'shop window'. As with all selling, first impressions are most important, and you are (in your advertisement) seeking to 'sell' your company and the job you are offering. The presentation of your advertisement will determine just how many people notice it in the first place and its effectiveness depends upon whether the content prompts enough of the readers who match your specifications to apply. To help formulate your ad, we'll give you a mnemonic in a lady's name, AIDA:

- A is for *attention*. Does your ad attract attention from the person who matches your specification? How will your ad attract attention? The layout needs to be interesting, even original. Several things will *attract*: a bold heading (perhaps the job title or some feature or benefit of the job), a good bold border, the logo of your company and perhaps a sketch/picture of some eye-catching item of interest (your product or a 'status' symbol).
- I is for *interest*. Does your ad (having attracted attention) create

interest in the job? Descriptions which are too verbose or in dreary language will just be a 'put-off'. Information about benefits or some exciting feature will create interest. Never cram in so much print that your ideal prospect is not motivated to read it—applicants do not want to read editorial. Ads which are just 'words' from top to bottom are rarely read.

Remember the rule for attention and interest—make use of S P A C E around words to make your message s t a n d o u t. Use space effectively.

- D is for *desire*. Does your ad (having created interest) generate a desire for the job? The reader may need the job but must also *want* the job. This is down to how you describe it. The result can be either enthusiasm or apathy or, if the reader applies, just lethargy and no real enthusiasm.
- A is for *action*. Does your ad compel the person who fits your specification to reach for the telephone or writing pad? Attracted and interested he or she may be, but not activated. Therefore, encouraging words with a 'do it *now*' message or the opportunity of an 'informal chat' over the telephone can help.

Responses We hope your advertisement will produce enough applicants for you to have sufficient people on whom to base your selection—one-from-one is not a very sure way of knowing that you have the right person. The level of response depends upon a combination of how you present your ad, whether you reach your *target* audience, and how many of the *right* calibre are seeking your kind of vacancy, so here are a few more hints:

Your description should not be so precise as to attract only one or two applicants and exclude many who would otherwise consider it, yet not so broad and vague as to prompt hundreds of applicants, 95 per cent of whom are unsuitable. In the job marketplace there are many 'square pegs' who try to fit into round holes and you should not have to waste your valuable time 'weeding out' countless unsuitable applicants.

You also need to be careful *where* you place your ad. There are countless newspapers and journals eager for your custom, yet may not produce your desired results (it is not unusual for there to be 'zero response'). So do not be pressured by a particular advertising media, but instead consider carefully which publication is aimed at, and *reaches*, your target audience?

Where to advertise, and cost
These are crucial matters to all sizes of businesses. An appropriate medium for one company can be totally inappropriate for another,

while 'too expensive' for one company can be 'too cheap' for another.

The media in which to advertise are almost limitless and include: national, regional, local and 'free drop' newspapers, trade magazines, Jobcentres, careers centres, libraries, Professional and Executive Register, the Employment Department, local Training and Education Councils (TECs), and Job Clubs. The very high rates of advertising in the larger newspapers and journals may be within the budget of large companies, but not of small businesses. Your local 'free drop' newspapers provide cheaper advertising, are usually value-for-money, have a longer shelf life, and may reach your *specific* catchment area. You have to make the choice.

But there is a way to *save money* on advertising altogether—try passing your ad details to your local Jobcentre or Job Club. They have many hundreds of job hunters and are usually very helpful. But beware, their role is finding jobs for people. They may not be so selective and may send someone for interview just because that person is looking for a job and has said 'I want to go for that one'.

Employment agencies, conversely, whose role is finding people for jobs, only get paid if they provide the 'right' person for the job, and there is normally a rebate of fees if, after all, that 'right' person turns out to be unsuited to the job (or the job to them) within an agreed period of time.

However, cost again being a crucial matter, you need to bear in mind that agencies charge fees (depending on the job category) of between 7 and 25 per cent of the first years wage/salary upon successful placement of someone with you. However, consider the benefit of paying a fee to an agency against a large fee for an unsuccessful advertisement.

So, weigh up the options, and make your choice.

Screening

You will not want to waste your valuable time interviewing every single applicant (unless the number is so small that you have no choice), and so you will need to 'screen' them in order to select an initial interview group.

The application form

An application form is very helpful, but how will you decide upon the format? This depends on the nature of the job on offer. Some companies have only one form, which can produce problems, while others have different forms for different types and levels of jobs, e.g. shopfloor, clerical/secretarial, management/supervision. The choice is yours, but you should ensure that the form will ask for information which is appropriate to the job. It should not be so brief as to omit essential information without which you could make an incorrect selection and have to dismiss later, nor should it ask irrelevant questions or be so vast and overwhelming as to put your candidate off. There is no restriction as to the kind of question you may ask in an application form, but you may not use any of the information gained in a prejudicial way against a candidate, e.g. sex, marital status, whether pregnant, race, etc. An example of an application form is given in Appendix A.

How do we screen?

A completed application form will tell you much about the job applicant. You have a legal obligation (under health and safety law) to employ only 'competent' workers, and your person specification which you drew up earlier comes in handy again as you compare applications with the person specification to assess which candidates most closely match the type of person you decided you want in the job.

Your first selection will be on the basis of qualifications (if needed), then relevant experience, then other factors.

- First of all the appearance of the form: does it appear as if a spider wrote it with a paint brush or is the writing neat and tidy? (Graphologists tell us that people's handwriting says much about them.) Does the form look as if it had last night's fish and chips in it or is it clean and neatly folded? (This tells much about the tidiness and conscientiousness of the applicant.)
- Secondly, what interests do they have—do they indicate something about their likelihood to be suited to the job, e.g. hobby skills? And what does the form tell you about their personality, are they likely to establish good relationships and 'fit in' with you and your other employees? (This is very important, as you want a harmonious workforce who can work together.)
- Finally, are you (or your existing employees) concerned about smokers? Are you concerned about an applicant who has children at school and whether crèche or other arrangements have been considered? Are they colour blind? Do they drive? Have they any restrictions due to health problems? Complete a checklist.

Note: You cannot refuse a job to a person simply on the grounds that they have children.

How many should you interview? That will depend upon the nature of the job, how many vacancies you have and how many apply. But a suggested ratio of six interviews to one job vacancy (6:1) would seem about right or if you have two similar vacancies, say about nine (9:2).

Short listing

You may select the one you want from those you interview or draw up a short list of two or three for a second and final interview, perhaps involving someone else (partner/another manager) in the final decision process—two heads being better than one. Short listing is more important at higher levels or in more technical or key functions.

Remember, the better your advertising skills in attracting the 'right' persons to apply and the better your screening skills with application forms, the less lengthy and arduous will be the selection and interviewing process.

Interviewing

The interviewing process is not the first key factor, but it is the most important of all. Whether you select the 'right' person and whether that person accepts your job offer, will depend very much upon how you conduct the interview. We want you to make a good job of it, so we shall give you plenty of hints, taking you through in stages from invitation to final appointment.

Invitation to an interview

Remember that you will be selected by the applicant as well as the applicant by you. For this reason, today, many organizations invite high-level job applicants for 'informal meetings' prior to the formal interview (which can also prove helpful for in-house applicants, as well as candidates from outside). This gives applicants an opportunity to ask questions with no questions asked of them, to get to know about the job, the people and the place, and to 'break the ice' with no pressure on either party. Applicants also have the opportunity to say 'No, I don't think I like that job/place' (better to find out now than after joining). You may like to consider this, e.g. if you decide to recruit a deputy, a partner in your business, or maybe another less senior but key position.

The interview letter which you send will influence the applicants very much (it is your application to become their employer—sounds daft, but in today's employment market, it is very true). The design of the letterhead and quality of the typing will indicate much—a letter with typing mistakes gives a poor impression of your company's work and quality standards. Is your letter friendly and informative, or curt and formal rather like a bureaucratic telegram? What about some directions? A map is most helpful and will show that you care. Also, are you going to reimburse all or part of applicants' travel expenses—bus/rail/taxi fares?

It will be helpful to you to ask persons to confirm their attendance, making sure they contact you (or your deputy), perhaps by a reply-paid answer-card which you can send—your time is too expensive to waste sitting around waiting for someone who is not going to turn up.

Preparation for the interview

You want to achieve your stated objective, i.e. to recruit 'the person most likely to succeed'. Thus it is most important that the interview is conducted correctly, otherwise you may give yourself many problems through mis-selection, or in discouraged applicants. So this will mean good preparation. You want to achieve three things:

1 To select the 'right' candidate for the job. This, at best, is only going to be 'the person most likely to succeed' even with the most sophisticated selection methods of psychometric testing and other systems available to larger firms.
2 To 'weed out' correctly those unsuitable and those who are really just 'professional interviewees' who are very good at talking about what they say they can do yet poor at doing it.
3 To encourage those candidates who may, conversely, be very good at what they can do, but are poor at communicating it to others. There are many people in this category, and it would be a shame to reject a good person just because he or she was poor at being interviewed!

So we are going to take you through a full interviewing technique in detail, which will help you to achieve those three objectives and also help you to select the employee and keep him or her as a loyal employee for a long time. Then we'll mention a few items of 'law' which must be remembered.

Preparation for the interview starts before the interview, so, before the interview there are some arrangements you need to make:

- *Diary*: ensure you have the time and date clearly entered in your diary (or that your secretary has the appointment in his or hers). You do not want to make the wrong first impression by forgetting it—that has been known to happen. Also, allow adequate time.
- *Calls*: ensure that *all* telephone calls are diverted to another office during the interview (except in a real emergency)—there is nothing more off-putting to an interviewee than constant interruptions. 'The impression of being busy or important' will not impress, but will rather give signs of being disorganized.
- *Seating*: arrange the seating in as informal a manner as possible,

preferably without a desk between you and your candidate (better a coffee table). Position the chairs so that they are at an angle of about 90° to each other—never so that you are eyeball to eyeball, as this is confrontational and can be very intimidating.
- *Desk*: clear your desk of all unnecessary items and arrange what is necessary in a tidy manner. Make sure that your 'necessary' items include the application form, a note pad and pens. (*Hint*: remember, when taking notes, that many people can read upside-down!—so be careful what you write in the presence of the applicant. Better to make notes afterwards, if memory permits. The author found shorthand very useful in this situation and those managers with that skill may find it helpful, too.)
- *Reception*: there are a number of important points about the reception you give to your candidate:

  – Make sure that someone other than yourself (your receptionist if you employ one) knows that your candidate is coming—it is reassuring and shows organization. And what about the 'reception' area? Being told to 'hold on' and stand in a passageway for half-an-hour will put the candidate off and worsen any nerves, so what about an area set aside (even if it is just the corner of an office) with a comfortable chair, small table, magazines, and perhaps a plant? Remember 'first impressions' are so important.

  – Do make sure that *you* receive the applicant on time and that your assistant doesn't have to search for you. If you keep him or her waiting for half-an-hour or longer, do not be surprised if he or she gets up and walks out!

  – Greet the applicant with a friendly smile and sincere handshake (not a 'wet fish'), and how about the offer of a cup of coffee or tea? Your candidate will appreciate your kindness and feel more relaxed. Oh, and don't forget—avoid smoking during the interview.

The interview itself
Your skill in interviewing will help you to select the person 'most likely to succeed' so that you do not take on a problem employee, or have to recruit again prematurely. So here are a few tips on *how to conduct the interview*:

- *Put at ease*: it is important that you start by putting your candidate at ease, not by launching into the attack with the first formal question. Introduce yourself (name and appointment) and help the candidate to relax by enquiring about his or her journey, remarking upon the weather or any other topical items. Then lead gently into a review of the application form by asking a 'tell me about . . .' question from something of interest on the form—perhaps a hobby or interest which you also share ('I noticed that you like voluntary work—tell me about that'). Finally, outline how the discussion will proceed. Speak about 'our discussion', not 'interview', as this will help to remove tension.

- *Questions* are very important and the way you ask them will determine whether you discover all you want to know, or finish with a feeling of frustration. So here are some do's and don'ts:
First the 'don'ts:

 - *Don't* ask questions which will attract 'yes/no' answers, they will kill the conversation stone dead with answers of convenience.

 - *Don't* ask leading questions, i.e. putting words into your candidate's mouth to give you the answer they think you want.

 - *Don't* criticize. You cannot know all the background, and this will give a poor impression of you as a critical boss.

 - *Don't* maintain eye contact too long; it is intimidating and can be offensive to those of the opposite sex. A suggested maximum is 10 seconds—maintaining frequent eye contact when speaking and looking slightly away when listening.

 - *Don't* bring your candidate back too abruptly to the point of your question if he or she strays a little ('that's not what I was talking about!'), wait for a pause to interject a relevance and lead the conversation gently back.

 - *Don't* raise delicate, personal matters too soon, but rather encourage a relaxed atmosphere into which to introduce them.

 - *Don't* ask gimmicky questions, you'll only confuse or mislead, or give a 'smart Alec' impression.

 - *Don't* keep looking out of the window, at your watch or at the ceiling, as this will suggest disinterest or impatience.

And the do's:

 - *Do* ask 'open-ended questions', the ones that begin with the words who, what, when, where, which, how, or why. This way your candidate has to give quality answers and cannot evade answers with 'yes/no'. (Notice that these 'all contain Ws').

- *Do* ask 'tell me about . . .' questions in the body of the interview, like the ones suggested to help your candidates be at ease. This will attract descriptive answers which are more likely to be full of what you want to know, though beware of allowing them to become verbose and irrelevant.

- *Do* 'pause' after your candidate has spoken before speaking again, this will allow time for thought by both parties, and avoid the impression of 'jumping in hastily'.

- *Do* repeat back short answers to your candidate with a raised intonation of voice to obviate a 'question', so that he or she will know you are interested and want more information, (e.g. candidate: '. . . in complexity', you reply: 'complexity?'

- *Do* show your candidate that you are interested. This is best done by leaning forward rather than back and by maintaining eye contact for brief periods.

- *Do* maintain control of the interview, not allowing your candidate to dominate the proceedings. Allow the ratio of conversation of about 50:50.

- *Do* ask relevant questions about those qualifications and experience which are important. To help you, have a checklist and refer to it.

- *Do* get the candidate to talk about himself or herself, preferably early in the interview, perhaps a potted career history and reasons for choice of career, likes and dislikes, and hobbies.

- *Do* round off the interview by asking if the candidate has any questions, or anything else he or she wants to add/modify.

- *Do* remember that you can continue the interview on the way out; indeed, this 'off guard', relaxed time can be useful.

- *Do* conclude by letting the candidate know what your next step is.

- *Do* follow up the interview. Nothing can be more frustrating and cause a worse impression than weeks or months of waiting with no news as to the result of the interview.

- *Do* let your candidate know if delays occur in your making the final decision, it will encourage the candidate, and perhaps keep your choice interested (otherwise you may lose him or her).

Selecting

Finally, here are a few tips to help you in assessing your candidates:

- *First impressions:* your first encounter will tell you much. Appearance—are they neatly/tidily/cleanly/smartly/attractively dressed? Does their appearance tell you something about their personality and whether you could have them working with you 'looking like that'? Do they smoke? Do they drive?
- *Intelligence*: what would you estimate their intellect to be? Above or below average? Above or below the level required for your job? Do they seem like a candidate for MENSA, or perhaps of a very low IQ (though not measured, you can reasonably assess)?
- *Communications*: what is their verbosity score? Talk too much or mute? Communicate clearly or hesitantly and vaguely?
- *Motivation*: what is the level and nature of your candidates' motivation? How enthusiastic are they? What is it about the job or type of work which interests them? (See also Chapter 7—Motivation.)
- *Learning styles*: you will need to train your new employee when in position. Everyone has different learning styles. What will be their best way of learning? (For guidance, see Chapter 6—Training and development.)
- *Ambition*: do they have any ambitions, if so, for what and why? How far do they want to go? Not far enough for this job or are they too ambitious and would not stay long? You will need to weigh this against the job requirements.
- *Are they likely to stay*? Four things will suggest that they are likely to move too quickly out of the job:
    - ambition beyond what you can offer
    - just using you as a 'stop gap'
    - history of too-rapid job changes
    - would extra hours (when condition demanded) be a problem to them?

    So the advice is check the application form, and question candidates well on this aspect.
- *Energy and stickability*: do they seem the kind of person who will work at the appropriate speed and stick at a job until its completion, or are they likely to approach work with lethargy?
- *Initiative*: do they seem to have initiative and ability to act independently when necessary, or will they need you at their side throughout every move? (You cannot afford them the luxury of constant close support and supervision.)
- *Stress tolerance*: what would you judge to be their ability to stand

up against stressful situations (if required by the job)? Do they have emotional maturity, or are they whimpish?
- *Relationships*: what does their information about their past jobs (and their interaction with *you*) tell you about their interpersonal relationships with bosses, peers or subordinates? Did they leave the last job because of a row with the boss or because of 'not getting on with work-mates'? Why? Are they 'loners'?

You will find it helpful to prepare an interview checklist, based on the above, to guide yourself through the discussion. Ensure you cover all the important points, and facilitate note taking. A suggestion for a checklist is given in Appendix B.

Discrimination
We need to re-emphasize a few principles which were mentioned in the section on advertising, because the law extends beyond your 'sits vac' advertisement into interviewing, recruiting and employing. So, here are some further important points of law.

Sex Discrimination Act   You must not apply discriminatory practice by imposing any requirements or conditions which directly or indirectly discriminate against either sex (s.37) (see the earlier paragraph on advertising), nor by offering employment in a discriminatory way to either sex (s.6(1)), except when the job is clearly one where specifically a male or female must be employed as a 'genuine occupational qualification' (s.7).

Never ask a female applicant 'are you, or do you intend to become pregnant?', as (apart from the fact that she may not know) this could be construed as sex discrimination.

However, it may be pertinent in certain specified occupations to seek the information, i.e. where her unborn child or the woman herself would adversely affect, or would be adversely affected by, the work undertaken. It would also not be unreasonable to refuse employment to a pregnant woman in those circumstances, but *only* those circumstances.

You must not discriminate against a person of either sex because they are married (s.3), though you may ask about marital status (for insurance or pensions purposes, or for next of kin records).

You must not penalize a person who takes action against you on the grounds of sex discrimination (in this context, one who feels that you discriminated against him or her in the selection process), *unless* such action is vexatious and false (s.4).

Race Relations Act   In the interview situation you must not treat a person less favourably on racial grounds than you treat or would treat others (s.1).

You must not apply conditions to a person on racial grounds which you would not also apply equally to others and to which the smaller racial group could not reasonably be expected to conform, unless you can justify such a condition regardless of race, colour, nationality or ethnic origin—or which is detrimental because they cannot comply with it.

So, the golden rule applying to both sex and race discrimination when recruiting is not to ask questions the answers to which cannot be given as you require. Nor must you expect candidates to do things which they cannot reasonably be expected to do, by reason of their sex or racial origin.

The job

You will need to include in the discussion an outline of the job and its conditions, together with details about your company: your history, size, industry/product/service, who's who, methods of operation, etc.; although there is no rigid rule as to which stage of the interview process you should introduce this. It is suggested, however, that you introduce an outline and brief discussion of the job early in the interview—perhaps when discussing the candidate's qualifications and experience, so that you can relate to them.

Then it would probably be appropriate to outline the conditions of the job right at the end of the interview, being careful to include all the relevant aspects, e.g., days and hours of work, breaks, welfare facilities, 'perks', annual and public holidays—how and when taken, pension, life assurance, remuneration, bonuses, future prospects, etc. By the way, do beware of applicants who want to major on the conditions right at the beginning of the interview, side-step the issue for *you* to deal with later and check their motivation.

Panel interviews

Perhaps you would not feel comfortable interviewing a candidate alone, particularly if you have no experience. Interviewing is not always easy and it takes skill to feel certain that you have selected the right person. You might consider a 'panel interview' in which someone assists you by sharing the questioning and assessment, e.g.:

- Someone else in your company in a responsible capacity (perhaps a co-manager or your secretary?)
- An external adviser (perhaps a suitable consultant who knows you, your company and your situation)—but be careful to ensure that costs are not too high.

If you are not already trained, you may consider attending a seminar to equip yourself with the skills in interviewing and selection. The initial cost could prove considerably cost effective in the longer term.

The job offer

You have now completed your interviews and have a clear choice in mind as to whom you want to come and work with you. That means an offer of the job. A job offer can be either verbal or in writing, the law of contracts makes no distinction—a verbal agreement between two parties is a legally binding contract.

The problem is that verbal contracts are hard to prove and in a court of law, it is a matter of whose version of the facts is believed. So, the best rule is to make the offer (or confirm a verbal offer) in writing. Make sure it has in it those conditions which you outlined in the interview situation, plus a date and time of starting.

The Institute of Personnel Management (IPM) has a 'Code of Professional Conduct' and the 'IPM Recruitment Code', which are very helpful and to which IPM members are expected to adhere. Copies may be obtained by sending a stamped addressed envelope to: Institute of Personnel Management, IPM House, Camp Road, Wimbledon, London 4UX SW19.

That concludes Chapter 2—Recruiting your employee. We are now ready to progress to Chapter 3—Employing. But first, to help you plan and carry through your first or next recruitment, we have drawn up another health checklist.

Health checklist for recruiting your employee

1 Your advertisement: is it 'legal, decent, honest'? Will it give offence to an average person? Will it discriminate against sex or race? If so, amend it. Does it represent the true nature of the job? Is the presentation good? Will it be effective? Have you incorporated 'AIDA'? Where will you place your ad to reach *your* target audience; to get the best response; to save money?
2 Application form: have you designed one? Is it effective?
3 Screening: how will you screen your applicants? How many do you want on your short list for interview?
4 Reception: have you prepared for the interview? Diary? Are all calls diverted? Have you a pleasant 'reception' area? Is seating for the interview arranged properly? Is your desk clear? How will you receive your candidate? Is everyone briefed?
5 The interview itself: put at ease, ask open-ended questions, remember the do's and don'ts; remember first impressions—theirs and yours; what are you looking for—intelligence, communication abilities, qualifications, experience, confidence, personality, motivation, ambition, staying permanently, initiative, tolerance, learning styles?
6 Finally, avoid sex or race discrimination.

3 Employing*

Your advertising has brought the desired response. You have conducted a professional interview, asked the right questions, and you have recruited the 'person most likely to succeed'. Are you ready to put him or her to work? Well, not quite yet. There is still much to do before employment actually starts.

Laws and regulations have no sympathies for business problems and do not interest themselves in business, per se. *The law is seen as a nuisance by many, but we cannot in any way bypass it. Short-cuts, especially where the law is concerned, are at best risky and at worse cause confusion and cost money.*

Getting the preliminary details right will save many problems later. So, we'll try to keep you on the right side of the law from the start, beginning with those important legal requirements which impinge from day one.

3.1 Legal requirements

The law places certain statutory obligations on employers which must be fulfilled. These obligations depend on the numbers of persons employed, with the director or owner-manager being 'number one' (see Table 3.1 overleaf).

3.2 Contracts, terms and conditions of employment

Everyone in society enters into a 'contract' at various times and in various situations. It may be for the purchase of grocery items or a car, advertising space in a journal or the loan of money; it may be a marriage or it may be employment. A contract is deemed to exist when there is an agreement between two parties for any particular purpose which the law will enforce.

A contract of employment is regulated by the same basic law which governs all other contracts. As with other contracts, the law has intervened to give one party to the contract minimum rights, in the case of employment, these rights go mainly to the employee. It is very important, therefore, when drawing up an employment contract, that

---

* Other aspects of employment law outside those covered in this chapter, being specialist in nature, are dealt with in later chapters.

Table 3.1 Statutory obligations of employers

Numbers	Legal requirements
1	No special requirements but see important point in Chapter 5—Health and safety.
2–4	Register with Health and Safety Executive or Environmental Health Department, as appropriate (see Chapter 5). Poster: 'Health and Safety Law—What you should know' must be displayed. All Health and safety legislation including 'COSHH', noise, electricity, environmental pollution, etc., must be complied with (see Chapter 5). Register with Inland Revenue and DSS (PAYE/NIC) (see Chapter 5). Obtain employers' liability insurance cover: certificate must be in-date and displayed (see Chapters 1 and 5). Obtain public liability insurance cover: certificate need not be displayed. Fire Precaution Act 1971 must be complied with (but no fire certificate required, yet) (see Chapter 5). Jobs must be open to all, regardless of sex, race or marital status (see Chapter 2). Contracts of employment, with terms and conditions of employment must be issued to all employees: • if working 16 or more hours per week, within 13 weeks of commencement • if working 8 hours or more, after 5 years' continuous employment (see page 41). Disciplinary rules need not be included (see below). Itemized pay statements must be issued (see Chapter 4).
5–9	Health and safety policy: must be written, displayed and communicated to all employees (see Chapter 5).
10+	Fire certificate required (only if more than 10 employed above ground floor level) (see Chapter 5).
20+	Fire certificate required if more than 20 employed at ground level. Must fulfil 3 per cent quota of disabled employees (Chapter 2). Must include disciplinary rules in terms and conditions of employment.
10+ to 100+	Redundancies, minimum notice periods to Secretary of State and for union negotiations (see Chapter 9—Redundancy).

you do not enter into one in which you, the employer, have no meaningful benefit. We shall give examples of agreements later.

What creates a legally enforceable agreement?

Regardless of any trade union collective agreement which may be in force, a contract of employment is regarded in law as existing between an individual employee and his or her employer. There are four essential ingredients to any contract, including that of employment, in order for it to be legally enforceable in a court or tribunal. The law says:

1 There must be both an offer and an acceptance.
2 There must be a clear intention by both parties to create a legally enforceable relationship.
3 The terms and conditions agreed in the contract must be sufficiently certain (no impracticalities or false situations).
4 The agreement must be 'supported by consideration' (i.e. it has the effect of making the agreement a legally enforceable contract).

Apart from being covered by common law and contract law, contracts of employment are governed by the Employment Protection (Consolidation) Act of 1978 (EP(C)A 78), as amended by the Employment Acts of 1980 and 1982 (EA 80 and EA 82), with some input from the Trade Union and Labour Relations Act of 1974 (TULRA) and the TULRA Amendment Act of 1976 in the case of collective agreements. Very small firms are unlikely to be affected by the latter.

As with other forms of agreement, a contract of employment can be made verbally. If two agree on the matter, that is a contract, and (in theory at least) is enforceable in law. However, there is the burden of proof and employment law has gone one step further and states that (even where there is a verbal agreement) the employment must be confirmed in written particulars (or contract) of employment, and that these written particulars must be provided to the employee within 13 weeks of commencement of the employment.

These written particulars must reflect the agreement reached with the employee before employment commenced. The employer cannot impose terms and conditions different from those agreed without the full consent of the employee. So the advice is: get it right before your employee starts.

Neither employer nor employee can regard himself or herself as 'exempt' from the terms of a contract of employment in the intervening period between verbal agrement and written confirmation, and failure to provide written particulars does not render the original verbal contract of employment void or unenforceable. The verbal contract still holds valid (providing one or the other can give proof) and usually it is what a 'reasonable person' says on oath which carries weight in a court of law. If you fail to furnish these written particulars within 13 weeks, or thereafter, you as employer lay yourself open to the rigours of the law in either an Industrial Tribunal or the civil courts. Additionally, where no written evidence of a contract exists, the courts may (in deciding rights of parties) imply terms based on assumption.

What should the written particulars (or contract) contain?

You may include in the written particulars (or contract) of employment anything to which two parties agree. But the law lays down the *minimum* which these particulars must contain. You must:

1 Identify the parties to the agreement (employer/employee).
2 Specify the date on which employment commenced.
3 Specify the date on which continuous employment began (taking into account previous service with existing or previous employers).
4 State the scale or rate of remuneration or the method of calculating remuneration.
5 State the intervals (weekly, monthly, quarterly, annually) at which payments are to be made. This may include an 'annual salary in 12 monthly payments'.
6 Specify conditions relating to hours of work, including normal working hours, overtime, other hours (e.g. standby, call-out) and whether additional hours outside normal working are paid.
7 Specify holiday entitlement, including public holidays, holiday pay and accrued holiday pay. Provisions for special leave (e.g. compassionate, paternity, etc.) may prove pertinent here, too.
8 Specify any pension arrangements, whether company scheme or employees' own scheme or combination. Do bear in mind the options open to employees, as outlined in Chapter 1 and page 103 of Chapter 4—Payments and deductions.
9 Specify lengths of notice required from both employee and employer for either to terminate the agreement. These must be at least the minimum required by law (see Chapter 11—Dismissals).
10 State the job title of the position held by the employee (see Chapter 1).
11 Give details of the disciplinary rules which affect the employee. You may simply refer the employee to a document which is reasonably accessible (see Chapter 8—Discipline and grievance). This requirement does not specifically include health and safety rules; though, of course, the general requirement to obey the law and company rules on health and safety may be included (see Chapter 5—Health and safety).

Note: If a company employs fewer than 20 people, there is no

legal requirement to supply copies of disciplinary rules to employees who commenced on or after 26 February 1990 (EA 89).
12 Specify the person to whom the employee should apply in the event of dissatisfaction with any disciplinary matter concerning themselves and similarly to redress any grievance they may have. Your disciplinary and grievance procedures must be outlined in a document which is reasonably accessible (see Chapter 8—Discipline and grievance).
13 State whether a 'contracting out certificate' is in force for the employment referred to in the contract (see page 99, and page 240). Although not 'statutory', you should also include such items as: company sick pay, Statutory Sick Pay, rights during maternity leave, sickness and absence rules, records and administration, use of company property, pay in lieu of notice, and any matter which you consider important.

Note: You may not include any clause which prevents individual membership of a trade union (see Chapter 12—Industrial relations).

What form should 'Written Particulars' take?

There is sometimes confusion of terminology, when the law speaks of 'written particulars of employment' and 'contract of employment'. The terms are really synonymous. This is further complicated by the phrase 'terms and conditions of employment'. Companies often use differing terms to describe the same article. Also, there are different views of what constitutes a 'contract of employment' document *per se*.

What you call the agreement is not important and there is no particular required format. What is important is what is in it. However, the styles of agreement that follow have been tried and proven effective for many companies, large and small. These are suggestions only, it is for you to design your own contracts. We suggest four types; the first is in two parts which you may find more convenient to administer:

1 Written Particulars, consisting of:
   (a) Contract of employment;
   (b) Terms and Conditions of Employment.
2 (Special) contract of employment.
3 Collective agreement.
4 Apprenticeship agreement.

Written Particulars of Employment
This agreement must incorporate those items 1 to 13 listed above, but it is suggested that it would be better divided into two parts, i.e.:

- Contract of employment—that specifically agreed between employer and employee, which is peculiar to an individual employee (job title, department, start date, remuneration, company car, any special conditions, continuous employment, etc.)
- Terms and Conditions of Employment—those terms and conditions that apply to every employee (or a particular group of employees) within a company.

These written particulars are enforceable under the EP (C) Act 78 as amended by EA 80 and EA 82. Ensure that your contrcts include a reference to obeying the company's terms and conditions of employment as a part of the contract. (Examples of these agreements are given at Appendices C and D.) For small firms, pre-printed forms titled 'Employment Protection—Main Terms and Conditions', carbon impregnated, are available from many main high street stationery shops and will save on costs.

Special contract of employment

This agreement normally relates to senior or key jobs with conditions outside normal statutory requirements. A typical example of this would be a sensitive position where you specify special terms such as: a minimum contractual period of notice of three or six months or maybe one year, undertakings regarding secrecy of company information or not working for a competitor within x years of leaving the company.

But beware! This form of contract cannot supersede the statutory rights of the employee under employment legislation and is not enforceable through an industrial tribunal. Your only recourse would be via a civil court with no guarantee of satisfaction. For example, if the contract has a three months' notice period but the employee leaves after only one week's notice, you can sue for loss and/or salary in lieu of notice only in a civil court, with enforcement in reality subject to the financial status of the offending employee; yet the employee would be able to enforce the three months' notice period against you if you dismissed him or her. In other words a special contract of employment may give all the benefits to the employee but little or none to you. (An example of a special contract is given in Appendix E.) Pre-printed forms are not appropriate here.

Collective agreements

A collective agreement is an agreement between one or more trade unions (representing the employees) and an employer, group of employers or an employers' association. These are not generally legally binding agreements between the parties and contain a clause to that effect because they do not fulfil the conditions for an enforceable agreement (above). Each employee retains an individual relationship with the employer with rights under employment legislation.

Collective agreements will include those details listed under 'Written particulars of employment' (above), plus: sick-pay schemes, disputes procedures, working practices, time-off arrangements (e.g. for trade union duties), disclosure of information, and anything else included in the agreement.

Apprenticeship agreements

An apprenticeship agreement must be in writing and signed by all parties to it. Such signatories would normally be the employer, the apprentice and his or her parents or legal guardians where the apprentice is under 18 years of age. It is usually in the form of a deed. While possibly having limited enforceability this agreement does give status to the training, establishes a long-term relationship between employer and apprentice with two-way loyalties and exempts the apprentice from any involvement in official trade union disputes. (An example of an apprenticeship agreement is given in Appendix F.)

Statutory conditions of employment

The law provides important considerations to protect the interests of all employees. These are mostly provided for under the Employment Protection (Consolidation) Act 1978, as amended by the Employment Acts of 1980 and 1982. They govern qualifying status and time off (below), dismissal and notice periods (see Chapters 8—Discipline and grievance, 10—Retirement, 11—Dismissals, and 13—Industrial Tribunals).

Status

For the purposes of status, any employee who normally works 16 hours or more per week is entitled to the full benefits of the terms and conditions of employment, including notice periods. Similarly, any employee who has worked for 8 hours or more (but less than 16 hours) per week for one employer for not less than 5 years is afforded the same privileges as a full-time employee.

Time off

The law gives rights to employees for reasonable unpaid time off for public duties, including magistrates and members of boards of visitors for prisons, remand centres and young offenders' institutions. Jury service is, of course, a mandatory order by a court.

The law does not recognize 'temporary' or 'casual' employee

status (not to be confused with temporary workers through an agency), unless there is a fixed-term contract covering that employment. A temporary employee on a fixed-term contract of less than one month but extended to be continuously employed for three months or more, has the same rights in that employment as other employees. (Non-permanent employees are dealt with later in this chapter, but see also Chapter 1.)

Breach of contract

Breaches of contract by either employer or employees can, of course, be dealt with in the courts. However, the Secretary of State has indicated that an Order is likely to be made which will confer jurisdiction on industrial tribunals to deal with breaches of contract of employment, which arise or are outstanding on the termination of a claimant's employment. This order has yet to be made as at the time of printing.

3.3 Restrictions on conditions of a contract

There are restrictions which can inhibit or frustrate a contract of employment for either employer or employee.

Some may be necessary restrictions, e.g. prevention of infectious diseases in medical and catering establishments, what happens when an employee fails to qualify within a specified period required by law or a travelling salesperson loses a driving licence or leaves to work for a competitor within a certain number of years of leaving?

Some are unnecessary and unlawful restrictions placed on employees, e.g. must reside within a specified district or radius of the firm, or which preclude their statutory rights, e.g. trade union membership (see Chapter 12).

There are also restrictive practices on the part of employees which are unlawful and which frustrate contracts of employment.

It is a matter of what the law lays down and/or what you have agreed with the employee in the contract of employment.

Restrictions by the employer

You cannot incorporate a restrictive clause in a contract which:

- would restrict personal liberty under common law, e.g. stating that employees must not engage in certain activities—unless those directly affect the employee's ability to fulfil his or her contract or would adversely affect your business;
- would be regarded as 'unreasonable' in the circumstances;

- has not been agreed with the employee as part of the contract and/or terms and conditions of employment;
- precludes individual membership of any trade union or of a trade union of their choice (GCHQ, Cheltenham is an example of an unlawful restriction being imposed) (see Chapter 12).

Finally, you cannot dismiss someone simply because he or she refuses to sign a clause of a restrictive covenant.

You can incorporate a restrictive clause which:

- protects secrecy in design, development and processes of your product and/or services;
- protects your company from competitors' inquisitiveness;
- prevents exploitation and abuse or misuse of company property;
- prevents you or the employee from breaking the law, e.g. not driving without a valid licence or while disqualified;
- makes it clear that if an employee becomes unable to fulfil his or her contract of employment due to non-routine circumstances, e.g. the employee loses his or her driving licence after a drink-driving offence, the result will be either dismissal or transferral to another job subject to availability;
- prevents your employee from setting-up in competition with you within a given period of leaving and/or within a given radius of your premises.

Note: A salesperson, required to drive a company (or own) vehicle, who becomes disqualified from driving is regarded as frustrating his or her contract of employment. An exception to this may be that such a person is able (through insurance protection) to arrange the services of a chauffeur, and is thus *not* prevented from fulfilling his or her duties. This exception may not apply if your company does not agree to non-employees driving company vehicles.

Restrictive practices by the employee

Employees cannot impose restrictive practices in which:

- they refuse to work outside certain 'lines of demarcation', unless clearly agreed in a contract or by negotiation. The advice here is to have job descriptions drawn up and agreed (see Chapters 1 and 5).
- they refuse to obey health and safety rules, whether those laid down by statute or those in company policy.
- they would be carrying out secondary action or blacking, as in Chapter 12.

3.4 Maternity leave and returning to work

A female employee who becomes pregnant has the statutory right to take 'maternity leave' and to return to work after her confinement, subject to certain important conditions. The rules are different to those for Statutory Maternity Pay (SMP) and are listed below.

Entitlement qualifications

1 She must have been an employed person for the purpose of Class 1 NIC* (as for SMP—see Chapter 4).
2 She must have been continuously employed with the same employer for not less than:
   - 2 years, working for 16 or more hours per week
   - 5 years, working for 8 or more but less than 16 hours per week,

   up to and including the twelfth week* before the expected week of confinement (EWC), so commencing maternity leave in week 11 before the EWC—but see comment B in Example 3.1.

   This includes those on 'irregular' working patterns who are available for work though not actually working in every week, e.g. part-time or temporary workers, supply teachers, agency employees. If an 'irregular' employee is not available in any week, she does not qualify.
3 She must have given notice *in writing* of:
   (a) her anticipated absence;
   (b) her intention to return to work;
   (c) her EWC.
   (Verbal notice is not acceptable here.)
4 She must confirm her intention to return to work, within 14 days of receipt† of a letter from her employer asking for such confirmation. This letter must be sent *not less than* 49 days after her notified EWC.
5 She must implement her return to work no later than the twenty-ninth week after her EWC (regardless of the actual date the confinement took place).
6 She may extend her maternity leave by a maximum of four weeks beyond the twenty-ninth week, due to incapacity. However, this incapacity *must* be supported by a medical certificate, and she will be permitted only one postponement. Any postponement beyond the first will result in loss of entitlement.

* Unless 'fairly dismissed' prematurely because of pregnancy, in which case the weeks not worked count towards qualification.
† Advise that the letter is sent by recorded delivery for proof of delivery.

Thus, in Example 3.1 we graphically illustrate maternity leave and the right to return to work.

Example 3.1 Qualifying periods for maternity leave

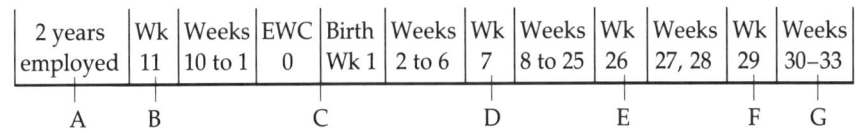

2 years employed	Wk 11	Weeks 10 to 1	EWC 0	Birth Wk 1	Weeks 2 to 6	Wk 7	Weeks 8 to 25	Wk 26	Weeks 27, 28	Wk 29	Weeks 30–33
A	B		C			D		E		F	G

Key: A She must have been continuously employed for a *minimum* of two years *before* the eleventh week before the EWC.
B Earliest week in which she can commence maternity leave (there is no 'latest' date but delays will reduce SMP entitlement if she starts later than the sixth week before the EWC).
C EWC and actual week of birth may (or may not) be the same. Begin to count 29 weeks from the EWC (or the week of birth *if earlier* than the EWC, but not if later than the EWC).
D Employer may write in, or after, week seven for confirmation of her intention to return to work.
E The latest week by which she must exercise her right to return to work by giving *written* notice.
F Latest week by which she must return or be offered her job.
G Maximum extension of maternity leave due to incapacity with medical evidence. Maximum *one* extension only.

Note: Special rules apply for business employing fewer than five people (see Note 3 below.)

Your obligations

There are a number of obligations placed upon you as the employer:

1 You must permit her to return to the job which she was doing prior to departing on maternity leave on the same terms and conditions and at the same rate of pay, unless it can be proven to be impracticable or the job is genuinely redundant (but see Note 3 below).
2 You must make her employment available to her within three weeks of her giving written notice or reply confirming her return to work, in any case by not later than the twenty-ninth week after the EWC (not necessarily the week of birth).
3 If it is impracticable (see Note 3 below) to offer her original job to her again or it is genuinely redundant, then you must offer her a job similar in status, terms and conditions and earnings.

If you fail to fulfil these conditions the employee will have the right to pursue a claim for unfair dismissal and/or sex discrimination at an industrial tribunal.

Notes:

1 You cannot declare a woman on maternity leave 'redundant' simply as a means of preventing her return to work as this will render you liable to a claim for 'unfair dismissal'.

2 You cannot refuse to take her back because you took a dislike to her nor because she is now a mother and may need time off to care for her child's needs. This could lead to a claim of 'sex discrimination'.

3 In the case of a company employing five or fewer people (including associated companies and the pregnant woman herself) she does not have the right to return to work if it is impracticable either for her to return to her original job or to another job of similar status (see also item 3 above). It is for you the employer to prove such impracticality, and any unfair refusal to allow her to return to her original job can lead to a claim for unfair dismissal.

We trust that the foregoing summary of maternity leave and the right to return will prove a useful guide. You should refer to official DSS literature for necessary detail and up-to-date factors such as entitlement and time scales, although these do not change frequently.

3.5 Non-permanent staff

For a diversity of reasons, companies often find it more convenient to take on non-permanent employees. Temporary assistance in its various forms can be quite advantageous. You may not have the volume of work to justify a permanent placement, your cash-flow situation may not permit permanence, conditions may be more amenable to both hirer and the hired, or you may need specialist help and advice in a particular circumstance in the short term. Also, training establishments may offer you certain benefits in taking their employees or students for a period of time. We shall outline here the 'pros' and 'cons' of taking on non-permanent staff.

First of all to dispel a myth—that companies are not responsible for those whose services they employ on temporary arrangements. Under regulations issued under ss.2 and 3 of the Health and Safety at Work Act 1974, you are responsible for the health, safety and welfare of non-employees and non-permanent employees. Under common law you are responsible for those whom you employ, permanent or non-permanent, and for their actions. Thus, you are responsible for the following:

- The legality of what the person whom you engage does if it is done knowingly to you, including tax evasion, claiming state benefits to which he or she is not entitled, and drug and solvent abuse (1990 Regulation). While individuals are accountable for their own acts and omissions, those who engage them have a liability for aiding and abetting.
- Health and safety: there is a responsibility upon you for their health, safety and welfare and for what they do which affects the health, safety and welfare of others (employees and non-employees).
- Employers' liability insurance, which is required for non-permanent workers as for other staff, except for self-employed who would be covered by your public liability insurance.

Temporary fixed-term contract

A person may be engaged on a temporary fixed-term contract of any duration. The contract will stipulate a starting date and either a period of time, e.g. six months, or a specified finishing date. In this case, notice of termination is not necessary.

However, if you do not intend to extend the contract beyond its final date you should make sure that it is clear to the incumbent person that this is so. If the temporary employee is allowed or encouraged to continue to work beyond the final date of the contract, the contract may become an indefinite contract by implication. If the contract further extends beyond the qualifying service period for protection under employment law (two complete years as at 1991/92), the incumbent could lodge a claim for unfair dismissal at an industrial tribunal if he or she later felt aggrieved at his or her dismissal.

Thus, if you intend to permit the extension of the fixed-term contract you should confirm this in writing, revising the final date, and specify any notice period which may become appropriate.

Beware of using a succession of short fixed-term contracts as a means of avoiding giving permanent employment to someone. If you retain a person for a continuous period of two years or more under successive short fixed-term contracts and then dismiss that person, he or she may claim unfair dismissal. An industrial tribunal would not look favourably on this and may regard the incumbent as permanent.

Temporary open-ended contracts

This type of contract is very useful for 'supply' workers who provide a valuable temporary 'on tap' source of labour such as supply teachers, temporary clerks and secretaries, market research and sales demonstrators. They undertake to make themselves available for work and the employer calls upon their services as and when required, paying them only for hours or weeks actually worked. PAYE and NIC are deductable from earnings subject to normal conditions.

These workers, once employed for extended continuous periods of time, may become entitled to protection from unfair dismissal (not redundancy) and may qualify for SSP and SMP (see relevant sections of Chapter 4—Payments and deductions).

Agency workers

Agency workers are employed by the agency for whom they work, normally a registered 'employment business' licensed by the Employment Department, as distinct from an employment agency which finds workers for employers.

- *To the agency itself*: the principles apply as for 'temporary open-ended contracts', above, with the same advice given.
- *To a client of the agency*: you have no obligation towards the workers other than to ensure their health, safety and welfare, and to fulfil agreements. You pay the agency for their services (which may be subject to VAT). The agency is responsible for all payments to employees, including Statutory Sick Pay and Maternity Pay, and for deductions/payments of PAYE and NIC. Should you offer a job to the agency worker you may pay a financial penalty, but of course you have saved the costs of advertising and interviewing (see Chapter 2—Recruiting).

Youth Training (YT)

Youth Training (YT) can be a valuable form of training for young people between the ages of 16 and 18 years and is a means of assistance with some of the costs of training for the employer. The scheme has previously been known as Youth Training Scheme, Training for Skills, and YTS. It succeeded the Youth Opportunities Programme of the early 1980s.

Many companies employ their own YT trainees and 'top up'*

---

* Where top-up payments are made, these will be subject to PAYE and NIC deductions, depending upon age and whether Minimum Earnings Levels (MELs) are reached (see relevant section of Chapter 4—Payments and deductions).

their training allowance (see below) to wage or salary levels, but the majority of YT trainees are employed by managing agents who act on behalf of Training and Enterprise Councils (TECs) (formerly Training Agency)* (Local Enterprise Companies (LECs) in Scotland) set up by the Training, Enterprise and Education Directorate (TEED).

The objectives of YT are: to provide training opportunities in relevant skills for young people and to train for recognized qualifications to the equivalent of 'level II' of the national vocational qualification (NVQ), within a flexible framework, to meet individual and local needs.

From the age of 16 years, trainees normally undertake a two-year term of education, off-the-job training and placements for specified periods of time in sponsoring companies to undergo on-the-job training and work experience. Those trainees leaving school at 17 years undergo a one-year programme of similar design.

Many firms who sponsor trainees employ them permanently, post-training.

It is not a general practice for trainees to spend their entire training period in one company (except those of 'employed' status), though this may occur. There has to be a clear training element in the employment with the sponsor and YT trainees should not be regarded as a source of 'cheap labour'.

Should you take on such a trainee, you would be required to pay a weekly sum to the managing agent for their services. You are not required to pay the trainee (unless of 'employed' status), though you may like to contribute to certain expenses. The agent (or employer) pays the trainee a 'training allowance' which is reviewed annually; they are a first-year allowance (£29.50 in 1991/92) and a second-year allowance (£35.00 in 1991/92) payable from the start of the second year or the trainee's seventeenth birthday if earlier. The same allowances are paid for three months and nine months respectively for one-year trainees who start later after an extra year at school or sixth form college. You may top up the training allowance if you wish.

Note: Payments (including for overtime) which exceed £15.00 per week are regarded by the IR as outside the terms of YT, should be under a separate contract of employment and are taxable under Schedule E.

Although trainees placed by a managing agent are not your employees but sponsored only, you nevertheless have a clear

---

* The role of the Training Agency has been assumed by the recently established TECs (or LECs) who are largely sponsored by donations from participating companies in industry and commerce.

responsibility for their health, safety and welfare under s.2 of the Health and Safety at Work, etc., Act 1974 and in recent regulations under the Act (see Chapter 5—Health and safety).

Training credits

A pilot scheme commenced in April 1991 in which approximately 45,000 YT trainees have been given training credits which they carry with them to a prospective training provider or sponsor company. These training credits have a monetary value to a provider or sponsor and the trainees 'purchase' their training with them. (see Chapter 6—Training and development)

Employment Training (ET)

Employment Training (ET) is a little similar to YT. It is described as a 'unified training scheme' of 12 months' duration for older people who have been unemployed for:

- not less than 6 months (but less than 12 months) if aged 18 to 24 years; or
- not less than 2 years if aged between 18 and 50 years.

By implication, those aged between 18 and 24 years but who have been unemployed for between 1 and 2 years or those who are over 50 years of age are precluded.

Entry into ET is normally via a Jobcentre or 'Restart' interview.

There are three processes in ET.

1 The trainee is first referred to a training agent (TA) who assesses each individual's aptitudes and draws up an individual training plan.
2 The TA then refers the trainee to a training manager (TM) who arranges the training programme.
3 The trainee spends one to two days per week in the TM's training centre for practical instruction and education, plus four or three days per week in a sponsoring employer's premises (as in YT).

Note: The TA and TM are invariably the same organization. Some larger employers are themselves accredited as TAs and/or TMs.

The trainee receives a fixed allowance (£10.00 in 1991/92) above the normal social security benefit entitlements and employers are not permitted to top up the allowance as with YT; to do so would create problems with the DSS as trainees are in receipt of 'benefits'. Also, ET trainees receive up to £4 per week for travelling expenses and for lone parents there is assistance towards the costs of child care. The TA and TM are paid fees by TECs (or LECs in Scotland) for their services.

The sponsoring employer pays a fee (not a wage or salary) to the TA, plus VAT. The conditions for ET are slightly different to YT in that whereas YT does not commit the sponsor to employ the trainee and may often be programmed to work with different sponsors for variety in their experience, with ET the trainee would hope to remain with one sponsor with the expectation of being offered permanent employment on completion of the training.

The skills range in ET is much narrower than in YT and is trainee-led. You may need to assess carefully what skills are taught, to what level and whether they are pertinent to your needs as a company.

Self-employed

A useful and valuable source of input to an organization is by the employment of people who are genuinely 'self-employed'. There are frequent situations where a need for specialist knowledge and skill is required but is not available within the company and to recruit a full-time permanent employee for the purpose would be unaffordable or unjustified. Even a part-time employee may not be a suitable solution.

The self-employed person may provide anything from accounts work or secretarial services, through marketing or production engineering to employment law, training or health and safety specialisms or sub-contracting services to someone in the building trade.

In this situation, a person contracts to work for you for a fixed or indefinate period of time (full time or part time, on your premises or in their own) and is paid a 'fee'. Such a person is responsible for declaring his or her own earnings for tax/NIC/VAT purposes and for preparing annual accounts for Inland Revenue.

There are three categories of self-employed:

1 The genuine 'freelancers' who offer their services in a particular specialism. They will undertake work for several companies either concurrently or consecutively, dividing their time between each client.

   They will be registered as self-employed with the Inland Revenue for income tax and Class 4 NIC and with DSS for flat-rate class 2 NIC payments. If you utilize the services of a self-employed person, you should maintain details of names, addresses, amounts and dates paid, etc., and ensure that a Schedule D tax reference number is in existence. Do they have an accountant whom you can contact? Their accountant or local tax inspector can verify a reference number.

2 The person who is self-employed but who works permanently as a contract worker for one particular employer. The advantages of this person are:
   (a) you have no permanent contract and can thus terminate the person's contract at any time with only civil contract laws applying;
   (b) you do not pay the employer's portion of NIC. The situation is exactly as for item 1 above.
3 The 'casual' worker. They may genuinely be in categories 1 and 2 above and can provide evidence of who and what they are. But they may be the typical 'I can tarmac your driveway for you, cash, no questions asked, know what I mean guv.' type of person. These are the many who constitute the 'black economy', who try to evade income tax, NIC and VAT and have no letterheads, invoices, receipts and perhaps not even a business card.

   Not only do these people break the law, but they put an added burden on those in the workforce who do pay their share of taxes. The employer also risks prosecution for fraud (or aiding and abetting) and will always be responsible for any unpaid tax when an audit inspector highlights the error.

Notes:
1 There is no statutory definition of self-employed.
2 The courts have found that there is no hard and fast rule for determining whether someone is employed or self-employed and each case must be decided on its facts.
3 The IR and DSS look for certain criteria to determine whether someone is self-employed, i.e.:
   (a) Are they able to determine their own hours?
   (b) Are they expected to provide their own tools?
   (c) What type of work will they do, i.e. a particular contract for particular work and not just any work?
4 To satisfy yourself, you should refer to IR booklets: IR.56—*Employed or Self-employed?*, and IR.53—*Thinking of Taking Someone On*?
5 Your local tax and DSS offices will be pleased to give a decision on employment status either to the person being engaged or to the employer engaging him or her.

Consultants

There are times when a company needs the expertise of a professional in particular fields, probably similar to that described above. They may be in the category 1 of self-employed or part of a larger company.

The consultant will come in, do a highly skilled job for you and leave you with a resolved situation, a new system or some staff trained to better skill levels. He or she may also be able to take a 'detached' view of, and provide valuable insights into, your organization which you—being *in* it—cannot see, often 'not seeing the wood for the trees'. Also, you may know the problem but may not be able to provide the solution. The differences here are cost and credibility.

- *Cost*: consultants can be expensive, but they can do an excellent job for you in a sphere in which you have neither the time nor the expertise to devote to it. They may also reap high dividends in benefits to your company.

    Fees vary widely between consultants, depending on 'image' and overheads. The small consultancy has fewer overheads than the larger one, the freelance consultant perhaps fewer still, and can thus set lower fees for smaller client firms.
- *Credibility*: don't be fooled; it is not always the large consultancy which is necessarily the best. A small firm of consultants, perhaps even the freelance consultant who is a self-employed 'one man band', can provide you with excellent services at very reasonable cost. Also, because they are themselves a 'small business', and suffer the same pressures as other small businesses, they are often able to appreciate and understand firms' problems.

    On the other hand, some areas of need may require an organization with the flexibility and size to supply a series of skilled consultants to tackle your particular problem. But beware cost.

    Perhaps a government initiative, e.g. Business Growth Training (BGT) might provide a helpful subsidy—contact your local Training and Enterprise Council (TEC). As with all walks of life, the advice is 'shop around' and evaluate who will be cost effective and value for money.

3.6 Data protection

Various laws lay down certain requirements to protect individuals and this is so with the Data Protection Act (DP Act) 1984, which regulates the use of 'personal data' in electronic information storage and retrieval systems. The two types of system are computers and word processors.

If you do not have an electronic system on which personal data are maintained but keep records in files, books or registers in paper form, then the DP Act does not *apply to you.*

Your responsibilities

You must register your business with the Data Protection Registrar. If you fail to register when you clearly are retaining personal information within an electronic system, you or your company may be subject to severe financial penalties.

If the data kept are for your own business purposes only and will not be used or supplied to any other person, then you need not register, although parts of the DP Act could still apply to you, e.g. supplying information on data held.

You also do not have to register if the only information that you maintain in electronic form is names, addresses and business types, e.g. for a mailing list.

The principles of data protection

There are a number of principals that data users must observe in accordance with the DP Act:

1 Personal data (data) must be obtained and processed fairly and lawfully and shall be for specified and lawful purposes.
2 Data shall not be used or disclosed in any manner incompatible with the purpose of their retention. (The Court of Appeal ruled on 24 October 1989 that disclosure of pay details under a legal enactment or rule of law is not in breach of the DP Act.)
3 Data shall be adequate, relevant, accurate, up-to-date and not excessive in relation to the purpose of their retention.
4 Once data are no longer relevant to their intended purposes they shall not be kept.
5 Appropriate measures must be taken against unauthorized disclosure of data.

Failure in any of the above respects may result in the refusal by the Registrar to grant registration, or the issue of an enforcement or prohibition notice, or a deregistration notice.

Individual rights

An individual is entitled to the following:

1 To be informed if you maintain any personal data about him or her in an electronic system.
2 To be supplied with a full copy of all personal data so held.
3 To be given, where the data is coded or in terms which require explanation, an explanation of those codes and terms.

Refusal

There are certain conditions which if not fulfilled are grounds for refusing to release the data. They are:

- A request for a copy of data held by you must be in writing, though you may agree to give it upon verbal request.
- You may insist on a fee within the maximum allowed (£10 in 1992).
- You may require satisfactory evidence of the identity of the person requesting the information.
- You may refuse to give the data if to do so would breach confidentiality of another person also named in the data, unless permission of that person is obtained.
- You feel that, having regard to the nature and purpose of the personal data held, the requests are too frequent.

If you are satisfied by the above conditions; you must provide the data within 40 days of the request being made.

To summarize and apply to your situation, if you maintain any personal data concerning your employees you must furnish them with that information should they request it in writing, within the conditions set out above. We suggest that charging a fee for the data may not be good for employee relations, though that is a matter for you to decide.

That concludes our discourse on the legal aspects of *employing* people. Remember that laws and regulations constantly change, you should refer to the sources mentioned (guides, leaflets, and/or the IR, DSS and Employment Department themselves) if you need more detailed guidance. The FSB will, of course, always be willing to advise the self-employed and small businesses.

Before we move to the financial aspects of employing people, here is a health checklist to help you assess what action or reading you need to do to come through this part of our 'minefield' unscathed.

Health checklist — employing

1 Have you complied with all legal obligations appropriate to you?
    Registered with HSE (or local authority EHO) (see Chapter 5)?
    'Health and Safety Law—What you should know' poster displayed (see Chapter 5)?
    Registered with IR and DSS for PAYE/NIC (see Chapter 4)?
    Employer's and public liability insurances both current (see Chapter 5)?
    Fire regulations complied with or fire certificate (see Chapter 5)?
    Health and safety policy written (see Chapter 5)?
2 Have you issued contracts/terms and conditions of employment?
    Do they conform to all the requirements of the law?
    Have you made sure there are no unreasonable restrictions?
3 Do you understand the maternity leave and right to return scheme?
    Have you acquired the DSS forms and literature (in case!)?
    Have you a maternity leave policy (in case!)? If employing five or fewer, contact DSS if right to return requested.
4 Have you considered non-permanent employees/staff?
    Temporary fixed-term or open-ended contracts?
    Agency workers ('temps')? YT or ET trainees?
    Self-employed contract workers or consultant?
5 If you have self-employed staff, are they legal?
6 Are your employees free to exercise their trades union rights?
7 Do you store personal data electronically other than mailing lists?
    If so, have you registered with the Data Protection Registrar?

4 Payments and deductions

Having successfuly recruited your employee and got all the legal aspects right, there now come the rather complex aspects of actual payment to your employee, what deductions you must or can make and all the documentation and forms which impose upon an employer immediately you take on just one employee. To complicate things further, other payments like Statutory Sick Pay (SSP) when an employee is sick or Statutory Maternity Pay (SMP) when a female employee leaves to have a baby, are statutory requirements.

A mistake in those aspects outlined in Chapter 3—Employing, innocently or honestly made, is easily remedied. But errors in payments or deductions can prove immediately embarrassing and in the longer term costly in legal repercussions. So it is important to get things right.

We shall take you systematically through the procedures, with 'signposts' along the way to point you towards those all-important documents, forms, literature and sources of help.

The dilemma involved in writing a general guide on matters like pay and deductions is that too much detail will totally confuse the layman or novice, while a concise gloss will disappoint those readers who look for something deeper. We hope to give sufficient detail to achieve a happy balance acceptable to all who study this chapter.

4.1 Payment for working

Whether you call the sum of money you pay someone for doing a job of work a 'wage' or a 'salary' is immaterial and academic so far as the law is concerned, the only concern here is 'earnings'. Normally, a 'wage' is variable, while a 'salary' is fixed. It is really a matter of status as the employee or the employer sees it, often, the gross wages for one person can total more than the salary for another, or vice versa.

Those already employing people will probably have settled on 'what to call it'. However, for those embarking upon becoming an employer for the first time, there are two useful categories (though not hard-and-fast rules) into which wages and salaries generally fall and which may be helpful to you in deciding what to call that payment made to your employee each week or month:

Status

Generally, a 'wage' is normally paid at the end of each week to someone in an hourly- or weekly-paid manual occupation such as shopfloor machine operator, driver or labourer. Sometimes it is paid a 'week in hand', i.e. earned in, say, the week ending 27 March 1993 but paid in the week ending 3 April 1993.

A 'salary' is paid to someone in a clerical, sales, managerial, or secretarial occupation, it is normally paid monthly in arrears (though some clerical staff are paid weekly) with no salary held 'in hand'.

There are instances where shopfloor employees are paid a salary, jealously guarding their 'staff' status and this is becoming the 'norm' in situations where harmonization of terms and conditions is agreed in new or developing situations. This can extend into 'annual hours contracts' where employer and workers agree an inclusive annual number of basic working hours, contractual overtime hours (paid whether worked or not), holidays, etc., reflected in a fixed annual salary (divided by 12 for monthly payment)—a popular trend in manufacturing operations with continuous-flow production where flexibility and commitment are important.

Occupation

If an occupation is directly concerned with production (hence the term 'direct wages'), a basic wage is calculated by the hour or minute and paid only for the hours and minutes actually worked (though note the exception of the annual-hours contract); there may also be a production or efficiency bonus paid, related to volume and/or quality of output. In your cash-flow and break-even analyses, you would have listed these under 'direct and variable costs'.

If an occupation is *not* directly related to production, normally a weekly or monthly salary is paid. Salaries are usually fixed, do not vary according to hours and minutes worked, and are usually with unpaid overtime (though in some lower-level situations, overtime beyond contractual hours may be paid). Commissions, incentive schemes, or bonuses (e.g. in sales functions) may be paid in addition.

In your cash-flow forecast and break-even analysis, you would have listed salaries under 'indirect and fixed costs' (except for commissions and/or bonuses to salaried people which would be added to variable costs). But do bear in mind the exception quoted above, in which the new 'norm' of shopfloor salaried staff status is, of course, also 'direct/variable costs'.

Note: You will note the potentially confusing 'either/and/or' situations with the options quoted above, but that is the reality in business today, with no hard-and-fast rules. These are just guides and examples; you will need to determine *your* situation and decide your ground rules, and you will need to be clear about what are *your* direct and indirect labour costs (for costing and pricing purposes).

Having decided how much you are going to pay your employee, for what work, by what method, and in what category, there then comes the weight of obligations upon you in the making of that payment. The Wages Act 1986 calls all earnings 'wages' and categorizes what is/is not 'wages':

- *Wages include*: payments for work actually *done*, i.e. any fee, bonus, commission, holiday pay, or emoluments pertaining to the employment; also SSP, SMP, guarantee pay, and those benefits in kind which can be exchanged for money, goods or services.
- *Wages do not include*: payments for non-worked items, e.g. lawful loans (such as car purchase) or advances of pay, expenses, retirement gratuities, pension fund contributions, payments in lieu of notice, redundancy pay, golden handshakes, or benefits which *cannot* be exchanged for goods.

Note: Pay in lieu of notice is a 'lump sum payment' and if entitlement is *in* the contract of employment, is taxable; but if *not* in the contract of employment, is *not* taxable.

Though employment law refers to 'wages and salary', the laws on PAYE and NIC make no distinction whatever between them nor are they concerned with how those payments are made up (except for enquiring into certain allowances, payment in 'kind' and extra non-regular payments), but call them all 'earnings' or 'pay'. Another term used by Inland Revenue (IR) and Department of Social Security (DSS) to denote pay and perks for tax and NIC purposes, is 'emoluments'. We shall not refer to 'wages, salary or emoluments', but to earnings or pay. We now commence a step-by-step brief on all requirements.

How will you pay your employees?

The old Truck Acts of 1831–1940, whereby employees could demand payment in 'the current coin of the realm' (i.e. cash) were repealed on 1 January 1987. Thus an employer is now entitled to pay wages/salary in whatever way he or she determines. Many employees are now paid by credit transfer or cheque.

However, firms which have employees who have been paid in 'cash' since prior to 1 January 1987 and now wish to change to cashless payment should check the contracts of employment; to insist on such change without prior agreement could lead to a claim for breach of contract.

Itemized pay statement

Every full-time employee (and part-time employee working at least 16 hours or more per week) is entitled to an itemized pay statement which should be issued prior to or at the time of a payment. It must be in writing (a verbal explanation of the amount in the cheque/pay envelope is not acceptable) and must contain the following information:

1 The gross amount of earnings.
2 The amount of any variable deductions, stating the purposes of each deduction (i.e. PAYE, NIC, pension).
3 The amount of fixed deductions, stating the purposes of each deduction, e.g. car lease; attachment of earnings; payments of purchase of safety footwear, overalls, tools or equipment; social club subscriptions or union dues; savings, insurance premiums or company sick-pay scheme.
4 The net amount of earnings.
5 The method of payment of net earnings, *if* the payment is by combined different methods (e.g. part bank-credit, part cash).

Notes:
1 The requirement for an itemized pay statement is separate and distinct from the details required in the contract/terms and conditions of employment (covered in Chapter 3).
2 Itemized pay statements are not required for self-employed persons with no contract of employment; part-time employees who work for *less* than 16 but more than 8 hours per week are entitled to itemized pay statements *if* they have worked for you for 5 years or more.
3 An employee who works 16 hours or more per week is regarded in law as full time with equal rights as for other full-time employees (as, for protection purposes, are those who have worked 8 hours or more per week for a continuous period of 5 years or more).
4 Although 'statutory', PAYE and NIC deductions must appear on the itemized pay statement.
5 You can 'top up' or take away small sums to round up or down to the nearest £1.00 or 50p, adjusting in a later pay statement.

Pay periods   There is no regulation of pay periods or intervals. You may pay your workers hourly, daily, weekly, fortnightly, four-weekly, monthly, quarterly or annually; the choice and decision is yours and for agreement with each employee.

Pay day Again, there is no regulated 'pay day'; but normally, hourly- and/or weekly-paid workers are paid on Thursday or Friday (often holding one 'week in hand'); while most monthly/annually-salaried workers, including shopfloor, are paid within the last three working days of each calendar month (some are paid mid-month). Where banker's orders, Giros, or credit transfer are used as a method of payment, you will need to arrange that sufficient time is given to the bank (three to five clear working days) to ensure that payment is received at your employee's bank account by the chosen pay day.

It is worth remembering that there are legal penalties for failing to provide a pay slip or for making illegal deductions.

Action on taking on new employees

First new employee When you first receive your new employee, *ask* the Inland Revenue (IR) (local tax office) for a 'PAYE System', as it will not automatically turn up on its own. If you do *not* contact the IR, it is unlikely that anyone will advise you of any anomalies in the first year, and thus errors could be made (see PAYE in the next section) which could leave you with tax and NIC debts, plus possible penalties.

All new employees You have engaged your new employee, decided whether a 'week in hand' is appropriate and have arrived at a 'pay day'. To calculate whether PAYE and NIC is appropriate, you need to know the taxation circumstances of your new employee. On engagement, he or she would normally have a 'P.45' (Leaving Certificate) from the last employer (or from the Department of Employment if unemployed), which should be handed to you. If a P.45 is *not* supplied, it is essential that you follow the P.46 procedure at Table 'B' in the IR *Employers Guide to PAYE*, or in the Instruction Card (Form P.8) which is an extract of that guide, i.e. complete and get the employee to sign either:

- a Starting Certificate (Form P.46), stating that *you* are the only or main employer; and a Tax Code Claim (Form P.15); or
- a Student's Declaration (Form P.38), stating that he or she is *still* attending college or university. (This will *not* apply to a person employed on a long-term full-time basis.)

If a person employed on a temporary or part-time basis is unable to give you a P.45 and *refuses* to sign a P.46 (or P.38, if a student), it is likely that he or she has some complication in personal tax affairs. In such circumstances, the law is quite clear: *all* earnings *must* be taxed at the basic rate (25 per cent in 1992/93)* until alternative instructions are received from your local inspector of taxes.

* 20% on first £2 000 taxable income (1992/93).

Disability Working Allowance (DWA)
One problem which discourages disabled persons from taking up employment is the loss of benefits which would leave them financially worse off. From April 1992, disabled persons on Invalidity Benefit (IVB) and Severe Disablement Allowance (SDA) will be able to work and, upon losing IVB or SDA, be paid a DWA if they work 16 hours or more per week. DWA will be income related in similar manner to Family Credit, but will be more generous.

Disability Living Allowance (DLA)
Also from April 1992 under the same regulations, there will be a DLA for those disabled and not able to work, payable under the same regulations.

Help
A DSS leaflet on DWA SDA and DLA is available by telephoning (free) 0800 100 123.

4.2 Deductions from gross pay

The only *absolute* rights which an employer has to make deductions from pay are for PAYE and NIC. The only exceptions to these are: if the deduction is a 'relevant provision' of the contract and/or terms and conditions of employment; or, the employee has previously given written consent. These rules apply equally to employees with a contract of service and to those with an apprenticeship agreement. The following notes will be helpful:

1 You need not detail each item of fixed deductions: *if* one sum is shown at the total of all deductions previously notified or agreed, *and* you have previously issued a detailed standing statement which contains details of these fixed deductions, i.e. the amounts, intervals, and purposes of each deduction.
2 A 'standing statement' of deductions is valid for a maximum of one year, after which it must be renewed and reissued. If you use these 'standing orders', you must annually: *check* with the employee for his or her agreement to any voluntary deductions; notify of your fixed deductions; and reissue the statement *in writing*.
3 You cannot make any deductions retrospectively, i.e. back-dated.
4 You must *not* make any deductions from pay which are not permitted by law. Thus (to quote one or two real-life examples) you must not: 'sell' your personal property to your employee and, verbally or otherwise, agree to deduct the price from his or her pay each week; nor must you deduct from pay the price of the

office 'sweep'. Even with the employee's full agreement, you are breaking the law.

You are, however, permitted to make the following deductions from pay:

1 Deductions for PAYE, NIC, or over-payment of SSP, SMP, where payment and/or refund to IR is required.
2 Recovery of over-payment of wages or expenses in relation to the employment (or those dishonestly obtained). But beware—if you make mistakes of fact or misinterpretation of legislation, a clerical error or 'received in good faith' mistake, you may *not* be able to recover these amounts, especially if the employee has left. The courts may not enforce such recovery in these situations.
3 Deductions as a result of disciplinary proceedings *under statute* (which does not include normal company disciplinary codes).
4 Where the employee has given written consent to trade union subscriptions (not those to a political fund where the employee has certified that he is exempt, which would be unlawful), pension fund subscriptions, payment into a savings account, or donations.
5 Deductions where an employee has taken part in strike action.
6 Deductions demanded by a Court Order, an Attachment of Earnings Order concerning unpaid fines, Matrimonial Order or community charge payment.

Note: These exceptions are only for the purpose of the Wages Act 1986. Under common law, *no* deduction can legally be made unless provision was made *in* the contract of employment. So there could be a conflict of law against law here, in which case the common law rule would apply, i.e. with the exception of PAYE and NIC, there should (strictly speaking) be an authority written into the contract of employment even for the deduction of fines, Attachment of Earnings under a Court Order or cases of over-payment of wages; though this is unlikely to cause problems for employers as the majority of affected employees raise no objections.

Deduction from Earnings Orders (DEOs)

In October 1990, the Government published its proposals on the welfare and maintenance of children in its two-volume discussion document *Children Come First*, out of which came the Child Support Act (CS Act) 1991 on 25 July 1991.

Two 1992 Child Support Regulations under the CS Act will establish the Child Support Agency (CSA) within the DSS from 1 April 1993, to act on behalf of the Secretary of State with powers quite separate from the courts. The tasks of the CSA will include tracing absent parents (see Inspectors below) and the issue and enforcement of Deduction from Earnings Orders (DEOs) ordering fixed deductions from pay specifically for the maintenance of children.

Regulations governing DEOs and related matters will take effect from April 1993. DEOs will be quite separate from any order which may be issued for spousal maintenance by a court, though further regulations may permit those Orders to be added to DEOs and thus relieve the courts of this responsibility.

Whereas Attachment of Earnings Orders are currently issued by a court for, e.g., spousal maintenance or payment of fines or local government tax (Community Charge), the CSA itself will have powers to issue DEOs. It is intended that these Orders will take priority over other Orders, with a priority system established to ensure that maintenance payments for children receive precedence over other matters, e.g. unpaid fines.

The possible priority may be:

- Priority 1—DEO for child maintenance issued by DSS.
- Priority 2—AEO for spousal maintenance issued by a court.
- Priority 3—AEO for payment of fines.

Attachable earnings As with PAYE and NIC, there will need to be a definition of what are 'attachable earnings' for the purposes of DEOs. There are differences in definitions, e.g. between Scotland and England and Wales; some of these differences affect superannuation; others payments to HM Forces, etc.

Protected earnings When a DEO is in force, there will be a level of protected earnings which cannot be affected by that DEO or other AEOs (but see Fees below). In cases where this would result in total or partial non-collection of the amount under the DEO, the oustanding balance would be carried forward to a date when the employee is in a position to afford the payments. Page 130 of the Regulations contains helpful tables of deductions, including attachable and protected income.

Multiplicity of Orders What happens when an employee has a string of orders for child maintenance, spousal maintenance, unpaid fines, etc? When protected earnings are taken into account, there will inevitably be some casualties among multiple Orders, but it is expected that (in keeping with the 'children come first' philosophy) DEOs for child maintenance take priority and should not become a casualty.

'Blocking' Orders A Community Charge Attachment of Earnings Order (CC-AEO), or Council Tax AEO (CT-AEO) from April 1993, has the status of a 'blocking' Order and may block payment of any later 'priority' Order (including DEOs) which may come into force *after* the issue of the CC-AEO (or CT-AEO in 1993). Thus, if a DEO for child maintenance is issued before a CC-AEO, it takes priority over all Orders, but if that DEO is issued after the CC-AEO, it has to wait until the priority CC-AEO has been fully paid before assuming priority. Thus, there are two possible scenarios ('R' indicating routine Orders in date order of receipt, and 'P' indicating priority Orders in date order of receipt), viz:

- *Scenario 1*: CC-AEO comes in after some routine AEOs (R.1, R.2 and R.3) but *before* two later priority DEOs for child maintenance (P.1 and P.2) are received:
  Priority Order: R.1, R.2, R.3, *CC-AEO* (blocking), P.1, P.2.
- *Scenario 2*: CC–AEO comes in after some routine AEOs (R.1, R.2 and R.3) but also *after* two priority DEOs for child maintenance (P.1, and P.2) are received:
  Priority Order: P.1, P.2, R.1, R.3, CC–AEO.

Employer information In some instances, the DSS may rely on employers for information about employees in order to issue and enforce DEOs. In such cases, employers' interests and employee relations situations will be given due consideration.

Inspectors The DSS will appoint inspectors, similar to those for state benefits, with powers to enter premises and question any person over the age of 18 years on those premises whom they think can assist them in either tracing an absent parent or obtaining necessary information about that absent parent's pay arrangements. It is stressed that inspectors will only exercise their powers in a last resort where other means of tracing persons or obtaining information have failed.

Appeals Employees against whom DEOs are issued will be able to appeal against those DEOs, but deductions from earnings *must* continue until after the appeal is heard.

Fees Employers are empowered to charge a fee of up to £1 for each Order from the pay of an employee against whom DEOs (or any other AEOs or CC-AEO) is issued. This can be taken from the 'protected' portion of the employee's income if need be. This is not in proportion to the actual costs of deduction, which can amount to between £10 and £15 per deduction, but current legislation restricts the fee to £1 per Order.

Practicalities Where it is proven to be impracticable for an employer to deduct regular, fixed amounts under a DEO from an employee's pay, arrangements can be made with the DSS for the employee himself or herself to pay by paying-in book. Such instances would include employees on irregular pay periods, short-term casual employees, seasonal workers, self-employed, supply teachers or agency workers.

Action Action on a DEO is required to be taken by an employer within seven days of its receipt. 'Action' in this context means taking action to ensure deductions, not actual deduction within seven days (which would be impossible with, e.g. monthly-paid employees).

Top-up Where an employee is on very high earnings, the DSS may apply to a court for a top-up in proportion to those higher earnings, in addition to standard child maintenance.

Additions Regulations will empower the DSS to add to a DEO such items as school fees and additional expenses incurred because of the disablement suffered by a child, in addition to standard child maintenance.

Note: It is stressed that this information on DEOs is tentative. Discussions are continuing through the CSA Employers' Panel and final Regulations and procedures will be subject to ministerial approval.

Community Charge Attachment of Earnings Orders

The Government proposes to make certain changes to Community Charge* Attachment of Earnings Orders (CC-AEOs) to bring them into line with DEOs for child maintenance (see above) and AEOs for spousal maintenance. It is hoped that these changes will ease administration for employers during the remaining life of the Community Charge. They may form part of the recovery procedures for the new Council Tax from 1993. In February 1992 the Community Charge Regulations were amended and Council Tax Regulations which will supersede these in April 1993, passed.

Changes These will include a prescribed Attachment of Earnings form; deductions based on percentages of earnings; no increase in deduction when unusually high aggregated earnings occur, e.g. holiday pay; amended definition of net earnings; and that CC-AEOs cannot be made against pensioners who are not in employment (thus relieving companies from the onerous task of making deductions from occupation pensions).

CC-AEOs are 'blocking' Orders, which means that they take absolute priority over any other priority Orders (e.g. DEOs for child

---

* To be known as the Council Tax as from April 1993.

Payments and deductions 67

maintenance, above) which may be made *after* the CC-AEO is awarded by the court.* CC-AEOs do not have 'blocking' status over any other priority orders which are made before the CC-AEO.

Note: As with DEOs for child maintenance under the CS Act, we stress that this information is tentative, subject to modification and subject to final Regulations and procedures receiving ministerial approval. When finalized, the Regulations take effect from 1 April 1993.

Income Tax (PAYE)

Income tax deducted at source from earnings is called 'Pay As You Earn' (PAYE). How much PAYE depends on personal allowances, as determined by personal circumstances. PAYE is linked with NIC deductions. (Self-employed persons pay tax under Schedule D after assessments and are not taxed under PAYE.)

Terminology

- Tax Code: a number (being the first three digits of the personal allowances, e.g. £3600 = code 360) and a letter representing the amount of tax-free pay which is allowed for the tax year. Most will have up to four digits (including zero) and a suffix H, L, P, T or V. A code 'NT' indicates no tax to be deducted; '344L' (1992/93) is for emergency use and must be applied on a 'Week 1' or 'Month 1' basis.
- P.38(S): completed by students employed during vacation periods (and only then) who wish to be paid without deduction of tax.
- P.45: a 'Leaving Certificate' given to an employee who leaves an employment. It contains details (for the tax year) of: the gross pay to date, the current tax code, and the amount of tax deducted, and the date/week-number of leaving. This enables the employer to commence deductions of PAYE and NIC from earnings.
- P.46: a 'Starting Certificate' completed for and signed by a new employee who does not possess a P.45, certifying that you are the only or main employer.
- Emergency code: the tax code (344L in 1992/93 year) on which an employer bases deductions of PAYE for a new employee who does not possess a P.45 for tax code authorization from the Inland Revenue.
- Tax tables: detailed IR guides for calculating income tax.

* Information and advice on DEOs, AEOs and CC-AEOs can be obtained from the DSS 'SSALE' (Sally Line') on 0800 393 539 and calls are *free*.

PAYE explained:

'PAYE' is the system by which the Government collects income tax from payments which the employer makes to people employed in their business. It is deducted from each payment (weekly, monthly, etc.) as they are paid; hence 'Pay As You Earn' (PAYE).

The Income Tax (Employments) Regulations 1973, as amended, state that 'it is the duty of the employer to deduct income tax (and by DSS Regulations, NIC contributions) from the pay of his employees whether or not he has been directed to do so by the IR'. If you fail to deduct income tax or NIC, the IR will hold you responsible for unpaid amounts.

If you take on an employee who has no P.45 or other documentation, you will need to deduct tax either at the basic rate or at emergency code rate (see cards 2, 4 and 5 of IR Forms P.8). To summarize, you must, per instructions on the P.8 Instruction Cards, deduct tax at 25 per cent on emergency code 'Week 1' or 'Month 1' basis plus NIC where appropriate.

Incorrect operation of PAYE and NIC can be a very costly exercise to unwary employers who will pay retrospective tax and NIC normally payable by the employee but will also incur penalties and interest on some late payments. Thus, if you take on an employee who does not have any documentation, you must deduct income tax at the emergency code rate and NIC, until you obtain a tax coding from Inland Revenue (as above), over- or under-payments to be remedied later.

How much PAYE tax?

Income tax is payable on taxable pay at either or both of two rates, called 'basic' and 'higher' rates. Taxable pay is pay left after deduction of 'free pay' (personal and other allowances). The lower tax band is the first £2000† taxable income, taxed at 20 per cent; the middle tax band is the next £21,700* taxable income, taxed at 25 per cent, while the higher tax band is any amount of taxable income over £23,700#, taxed at 40 per cent (1991/92 figures). Thus, two much simplified examples (for single persons) are shown in Table 4.1.

In this example, gross pay is *less* PAYE and pension fund contributions only.

Who pays PAYE?

Anyone who is 'employed', i.e. works for an employer, including all employees, office holders, directors and pensioners (not self-employed).

†*# See Table 4.1.

Table 4.1 Income tax payable on two different salaries

Gross annual salary	£11,995	£30,495
Personal allowances	£ 3,295 –	£ 3,295 –
Pension fund (p.a.)	£ 700 –	£ 1,000 –
Net taxable income	£ 8,000	£26,200
PAYE @ 20% (p.a.)	£ 400	£ 400
PAYE @ 25% (p.a.)	£ 1,500 –	£ 5,425*–
PAYE @ 40% (p.a.)		£ 1,000*–
Net annual income (before NIC)	£ 9,395	£22,670

In this example, gross pay *less* PAYE and pension fund contributions only.

What payments are covered by PAYE?

The list seems almost endless but basically includes earning (which can be from £1.00 upwards), fees, bonuses, commissions, pensions, 'perks', honoraria, sick pay (including SSP and SMP), maternity pay, vouchers which can be exchanged for *cash*, 'round sum' expenses, profit sharing, holiday pay, 'certain' expenses. (Payments in kind and 'fringe' benefits which have a monetary value are declared on form P.11D at the end of the year, for assessment or coding by the IR.)

What you *must* do concerning PAYE/NIC

You must pay to the Inland Revenue all PAYE tax and NIC which you have deducted in any month. You are permitted to deduct from this sum all SSP, SMP and NIC compensation on SMP (4.5 per cent in the 1992/93 tax year). Failure to render PAYE and NIC may result in penalties for you as employer; it may also cause *loss of benefits* to your employee, as NIC is benefit related.

Note: More insolvencies are brought about by the legal actions of the IR chasing non-payments of PAYE and NIC than any other source. See also Offences and Penalties below.

You must also maintain the following records for at least three years after the end of the tax year to which they relate:

- Pay records, which may be in paper, book or computer disk form.
- All official forms not sent to the tax office.
- Code-number lists provided by the tax office before the start of and during the tax year.
- Deductions working sheets.
- All documents relating to SSP and SMP.

What regular action must you take?
You must take action on PAYE on five *'Action dates'*. They are:

1 when an employee starts;
2 each time you pay an employee;
3 at the end of each tax month, i.e. on the fifth monthly;
4 at the end of each tax year;
5 when an employee leaves.

1   See earlier comment under Action on taking on new employee.
2   Each time you pay employees, calculate: how much gross pay you will pay them, including SSP and SMP, their 'taxable' pay (gross pay *minus* allowances) and how much tax and NIC they should pay. Methods of calculation (weekly/monthly) are given in:
   Form P. 8 (1991), cards 1, 2, 6 and 7, or in booklet form Tax Table A—*Free Pay after Allowances*;
   Tax Table B (Rev. May 1991) (*Taxable Pay on Basic Tax Band*),
   Tax Tables C and D (*Taxable Pay on 'Higher' Tax Band*) and
   Tax Table F (*Ready Reckoner for Tax Codes*);
   all of which are available from IR and which come in the IR Starter Pack when employers first register.
3   At the end of each tax month you must (within 14 days) pay all that you owe across to the Inland Revenue accounts office (which is in Cumbernauld or Shipley). This will include:
   All PAYE that you have deducted;
   All NIC you have collected;
   less:
   Any PAYE refunded during that month;
   Any SSP and SMP paid during that month (but see section on SSP below);
   Any NIC compensation (@ 4.5 per cent) on SMP payments.
3A *Small Firms* whose average monthly payments of PAYE and NIC deductions in a current year are likely to be less than £400 may elect to pay quarterly within 14 days of the end of each quarter.
4   After the end of each tax year (5 April) and *by* 19 May, you must send a Form P.14 tax return to Inland Revenue (Inspector of Taxes) local office *for each employee*. The individual forms—P.14 and overall summary—will contain details of:
   Total pay in the tax year (including any previous employment);
   Total tax deducted in the tax year (including any previous employment), plus the income tax code used;
   The employee's national insurance number;
   NIC deductions and deduction letter (i.e. A, B, C, or D);
   Earnings on which standard or contracted-out NIC contributions have been deducted;

SSP and SMP payments and dates;
Rebates of over-deductions of tax.
5   Follow the P.45 procedure.

Note: The IR will help with any problems, under the Taxpayers' Charter.

Repayment of PAYE   Where over-deduction of PAYE has been made and/or sent to the IR, there are ways in which rebate can be made to employee and employer. Where you have discovered an error in the current year, it is an easy matter to refund this to an employee; but once the year-end has passed, the rebate *must* come via the IR local office. Where *you* have paid too much to the IR, they will advise you of the adjustment automatically.

We have attempted to 'summarize' here all that is involved in dealing with PAYE. To attempt to explain further would be very complex. Full detailed and helpful information will be included in the starter pack, including Booklet P.7, Instruction Cards (P.8) and the above forms, available from the Inland Revenue local office.

National Insurance Contributions NIC

The official DSS guide to calculating NIC is given in DSS manual NT.269, 'green booklet number one'. The NI Tables are:

1   *Not* Contracted-out (Charts A, B and C).
1A Contracted-out (Charts D, E and C (special)).

NIC is calculated differently to PAYE. Like PAYE, NIC is paid by *all* employees including directors. NIC (Class 1) is paid by deduction from pay by all employees, though directors are treated differently and theoretically pay after the end-of-year accounts are declared but (in practice) pay cumulatively as the time of right to monies arises.

Also, whereas PAYE is charged on all earnings (with no limit) *after* deduction of personal allowance and approved expenses, NIC is payable by all employees on all gross earnings within the income bracket between the 'lower earnings limit' (LEL) of £2808* p.a. (or £54.00* per week) and the 'upper earnings limit' (UEL) of £21,060* (or £405* per week). Employers pay NIC on ALL employees' earnings, with NO upper earnings limit.

Earnings   For NIC purposes, 'earnings' are defined as 'any remuneration or profit deriving from employment' and include SSP and SMP. DSS legislation also stipulates that payments of earnings can be made either to or for the benefit of the employed earner.

* Figures correct for 1992/93 tax year.

Unfortunately, DSS definitions of earnings are slightly different from IR definitions.

Exclusions Under regulations, certain payments are disregarded from the computation of earnings for NIC purposes even though they are earnings under DSS legislation. One of the main types of exclusions are 'business expenses'. To be excluded for NIC purposes, a business expense must be a specific and distinct payment of, or contribution towards, expenses actually incurred by the employees in carrying out their employment. The other main type of exclusion is a 'payment in kind', usually something of no value other than by sale (e.g. a company car).

'Perks' Beware also, that certain perks count as earnings and are liable for NIC. These include: payments of bills (e.g. electricity, gas, rent, telephone, credit cards), gratuities paid by the employer and benefits in kind which have a direct value (e.g. payment of rent, giving rent-free accommodation or paying their Community Charge/Council Tax) or others which *can* be exchanged for cash.

NIC is *not* payable on benefits in kind which *cannot* be exchanged for cash. However, as at the 1992/93 tax year, the position for NIC is still a little uncertain with regard to various obscure benefits, but this will be clarified soon.

NIC on company cars

The Social Security (Contributions) Act 1991, passed by Parliament on 25 July 1991, applies employers' secondary NIC to company cars and to free fuel for the private use of company cars—called 'Class 1A NIC'. The rates will be on a sliding scale according to business mileage and/or employee contributions to cost. Class 1A NIC will be paid on cars provided for private use in each tax year commencing 1991/92 and annual payments will be due in June of each following year, commencing June 1992 (with an extension to July in the first payment year, 1992). A new IR guide 480 (1991) and leaflet Form CF.2 are available from the DSS Contributions Agency, Newcastle. Detailed Regulations on Class 1A NIC were issued in late 1991.

For companies with ten or more cars, a direct payment system via bank Giro can be operated in 1992/93 *only*—contact your local IR office.

There will be concessions for disabled drivers and shared cars, and instructions concerning change of car in mid-year—outlined in late-1991 Regulations.

Records You will be required to keep detailed mileage records for Class 1A NIC purposes. If your payroll and travel/transport departments are separate, Class 1A NIC returns may be submitted separately from the main NIC return. Detailed guidance on records is available from your local IR office.

Notes:
1 There will be penalties for late submission of annual returns.
2 Details will be in a supplement to the *green book* NI.269 (March 1992). Telephone SSALE line for a copy (0800 393 539).
3 The IR/DSS has *no* right of access to employees' mileage records. Therefore, adequate official company records will be important.
4 *Vans* are not included for employers' Class 1A NIC payments.

Directors
Directors are office holders and provided their earnings are (or would be but for IR concessions) chargeable to Schedule 'E' PAYE, are classed as being employees for NIC purposes.

While an employee's earnings period is usually the interval at which he or she is paid, special rules apply to directors—ask the IR for *Green Book* NI.35. These rules do *not* apply to a sole trader, proprietor or partner in a non-incorporated business. But in a 'private limited liability' (Ltd) company or a PLC, these rules apply to the directors.

Even if directors are paid weekly or monthly, their earnings period is *annual* or in some cases *pro rata*, i.e.:

- Directors appointed on or before the beginning of the tax year (6 April) have an annual earnings period, even if they cease to be directors before the end of a tax year.
- Directors who are first appointed after 6 April have a *pro rata* earnings period for that tax year, from the week of appointment up to 5 April. (There are always 53 weeks in a tax year for the purpose of working out the *pro rata* period.)

Employees pay NIC on actual weekly or monthly earnings which are not cumulative, but directors have an annual (or *pro rata*) earnings period, so their NICs are calculated on the *TOTAL EARNINGS* paid *TO DATE*. Thus, to calculate each NIC deduction due: determine first the *TOTAL NIC* due on the *TOTAL EARNINGS TO DATE*, then *DEDUCT* any NIC already paid in the current tax year, and the balance is the NIC due.

Note: No NICs are due on directors' earnings until they reach the annual (or *pro rata*) lower earnings limit. But once the total earnings to date reach the annual (or *pro rata*) lower earnings limit, then NICs are paid on *all* earnings at the appropriate percentages, as per NIC tables.

Adapting NIC tables   NIC tables are produced for employees with weekly or monthly earnings periods, but they can be adapted to the annual earnings period for directors by following the instructions given in DSS Fact Card NI.274 (April 1990). It is a simple matter of dividing the annual earnings to date by 12 to arrive at the 'average monthly income', if below the lower earnings limit for one month, no NIC is payable; if above the lower earnings limit, multiply the NIC due in the tables by 12 to determine the total NIC due to date; deduct the NIC already paid to date; the difference is the amount of NIC payable.

Employee contributions

Employee 'primary' contributions are fixed at a rate depending upon whether they are contracted-out, *not* contracted-out or on reduced rate contributions. (There is no such category as contracted-in.)

Contracted-out For an explanation, see section on pensions, page 98.

Not contracted-out For employees *not* contracted-out, no NIC is payable if their income is below the lower earnings level (LEL) of £2808* p.a. (£234* per month or £54* per week)—use the NIC A or B chart; but once they rise above the LEL they pay at 2 per cent* on the first £2808* p.a. (£234* per month or £54* per week), plus 9 per cent of all income between the LEL of £2808* p.a. (£234 per month or £54* per week) and the upper earnings level (UEL) of £21,060* (£1755* per month or £405* per week) (see Table 4.2).

Note: NICs are not calculated on a cumulative basis, but on a payment-by-payment basis. The extent of NIC liability and the earnings limits on which the employer calculates NIC liability depend on the employee's earnings period. Normally the earnings period is the interval at which the employee is paid.

Reduced rates Certain married women and widows who elected to pay reduced rates of NIC *before* 6 April 1977 and who hold a *valid* certificate CF.380 (which they *must* produce) may continue to pay at the reduced rate; charts B for weekly and E for monthly. However, no woman can now elect to do so nor can one who gave up that right return to it. If a woman cannot produce her certificate CF.380, she must pay the higher rate until the certificate is produced.

Note: The DSS is anxious to phase out the 'reduced rate' option.

Reduced rates are: *nil* if earnings are below £2808† p.a. (or £54* per week), then when earnings rise to or above that level they pay at a flat-rate of 3.85† per cent on all earnings up to £21,060† p.a. (or £405† per week). For women still eligible to pay reduced rate NIC, use

* Figures quoted are for the 1992/93 tax year.
† Figures correct for 1992/93 tax year.

Payments and deductions

Table 4.2 *Simplified* example for an employee *not* contracted-out

	Per month	Per week
1. Monthly (weekly) earnings	£ 233.95	(£53.99)
NIC deductable	NIL	NIL
or:		
2. Monthly (weekly) earnings	£1075.00	(£244.30)
NIC deductable: 2% of £234 (or £54)	£ 4.68	(£ 1.08)
plus: 9% of £841*	£ 75.69	
(*plus*: 9% of £190.30)		(£ 17.13)
Total NIC deductable:	£ 80.37	(£ 18.21)
or:		
3. Monthly (weekly) earnings:	£2166.66	(£500.00)
NIC deductable: 2% of £234 (or £54)	£ 4.68	(£ 1.08)
plus: 9% of £1521†	£ 136.89	
(*plus*: 9% of £351)		(£ 31.59)
Total NIC deducable:	£ 141.57	(£ 32.67)

* Difference between monthly LEL (£234) and gross monthly earnings.
† Difference between monthly LEL (£234) and monthly UEL (£1775).
  Multiply weekly LEL/UEL by 52 and divide by 12 to arrive at monthly LEL/UEL.
  No NIC deductable on earnings over £21,060 p.a. (£1755 per month) (£405 per week).
  All figures (except example one, nil NIC) rounded to nearest £ for simplicity.

NIC charts B (for weekly or monthly paid) to calculate NIC. (Chart C is an employer contributions table for retired persons.)

An employee who contracted out of the State Earnings Related Pension Scheme (SERPS) will pay no NIC on earnings below £2808* p.a. (£54* per week), but once the earnings exceed those levels they pay at a flat rate of 2 per cent on all earnings up to £2808* p.a. (£54* per week) plus 7 per cent of all earnings above those levels.

Note: Employees pay NIC *only* on pay up to the upper earnings limit (UEL), though the UEL may rise in the future, and do remember NIC due on company cars and free fuel mentioned earlier.

Employer contributions

Employer contributions (called 'secondary' contributions) are *VARIABLE* and have a lower earnings limit but *no* upper earnings limit. Thus, the employer will pay *nil* on earnings below £2808 p.a. (or £54* per week), but a rising percentage rate on *all* earnings from

---

* Figures correct for 1992/93 tax year.

£1.00 upwards once the employee's pay rises above the lower earnings level.

Note: From 6 April 1991, employer secondary contributions were reduced slightly following the SSP Act 1991 to compensate for the reduction in rebate of SSP (see section on SSP below).

Not contracted-out (A, B or C Charts) Employers NIC contributions on the inclusive earnings bands for employees *not* contracted-out are*:

Below £54 per week	*nil*
£54 to £89 per week	4.6% of all earnings
£90 to £134.99 per week	6.6% of all earnings
£135.00 to £189.99 per week	8.6% of all earnings*
£190.00 to £405.00 per week	10.4% of all earnings†
Over £405.00 per week	10.4% of all earnings.

(NI.1 Table CF.391 (red cover)).

Contracted-out (D, E, C (special) Charts) Employer NIC contributions on pay in the inclusive earnings bands for contracted-out employees are†:

Below £54 per week	*nil*
£54.00 to £89.99 per week	4.6% of £54 *plus* 0.8% of balance
£90.00 to £134.99 per week	6.6% of £54 *plus* 2.8% of balance
£135.00 to £189.99 per week	8.4% of £54 *plus* 4.8% of balance
£190.00 to £405.00 per week	10.4% of £54 *plus* 6.6% of balance
Over £405.00 per week	10.4% of £54 *plus* 6.6% of pay between £54.00 and £405.00, *plus* 10.4% of balance

(NI.1A Table (red cover)).

Effect of reduced rate for employers Employer contributions for reduced rate NIC payers will be as either of the above depending on whether the employee *is* or *is not* contracted out. There are *no* reduced rates for employers' contributions.

Under 16s: No NIC is payable by employees who are below 16 years of age, and there is *no* liability for employer's NIC contributions.

YT Beware YT trainees whose training allowance is 'topped up' by £15 or more—the IR may require PAYE and NIC on the top-up.

---

* Once £190.00 per week has been reached the employer's contribution will remain at 10.4 per cent. These figures are for weekly-paid employees; the same percentages apply to monthly-paid *pro rata* equivalents.
† Figures correct for 1992/93 tax year.

Pensioners in employment Pensioners do not pay any NIC but the employer pays secondary contributions at the contracted-out rate *only* (Chart C applies).

Failure to collect NIC

If you fail to collect NIC contributions by deduction from pay you, the employer, are still liable for them. If by genuine error you have not deducted (or have under-calculated) NIC, you may reclaim overdue NIC from the employee by deduction from his or her pay in addition to current normal deductions, but subject to two important conditions:

1 You *must* deduct them *in* the tax year in which they were due, otherwise when the tax year has passed you, the employer, might bear the loss.
2 You may *not* deduct an amount exceeding the current normal rate which the employee should pay, e.g. if an employee's current NIC is £9 per week and you are owed £34 in unpaid NIC, you may claim only at £9 per week for three weeks and one of £7. To deduct the whole £34 in one payment would be unlawful.

Failure to pass on NIC

You *must* pay across to the IR all NIC deductions from an employee's earnings plus the employer's NIC, together with all PAYE even though you may have failed to deduct NIC from an employee's pay—subject to the retentions outlined under PAYE. This is an important point, as NIC is *BENEFIT RELATED*. It is not only an offence to deduct NIC from an employee's earnings and withhold it or to fail to deduct any NIC, but to do so deprives employees of their right to full benefits.

Discretion

An additional point to bear in mind is that while PAYE assessments can be discretionary by IR as to what will/will not be allowed, NIC is a matter of rigid *law* in which a DSS inspector has no discretionary power.

Repayment of NIC

Where over-deduction of NIC has been made and/or sent to the IR, there are ways in which rebate can be made to employee and employer. Where you have discovered an error in the current year it is an easy matter to refund this to an employee, but once the year-end has passed the rebate *must* come via the DSS head office in Newcastle. Where *you* have paid too much tax or NIC to the IR, they will advise you of the adjustment automatically after the year-end P.35 return has been processed.

Equality of NIC

Several cases before the EC Court in March 1992 will rule on the legality of men paying NIC to age 65 while women pay NIC only to age 60 to receive the same rights 5 years earlier than men. Other cases to follow include: the *Heath* v. *Steeper* and *Coloroll* cases and deferred pensions before May 1990.

Offences and penalties

It is an offence to fail to send Forms P.35, P.14, SC.35 and SC.11 to the IR, or to send them late, i.e. after 19 May each year. Initial penalties for small firms with up to 50 employees can be up to £1200, with much larger sums for larger firms. From 1995, penalties for late returns may be charged automatically, with a 'period of grace' in 1995 only up to 19 July 1995.

Some helpful guides

IR.480—*Guide to Class 1A NIC (cars)*, available on request from IR.

NI.274—*Fact Card—Company directors NIC* (blue).

Card NI.275 (1991)—*Information for employers*.

NI.35—*NI for Company directors* (in detail) (green).

NI.268—*Quick guide for employers* (yellow).

Employer's Manual on NIC; plus supplement.

NI.269—*Guidelines on What Is/Is Not Included in Gross Pay for NIC*.

CF.391 (1991)—Table 1—NIC for *not* contracted-out contributions (See pages 92 and 97 below for Tables 2 and 3 for SSP and SMP).

(Most of the above will come in the *IR New Employers Starter Pack*; those not included can be requested.)

IR.56/NI.39—*Employed or Self-employed?*—guide for tax and NIC.

IR.53—*Thinking of Taking Someone On?*—PAYE for employers.

Taxpayers Charter—available from IR.

Help line!

The new DSS Contributions Agency has a Social Security Advice Line for employers and self-employed which provides guidance on NICs, SSP and SMP. The telephone number is 0800–393539 and calls are *free*. The DSS also provides excellent SSP/SMP seminars for employers nationwide—also *free*, details of which can be obtained by telephoning the advice line.

You may also contact your local DSS office or inspector of taxes for guidance.

4.3 Statutory Sick Pay (SSP)

Times change frequently, and along with them laws and requirements concerning people. This is very true with sickness and maternity benefits. In the 1980s there were far-reaching changes in these benefits with the introduction of Statutory Sick Pay (SSP) and other sickness and maternity benefits paid by the DSS. The scheme places the responsibility for the administration of payment of SSP to employees upon employers. Further minor changes augur well for the future, some of which we will outline in this section.

In summary, employees can certify themselves sick for absences due to sickness or injury of up to seven days (including Sunday), provide medical evidence for absence of more than seven days and be paid Statutory Sick Pay (SSP) by their employer for up to 28 weeks, provided all the necessary qualifying conditions are met. The employer pays SSP to the employee and reclaims 80 per cent or 100 per cent of it from the Department of Social Security (DSS) along with SMP (see next section), via the monthly returns to IR.

Terminology

- *Statutory Sick Pay (SSP)*: the levels of pay received when absent from work due to incapacity.
- *Self-Certification (SC)*: the certification by an employee that he or she is absent from work due to sickness and/or injury.
- *Period of Incapacity for Work (PIW)*: The period during which an employee is incapacitated from working due to sickness or injury.
- *Waiting Days*: the first three days of sickness which do not count towards a qualifying PIW.
- *Qualifying Days (QDs)*: Days of incapacity due to sickness or injury qualifing for payment of SSP according to working patterns.
- *Linking*: The period of 56 days *or less* between PIWs which link two or more PIWs into one without 'waiting days'.
- *Lower Earnings Limit (LEL), Upper Earnings Limit (UEL)*: as for NIC.
- *Sickness Benefit (SB)*: State benefit paid by the DSS when SSP is *not* payable by the employer.

Definition and responsibility

SSP is the payment which employers *must* make (it is statutory) to any employee aged 16 years or over who is sick for 4 days or more consecutive days (including Sundays) and satisfies the qualifying conditions. It is payable for up to a maximum of 28 weeks.

Who is not covered by the SSP scheme?

Some people are not covered by the SSP scheme, including mariners, aircrew, agency staff, HM Forces. Those not covered and who fall sick for four or more days in a row can claim state sickness benefit by filling in form SC.1. The employer is not required to complete form SSP.1 (see below) for the above people.

Who is covered by the SSP scheme?

Any employee who pays Class 1 NIC (see page 71) is entitled to SSP if he or she meets the satisfying qualifications, including those working within the European Community. An employer who is liable for Class 1 NIC and passes it across to the Inland Revenue is responsible for payment of SSP and may reclaim it by reducing future payments of PAYE and NIC to the Inland Revenue (IR).

Which employees cannot receive SSP?

Some groups of employees are *not* entitled to SSP, e.g. those who on the first day of the period of incapacity for work (PIW) whether or not linked (see below) are:

- Mariners on non-UK ships or on UK ships outside European Community (EC) waters and aircrew outside EC waters.
- Recent claimants of certain benefits with DSS 'linking letters' (see page 86) within 56 days of the end of a state benefit claim.
- Employees already paid a full 28 weeks' SSP by a former employer and who have an interval between their last and present PIWs of 56 days or less. (Refer to DSS for payment of state sickness benefit.)
- Employees earning *less* than the lower earnings level (LEL) (see 'average earnings' below)—refer to DSS.
- Employees on fixed-term contracts of three months or less, unless the contract is extended or the aggregate of two short-term contracts within eight weeks is more than three months.
- Employees working past the state retirement pension age (65 for men, 60 for women). (Employees who were *under* their retirement age at the beginning of a PIW will remain entitled throughout their PIW, including linking.)
- Pregnant women in their 18 weeks' 'disqualification period', i.e. the Maternity Pay Period (MPP) which began six weeks before their expected week of confinement (EWC) (see next section) and: are in receipt of either SMP or maternity allowance (MA), or are within six weeks before the EWC and are in receipt of sickness benefit (SB). (MA and SB are alternatives to SMP, where not qualified.)
- Employees involved or having a direct interest in a trade dispute, i.e. a strike, walk-out, lock-out or other dispute about work.
- Employees in police custody (unless voluntarily assisting with enquiries) or in prison.

- Those outside the EC on the day(s) of sickness.
- Employees who have not actually *worked* for you under a contract of employment, i.e. became sick before starting their employment.

In all these instances, complete and issue to the employee a DSS Form SSP.1 (Change-Over Form) and refer him or her to the DSS. (The abbreviations given here are those used by the DSS and IR in their publications.)

When does SSP end?

Employers' liability to pay SSP ends when:

- The PIW ends (e.g. the employee is fit to return to work).

or if, during a PIW:

- The contract of employment ends.
- The employee has been paid 28 weeks' SSP in the PIW.
- The SSP disqualifying period begins.
- The employee's linked PIW has run for three years.
- The employee is taken into legal custody.
- The employee goes outside the EC.

Notifications

An employee who becomes incapable of carrying out contractual duties because of physical or mental sickness, or injury, must in the first instance notify the employer that he or she is sick or injured. This notification may be by telephone, third party or letter as you, the employer, require.

Proof of sickness *You* must decide whether the employee is genuinely sick, but 'proof' is usually provided by submission of Form SC.1 or SC.2 (see below).

Self-certification (4–7 days)

DSS Self-Certification Form SC.2* covers the first four to seven days of sickness, including Sunday, is available from DSS offices and doctors' surgeries and may be made available at employers' premises. You, the employer, may, if you wish, provide Form SC.2 or your own self-certification forms, there being no legal obligation to use the official DSS form. Form SC.2* (or your alternative) must be completed by the employee on day one if your company's rules require certification for the first three days of sickness, and in any case by the fourth day of absence.

It is important that adequate procedures exist for ensuring that absence is genuinely due to sickness or injury, that DSS inspectors

---

* Form SC.2, employee's statement of sickness, superseded Form SC.1 from May 1990 and is specially for employers' purposes. SC.1 continues to act as a state sickness benefit claim form, though may still be used by employers.

are satisfied with your procedures and that you maintain full records including retaining Form SC.2 (or your own forms).

You may feel that employees may declare themselves 'sick' when in fact they are not and you just have to accept their word. The law allows you to say 'in my opinion you may not be sick', reject the self-certification and ask for proper medical evidence. You may request the DSS to obtain the decision of an adjudication officer. You may feel that you require medical evidence from day one but this may not be popular with doctors, is not a legally recognized practice, and will in any case be used only in extreme cases.

Medical certification (more than seven days)
Before paying SSP (for any period of sickness) you may ask for reasonable proof of sickness or injury. Where self-certification forms are *not* provided or, in any event, after seven days, a 'sick note' *must* be provided by the employee. A sick note may be a medical practitioner's certificate provided by a doctor or hospital or a certificate from an alternative non-medical authority acceptable to the DSS such as: osteopath, herbalist, or acupuncturist, but it is for *you* the employer to consider each certificate on its merits.

You cannot require that the certificate be submitted to you *before* a certain time on the due date; if it is in before cease-work it is 'on time' in law. Also in the case of delayed submission of certificates, you must use discretion as to whether the delay is reasonable in individual circumstances. If a certificate is 'in the post' you must accept the postmark or if not postmarked assume at least two clear working days since posting.

In cases of unreasonable or neglectful delay, you may withhold SSP until the date on which actually submitted. You may make your own rules which are strict at the onset of sickness and then relax them with a degree of discretion later—as long as your rules at least meet the needs of the DSS they will be acceptable, but if you have no rules or your rules are quite unclear then DSS rules apply.

Again, where you, the employer, have reason to doubt the genuineness of the sickness, you may request an independent medical opinion from a doctor of your choice. Alternatively, in certain circumstances, such request can be made via the regional medical service (RMS) of the DSS, although this will be very rare.

How does SSP work?
SSP is paid by the employer for the first 28 qualifying weeks of incapacity for work and for each successive period of 28 qualifying weeks intervened by a period of more than eight weeks returned to work unbroken by certified sickness. But first, each PIW must consist of 'qualifying days' (QDs) (see below).

Period of incapacity for work (PIW)

A period of incapacity for work (PIW) is a period of four or more days in a row, including Saturdays and Sundays, when an employee is away from work 'sick'.

Linking

Two or more PIWs in the same employment are 'linked' when gaps between PIWs when the employee has returned to work are 56 calendar days or *less*, including Sundays, i.e. they are treated as one PIW. For PIWs to be linked, there must be a minimum of 4 QDs in each PIW. Linking tables in SSP.55 are very helpful in working out linking periods.

How to calculate maximum entitlement to SSP

Examples 4.1 and 4.2 are simple examples of 28-week PIWs.

Example 4.1

Straightforward continuous (unbroken) PIW of 28 weeks, after three 'waiting days':

| 3 'waiting days' | 28* weeks PIW |

Example 4.2

Two or more straightforward continuous (unbroken) PIWs of 28 weeks, each after three 'waiting days', with more than eight weeks in between them:

| 3 'waiting days' | 28 weeks PIW | more than 8 weeks work | 3 'waiting days' | 28 weeks PIW |

Example 4.3

Broken into shorter PIWs 'linked' with periods of less than eight weeks between PIWs and which add up to 28 weeks in total. Examples of these are:

| 12* weeks PIW | 4 weeks at work | 7 weeks PIW | 3 weeks at work | 9 weeks PIW |

In Example 4.3, three 'waiting days' apply before the first* PIW but do not apply before the later PIWs because these PIWs are 'linked' by periods of 56 days or less. The exception to this would be a new employee with a form SSP.1(L).

A further complication may be very short PIWs of just a few days. Let's look at two possible scenarios (Examples 4.4 and 4.5):

* After three 'waiting days'.

Example 4.4
In this example days of PIW count towards the 28 weeks' SSP:

| 3 waiting days | 7* days PIW | 6 weeks at work | 4 days PIW | 3 weeks at work | 2 weeks PIW |

In Example 4.4, the first three days in the initial period of seven days PIW do *not* qualify for SSP, being 'waiting days'. However, the second PIW *does* qualify, as it occurs less than eight weeks after the previous PIW *and* is of four days; also there is no 'waiting days' rule in this four-day PIW.

It is possible for a single PIW which includes multiple 'linkings' to extend over a considerable period of time. In such cases the *MAXIMUM* period over which any aggregated 28 weeks PIW, including linkings, can extend is three years (see How to determine maximum entitlement to SSP, opposite).

Example 4.5
In this example days of PIW do *not* count in the 28 weeks PIW:

| 3 waiting days | 7* days PIW | 6 weeks at work | 3 days sick | 3 weeks at work | 3 waiting days | 2* weeks PIW |

In Example 4.5, the first three days before the initial PIW of seven days do *not* qualify for SSP (as in Example 4.4) being waiting days; although the second period of three days' sickness (after six weeks of working) fall *less* than eight weeks since the previous seven days' PIW, they are *not* a PIW for SSP as they are less than four days' sickness. The two weeks' PIW following the second period (three weeks) at work are after three waiting days, as it is more than eight weeks since the last qualifying PIW (seven* days) and is a new PIW.

Note: Unless an employee has been off sick for four days or more, this sickness does not count as a PIW.

To help you determine whether PIWs are linked, the DSS has produced tables in booklet SSP.55, revised annually.

Leavers
If an employee leaves your employment within eight weeks of returning from a PIW you must issue a DSS Form SSP.1(L) to the employee (giving details of the SSP paid) which the employee is required to pass to the new employer if he or she becomes sick again within eight weeks of joining the new company. (See Forms below.)

* After three 'waiting days'.

New employees

PIWs with former employers If you have been given a Form SSP.1(L) by a new employee, you can offset SSP paid by a previous employer against your maximum liability if the employee goes sick within eight weeks of joining you. So remember at the start date to *ask* your new employee for Form P.45, SSP.1(L) or linking letter, if no SSP.1(L) is given to you and the employee goes sick within eight weeks of joining you, contact the previous employer to ascertain if and when SSP was paid.

How to determine maximum entitlement to SSP

A period of entitlement (PE) begins with the first day of a PIW and ends with any of the following (see SSP Manual sections 73 to 78), i.e. when the employee:

- is fit to return to work, or
- reaches his or her maximum entitlement to SSP, i.e. 28 weeks, or
- starts the SSP disqualifying period, or
- goes outside the EC, or
- is taken into legal custody, unless voluntarily assisting police with enquiries, or
- leaves your employ and the contract of employment ends, or
- has a single PIW with the same employer which, aggregated, has run for three years.

Qualifying days

Qualifying days (QDs) are the only days for which SSP can be paid or which count as waiting days. The general rules are that there must be at least one qualifying day in every week, whether or not the employee is required to work in that week. QDs are usually the days which the employee is required to work under a contract of employment and are important in calculating daily rates of SSP due (see Rates of SSP and qualifications, later in this section).

QDs can be any days which you agree with your employees within the *NORMAL* working pattern, and are a matter for negotiation initially.

In the case of staff who regularly work a week of Monday to Friday, the choice is simple: qualifying days are Monday to Friday. But for more complex working patterns where different days (say, Sunday to Thursday, or 10 days in a 14 day cycle) are worked, you will need to work this out and agree with the workforce. QDs can be all seven days in one week or only one day; if an employee is *not* required to work in a particular week, the qualifying day is (by law) Wednesday unless you agree otherwise with the employee (see Example 4.6).

Example 4.6

	Week 1	Week 2	Week 3
Working pattern	M – T – W	No work	M – T – W
Qualifying days			M – T – W
either (by law)*	M – T – W	Wednesday	M – T – W
or (by agreement)†	M – T – W	M – T – W	

* Wednesday by law.
† Wednesday by agreement.

The DSS will be very happy to advise you in *your* particular situation.

QDs must *not* be defined by reference to actual days of sickness. Such agreements artificially increase the SSP due and are not permitted.

DSS linking letters

(These are not to be confused with 'linking' periods for PIWs.)

Linking letters are issued to people who are or have recently been in receipt of certain social security benefits. You should *ask* new employees if they have one when they start their employment with you.

If they produce one, DO NOT PAY SSP before the date shown on the form. If they do not have one and you have reason to believe (perhaps from information given in interview) that they have been in receipt of SB or IVB benefits, you should check with the DSS. If you pay SSP to an employee who is not entitled, *you* will be asked to repay it to the DSS and it will be UP TO YOU TO RECLAIM IT from the employee.

Note: The DSS has intended to abolish linking letters as soon as practicable. If or when this occurs, it will not alter your liability.

Withholding SSP due to late notification

There are several instances in which you may withhold and *not* pay SSP (whether linked or unlinked). They are:

- When there is *no* good reason for late notification of sickness or injury. Payment by you when notification is late is discretionary, but any SSP not paid for these PIWs is carried forward to later PIWs. 'Late' in this situation can be after the seven days laid down by DSS or if, for example, your stated company rules require notification on the third day and notification is not until fourth or fifth day.
- Those listed in Who is *not* covered by the SSP scheme, above.

Rates of SSP and qualifications

Rates of SSP There are two rates of SSP payable according to the employee's average weekly earnings in the relevant period, normally eight weeks *BEFORE* the first day of the first PIW (linked or unlinked). Average earnings are either in the upper earnings level (UEL) or lower earnings limit (LEL), with corresponding rates of SSP payable at the standard and lower rates, reviewed annually. (Refer to DSS leaflet SSP.55—SSP Tables.) Rates in 1992/93 are as follows:

Level	Average weekly earnings	Weekly rates of SSP
Standard	£185.00 or more	£52.50 (unchanged 1991/92/93)
Lower	£54.00 to £184.99 (£52.00)*	£45.30 (£43.50)*

The daily rate is calculated by dividing the weekly rate by the number of qualifying days in the week (see section 94 of DSS leaflet NI.270).

How to calculate average earnings Average earnings are normally calculated over the eight weeks immediately prior to the PIW for which SSP is to be paid, i.e:

- For weekly-paid employees, add the previous eight weeks' pay together and divide by eight.
- For monthly-paid employees, add the two payments in the last eight weeks before the PIW, multiply by six and divide by 52.
- For new employees, use the single payment received or (if not yet paid when the PIW began) the amount they would have been paid. Be careful to average out correctly.

Having calculated the amount of SSP payable, employers may then top up the SSP to the level of their own occupational sick-pay scheme (if any) provided in their conditions of employment, but such payments cannot be reclaimed from the DSS.

Earnings limits Employees whose average earnings fall below the 'lower earnings limit' are *not* entitled to SSP, *must* be given a Form SSP.1 (Change-over Form) and you should refer them to the DSS. (See 'Forms' (SSP.1) below.)

PAYE and NIC

All payments of SSP are subject to deductions of PAYE and of both employer and employee NIC payments in the normal way. However, SSP payments are not made by you, *per se*, but by you on behalf of the DSS and you can, therefore, reclaim part or all of SSP

---

* 1991/92 lower rates.

paid, but not NIC, from the DSS (see below). However, if you pay more than the entitled set rate of SSP, you *MUST NOT TRY TO RECOVER* this. As from 6 April 1991, employers are no longer entitled to reclaim employer-NIC from the DSS.

How to claim back SSP

You may recover amounts of SSP paid (but *not* top-up or over-payments of SSP) by deduction from payments of income tax and NIC paid to the IR, in the same way as SMP but at the following rates:

- Larger employers: 80 per cent of SSP paid.
- Small employers: 80 per cent of SSP paid for first 6 weeks, 100 per cent of all SSP paid from week 7 to week 28.

Notes:
1 Small employers are defined as those whose total of employer *and* employee NIC, including all NIC on SSP and SMP, paid in the previous tax year was £15,000 or less, called Small Employers' Relief (reviewed annually in November).
2 Guide NI.268 (1991) does *not* include this information.

Terms and conditions of employment

It would be advisable to include in the terms and conditions of employment a clause concerning repayment of over-paid SSP (and SMP for women), as to deduct without any contractual authority could render you liable to a claim for 'breach of contract'.

Forms

There are several DSS forms with which you will need to be familiar:

SSP.1—Change-over Form   This should be issued when there is *no* entitlement to SSP, when a PIW continues beyond entitlement to SSP, if an employee disagrees with amount of SSP paid or that no SSP is paid, or when an employee on SSP goes overseas. It contains a form which the employee can use to claim state Sickness Benefit (SB) or possibly Income Support if no entitlement to SB exists.

SSP.1(L)—Leaver's Statement   Completed for and handed to or posted to employees who have been paid at least one week's SSP within the last eight weeks of an employment (periods of more than three days count as one week). It must be issued within seven days of leaving (to be given to the next employer for use in the event of sickness again within less than eight weeks of joining their new employer). Failure to supply SSP.1(L) can result in financial penalties.

Note: You may if you wish provide your own computerized form SSP.1(L), but it must contain the following information:

1 Employee's name, NI number, works number and department.
2 First and last days of sickness which were counted for SSP.
3 The number of days (balance) of SSP payable.
4 Date of issue.
5 Your company's name and address.
6 Advice to the employee on how to use the form.

SSP.2—SSP Record Sheet This form is especially designed by the DSS for small businesses to operate SSP and is available free from your local DSS office. Use of this form is optional; you may purchase pre-printed forms from various printers or you may wish to design and use your own. (See also Records below.)

Records

You must maintain full and adequate records, as indicated earlier, and keep them for three tax years after the year in which SSP is paid. Failure to do so can result in penalties. These records should include the following:

1 Details of all PIWs notified by your employees, whether SSP was paid or not.
2 Details of any PIWs for which SSP was NOT paid—with reasons.
3 Details of the identified 'qualifying days' in each PIW.
4 Any leavers' statements (SSP.1(L)) taken in account.
5 Copies of leavers' statements (SSP.1(L)) issued by you.
6 Details of amounts of SSP actually paid on each pay day, together with PAYE and NIC deductions, etc.
7 Details of the *gross* amounts of SSP in column 2 *and* in column 1(f) of your Form P.11—deductions working sheet (either the official form or your own), together with details of NIC contributions. ('Total earnings' on Form P.11 includes SSP payments.) *RETAIN* Form P.11 and all SSP records for inspection for at least three years after the end of the tax year in which SSP is paid.
8 Details of the gross SSP paid in the tax year in Form P.14.
9 Details of the gross SSP and NIC compensation on Form P.35; both (9 and 10) submitted to the Inland Revenue at the tax-year-end.

You may also like to keep records of all the details contained on sick notes—for your future reference (e.g. in the event of a claim against your company). In this respect, the common abbreviations used by medical practitioners and others are listed in DSS booklet NI.270 and may be useful for reference.

Finally, a few 'signposts'.

Mistakes

In the current year If you record a wrong amount of SSP on the Form P.11 or your pay records, draw a line through the original figure (so that it can still be read) and write in the correct figure. (For how to correct errors in recording NIC compensations on SSP, see *Green Book One*, section 97.) If you over- or under-recover NICs, adjust your next monthly payment or your payment of any end-of-year balance due.

In past years If you discover a wrong amount of SSP or NIC compensation on the Form P.11 or your pay records for a year, *AFTER* the end-of-year returns have been sent to IR, you may still adjust the returns provided the IR Accounts Office still holds them. If they have agreed your returns and sent them to DSS Newcastle, you should contact your local DSS office for advice. (*Note*: You must *not* correct the error by decreasing or increasing your next monthly contributions payment—see *Green Book One*, section 97.)

SSP wrongly paid If you pay SSP to which an employee is *not* entitled, contact your local DSS office with all the relevant details. They will ask you to complete a form which will enable your employee to claim social security benefit.

Too much SSP paid If SSP was due but you paid it at too high a rate, you need not inform the DSS (see earlier comment). Whether or not you are able to recover over-payments of SSP from the employee, you must nevertheless adjust your records and deductions as described above.

Too little SSP paid (1) If you issue a Form SSP.1 (Change-over), contact your local DSS office with all the relevant details. They will check whether *they* have over-paid SB. Any arrears of SSP must be paid to the employee and your current Form P.11 corrected as above. (2) In other cases of under-payment, do not inform the DSS but pay the arrears to the employee and record them on the Form P.11 in the normal way.

Note: Do remember to adjust your employee's sickness records.

If a DSS inspector finds an error If an inspector finds you have wrongly paid SSP, correct it. If you disagree with the finding, you may ask the DSS adjudication officer for a formal decision. If the finding is that you have under-paid SSP, you must pay it to the employee within the fixed time given by the inspector, unless lodging an appeal.

Offences and penalties

There are penalties prescribed for described offences, under the Social Security and Housing Benefits Act 1982. Briefly, they are:

1 A fine up to £400 plus £20 per day of non-compliance after conviction for the following:
   Failure to pay SSP following a formal decision
   Failure to provide information when requested in writing
   Failure to keep required records
   Failure to provide an employee with prescribed information, i.e. Form SSP.1 (Change-over Form)
   Failure to provide Form SSP.1(L) (leavers' form).
2 A fine not exceeding £2000 and/or up to three months' imprisonment for:
   Producing any document or information, or allowing any document or information to be produced, knowing them to be false in their content, when recovering SSP and/or NIC.

More than one employer

Some employees have two or more contracts of employment with separate (or, in some cases, the same) employers. This would not affect your liability to pay SSP (or SMP—see Sec. 4.4) if the conditions in the contract of employment with you satisfy the criteria for payment of SSP (or SMP), i.e. UEL/LEL, etc. You do not need information from another current employer.

If an employee has more than one contract of employment with you, you may aggregate the earnings for determining entitlement to SSP (or SMP).

In the above situations, calculate SSP in the way outlined above.

Where to find help

We have endeavoured to summarize in 'layman's language' the main workings of the whole of SSP. Advice concerning queries on a particular employee's SSP is available from the DSS local offices who will be pleased to help.

The DSS Contributions Agency in Newcastle upon Tyne has established its Social Security Advice Line for employers and the self-employed. This is available to provide guidance on SSP, SMP, NICs, DWA, SDA and DLA, and you are encouraged to use this very helpful and friendly facility—anonymously, if need be. The telephone numbers are: for SSP, SMP and NICs: 0800 393 539; for DWA, SDA and DLA: 0800 100 123. Calls are *free*.

For employers, and others interested, guidance on how to operate the SSP scheme is given in the following documents which are available from local DSS offices:

- *Quick Guide—Key to National Insurance Contributions (NICs), Statutory Sick Pay (SSP), Statutory Maternity Pay (SMP)*—DSS leaflet NI.268.
- *Information for Employers*—DSS leaflet NI.275 (1991).
- *Employer's Manual on SSP*—DSS leaflet NI.270.
- *SSP—Small Employers' Relief*—DSS leaflet NI.278 (1991).
- *SSP Flow Chart*—DSS leaflet NI.271.
- *SSP Tables*—DSS leaflet SSP.55.

Copies of leaflets NI.268 and NI.270 are also available from: Leaflets Unit, PO Box 21, STANMORE, Middlesex, HA7 1AY.

A helpful FSB leaflet; *SSP—Employers: Do You Know the Costs?*, is available from Federation of Small Businesses (FSB), 140 Lower Marsh, Westminster Bridge, SE1 7AE.

4.4 Statutory Maternity Pay (SMP)

In summary, when a woman who has been working for the same employer for a period of time becomes pregnant she is entitled to Statutory Maternity Pay (SMP), subject to certain important conditions. If she does not qualify, social security benefits may become payable. SMP, which is paid by the employer but reclaimed from the DSS, is similar in concept to SSP and the following is a summary of SMP in layman's terms. We dealt with the right to return to work in Chapter 3—Employing, the rules being slightly different to those for SMP.

Terminology

- *Statutory Maternity Pay (SMP)*: the levels of pay received after ceasing work to have a baby.
- *Expected Week of Confinement (EWC)*: the week (Sunday to Saturday) in which the confinement (birth) is due, whether or not it takes place in that week.
- *Fairly dismissed*: dismissed wholly due to pregnancy because of the *risk* in the job to the pregnant woman and/or the unborn child, e.g. German measles, radiation, heavy lifting.
- *Qualifying Week (QW)*: the fifteenth week (Sunday to Saturday) before the EWC, leaving 14 weeks before (and excluding) the EWC.
- *Maternity Pay Period (MPP)*: The period during which SMP is payable.
- *Average Weekly Earnings*: the average of all earnings for SMP

purposes over the eight weeks ending with the last pay day before the end of the QW, calculated as for NIC.
- *Lower Earnings Level*: as for NIC.
- *State Maternity Benefit (MB)*: that paid by the DSS when SMP is NOT payable by the employer.

Who qualifies?
Any female who is pregnant and who is an employee for the purposes of Class 1 NIC (or would be if her earnings were high enough), including those from EC countries. Similarly, an employer who pays the employer's share of those Class 1 NIC payments is required to pay SMP.

How does she qualify?
To qualify for SMP a woman *must* fulfil the following criteria:

1 (a) She must have worked for the same employer for a minimum of 26 weeks into/including the qualifying week (QW) and have ceased working wholly or mainly due to pregnancy. (A previous maternity absence with exercised statutory right to return counts towards this period of continued entitlement.); or
 (b) she has been 'fairly dismissed' (see below), has worked for at least eight weeks, would otherwise have completed 26 weeks into/including the QW and would have worked into the QW; or
 (c) she has given birth *before* the QW and would have completed 26 weeks into the QW but for her early confinement.
2 Her average weekly earnings over the eight weeks ending with the last pay day before the end of her QW are not less than the lower earnings limit (LEL) for NIC* (Regulation 5 of 1990 Regulations).
3 She must have reached the eleventh week before her QW and still be pregnant or have been prematurely confined before the eleventh week.
4 She must have given notice, in writing if you require it, of her anticipated absence due to pregnancy not less than 21 days before her absence is due to commence (unless 'fairly dismissed'). You may, at your discretion, accept less than 21 days if you feel there are good reasons for late notification.
5 She must provide WRITTEN evidence of her 'expected week of confinement' (EWC), normally Form Mat.B.1 obtained from her GP or hospital, though other forms may be acceptable.

* £54 in 1992/93 tax year).

Example 4.7

QW				MPP commences											EWC
15	14	13	12	11	10	9	8	7	6	5	4	3	2	1	0

Note: Visual evidence of pregnancy is *not* acceptable. Documentation is required after the confinement to support reclaims of SMP payments from IR (by deduction from NIC remittances, or PAYE if NIC insufficient). A maternity certificate (Form Mat.B.1 or other) is *not* valid if it is issued more than 14 weeks before the EWC.)

6 She must remain *in* her employment for at least part of the QW unless 'fairly dismissed'.

7 She must actually have stopped working for you.

When is payment made?

Payment of SMP is made during the 18 week 'maternity pay period' (MPP) which is a 'floating' period commencing at the beginning of weeks eleven to six (inclusive) before the EWC, (see Example 4.7).

Thus if a pregnant woman stops work at the end of the tenth week before the EWC, her SMP will commence in week nine before the EWC and continue into the EWC and up to and including the eighth week after EWC (whether or not the birth actually occurs *in* the EWC). Her MPP *must* in any event commence no later than the sixth week before the EWC, but if the MPP is delayed she will lose weeks off the *end* of her MPP at the lower rate.

Notes:

1 The latest date up to which SMP can continue to be paid is the eleventh week after the EWC.

2 She will lose SMP for any week (or part week) worked in or after week six before the EWC.

How much SMP is paid, for how long?

Similarly to SSP, there are two rates of SMP but, unlike SSP, there is no daily rate.

Higher rate   If your employee was employed by you:

- for a continuous period of at least two calendar years into/including the QW, normally working for at least 16 hours or more each week, *or*
- for a continuous period of at least five calendar years into/including the QW, normally for eight hours or more (but less than 16 hours) each week,

she satisfies the employment rule for the higher rate of SMP. The higher rate is 90 per cent of the employee's average weekly earnings

Example 4.8

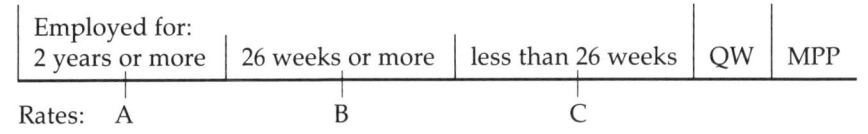

Employed for:				
2 years or more	26 weeks or more	less than 26 weeks	QW	MPP
Rates: A	B	C		

over the last eight weeks up to the QW, for a maximum of six weeks of the MPP. For the remaining (up to) 12 weeks of the MPP, the lower rate of SMP will be payable.

Lower rate If your employee has been employed by you for a continuous period of less than two years but of at least 26 weeks into/including the QW (regardless of the number of hours normally worked), she satisfies the employment rule for the lower rate of SMP. The lower rate is a set rate, reviewed each year (£44.50 in 1991/92; £46.30 in 1992/93; a little higher than SSP, the lower rate of which is £45.30 in 1992/93) and changes annually on the first Sunday after 6 April (not *on* 6 April as with SSP).

Notes:
1 A pregnant employee whose earnings are *below* the LEL cannot be paid SMP but should be referred to the DSS for MB.
2 Beware—SSP payments can *reduce* the average earnings to below the LEL for SMP and disqualify the employee.
3 Average pay calculations *include* bonuses, holiday pay, overtime, in the last eight weeks and may thus inflate SMP rates.

Thus, we can represent these rate levels in diagram form as shown in Example 4.8.

Notes:
1 If an employee satisfies the qualifying conditions with more than one employer, she can receive SMP from both of them.
2 The maximum number of weeks' SMP is 18.
3 The maximum entitlement (18 weeks) is reduced by any week (or part week) which a pregnant woman works after week six before the EWC, but the reduction will always be from the end of her MPP at the lower rate of SMP.
   Thus, for example, if a woman continues working into week three before the EWC (see Example 4.7) she will still receive six weeks at the higher rate of SMP (90 per cent of average weekly earnings), but only nine weeks at the lower rate of SMP (£46.30 in 1992/93).
4 You may offset SMP against your own occupational maternity pay payable for the same period. You can recover payments of SMP from the DSS (see below).

5 If a birth is *late* the maximum is still 18 weeks' SMP from the sixth week before the original EWC.
6 You may pay SMP weekly, monthly or in a lump sum. But beware, a lump-sum payment of SMP may cause a higher rate of NIC to be deducted (being calculated on actual payments of earnings) by both employer and employee than would otherwise be paid if spread over the 18 weeks.
7 A woman on sickness benefit or SSP immediately before payment of SMP will not lose her entitlement to invalidity benefit (IVB) if appropriate (Regulation 6 of 1990 Regulations).

Changes in circumstances

Your liability to pay SMP will end if:

- after your employee has been confined, she starts work for any other employer having been employed by you into/including the QW. Your liability will end on the Saturday of the week before she starts working;
- your employee goes outside the EC;
- she leaves your employment.

Change from paying SSP to SMP

Note: If an employee is receiving SSP when she commences to be paid SMP, complete Form SSP.1 (Change-over Form) to be passed to the DSS.

Recovery of SMP

You may recover amounts of SMP paid by deduction from the payments of NIC paid to the IR accounts office, or if insufficient NIC is available to offset SMP then from income tax, in the same way as SSP. NIC is payable on SMP by both employee and employer but you may reclaim your employer portion of NIC on SMP (but not SSP) from the DSS by deduction of the flat-rate percentage prescribed for each year (7.5 per cent in 1989/90, 7 per cent in 1990/91 and 4.5 per cent in 1991/92/93).

If refusal-to-pay SMP is disputed by employee

If you decide an employee is *not* entitled to SMP, give her a completed Form SMP.1 (see below). If she disagrees with your decision not to pay SMP, she can ask you for a written statement stating why you are not paying SMP. She can than ask the adjudication officer at her local DSS office to give a formal decision on her entitlement. If the adjudication officer gives a formal decision that she is entitled to SMP, you *must* pay that SMP within the stated period of time. Similarly, if the employee disagrees with the *amount* of SMP paid, complete Form SMP.1.

Forms

NI.257: *SMP Manual for Employers*, giving detailed instructions; issued by DSS and available from local DSS office.

NI.268: *Quick Guide to NIC, SSP and SMP*.

SMP.55: Booklet—*SMP Tables* (1991).

Mat.B.1: 'Maternity Certificate'. Provided by doctor or appropriate medical authority (e.g. maternity clinic or hospital).

SMP.1: 'Non-entitlement to SMP' (similar to Form SSP.1). Completed by the employer and handed to the employee.

SMP.2: 'Record Sheet'. Optional form devised by DSS especially for small businesses but useful also for other firms. You can, of course, produce your own Form SSP.2.

SMP.3: 'Checklist and Work Sheet'. Instructions: how to pay SMP, how to keep records of payments, NIC deducted, and reclaim from DSS. A valuable guide to the operation of SMP. (See also Records, below.)

Records

The following records *must* be maintained for inspection for not less than three years beyond the end of the tax year to which they relate:

- Dates of absence on maternity leave notified and actually taken.
- Weeks (dates, numbers) of SMP paid in the tax year.
- Amounts of SMP paid in the year.
- Weeks of SMP *not* paid in the year—with reasons for non-payment.
- Maternity certificates (Mat.B.1 or alternative), original or copy.
- SMP.2 (or SMP.1 if still used).

Help line

The DSS Contributions Agency in Newcastle upon Tyne has established its Social Security Advice Line for employers and the self-employed. It provides guidance on NICs, SSP and SMP to employers and the self-employed and you are encouraged to use this very helpful and friendly facility—anonymously if need be. The telephone number is: 0800 393 539 and the calls are *free*.

You may also contact your local DSS office concerning queries on a particular employee's SMP, MPP or any aspect of her maternity leave.

Small Firms Small employers with cash-flow problems—contact your local Inspector of Taxes (IR), you can receive SMP repayment in advance. Show SMP advance against SMP in P.35 records.

Maternity leave and the right to return are dealt with in Chapter 3—Employing.

4.5 Pension contributions

Until recently, many companies could have their own compulsory occupational pension schemes to the exclusion of other schemes; or in the absence of such a scheme employees could make their own private retirement pension arrangements until required to join a compulsory company scheme. (It was unlawful for members of company schemes to contribute to personal pension schemes).

There is also the state pension scheme combined with the State Earnings Related Pension Scheme (SERPS) funded through NIC. An employee was either in *the* SERPS *portion of the state scheme* or *contracted-out under specified conditions (see later comment)*. Males and females were treated quite differently and firms could retire male and female employees at different ages.

Since 1975 and particularly in the late 1980s, new laws have changed all of these schemes. Other changes were introduced in the 1989 Finance Act; they are rather complicated for a guide of this type, but we have included key points in this chapter.

Occupational pension schemes

You may establish an occupational pension scheme (called a 'fund') through any reputable fund of your choice, licensed under The Financial Intermediaries, Managers and Brokers Regulatory Association (FIMBRA) or The Life Assurance and Unit Trust Regulatory Organization (LAUTRO) (normally a life assurance/insurance company, or a broker). Rates of contributions from employer and employee to the fund, and the level and types of benefit to contributing employees, are matters for negotiation by the employer. However, a scheme will only receive tax approval if the employer is contributing at least 10 per cent of the payments (excluding AVCs—see below) going into the scheme. As with other areas of commodity purchase, the advice is 'shop around'.

Contributions

Normally, all eligible employees are encouraged to join a company's occupational pension scheme—but this is no longer obligatory. Employees' participation in a company scheme is now entirely voluntary; they may express a preference to make their own personal pension arrangements—see below. However, a *non*-contributory death-in-service scheme can still be made compulsory, though such membership does not prevent an individual from taking out a private pension plan.

Contributions by employer and employee are expressed as a

percentage of earnings, or the scheme may be non-contributory as above. In a tax-approved scheme, the term 'non-contributory' can, of course, only apply to employees—employers' contributions must be paid. You, as employer, may decide contributions, or you may wish to negotiate with your employee(s). Examples are:

- employer 7 per cent : employee 5 per cent; or,
- employer 9 per cent : employee 4 per cent;
- employer 9 per cent : employee 0 per cent, (non-contributory).

Employer contributions are tax-deductable from profits. Employees' contributions to an approved fund will attract income tax (PAYE) relief at standard rates, by deducting contributions from gross salary, then taxing net pay after deductions of allowances and pension contributions.

This way of giving tax relief is called the 'Net Pay Arrangement' and is explained in the *Employer's Guide to PAYE* (available from tax offices). In order to qualify for PAYE relief, the scheme must meet certain minimum criteria and be approved by the Inland Revenue.

Contracting-out The fund may also, subject to certain minimum criteria, be able to contract-out of SERPS, in which case employees will pay a lower NIC contribution to compensate (see NIC above). The test is: will the fund provide benefits at least equal to SERPS? To obtain approval for a proposed company scheme, you will need to contact your local inspector of taxes who will issue a 'Contracted-Out Certificate' for approved funds.

No pension fund contributions (of any kind) attract relief from NIC, although you will need to use the special Chart D or E for contracted-out contributions.

Benefits

What benefits you wish your fund to afford to your employees is a matter entirely for you as employer to negotiate with your chosen pension fund administrator and with your employees. There are two aspects to funds:

1 value of the funds, which depends upon the fund managers performances in the investment market; and
2 the types of benefits the funds give.

Aspect 1 is entirely speculative; deposit- or policy-based schemes tend to be secure and give fair returns, and unit- and investment-linked schemes can achieve spectacular gains but at a greater risk. With aspect 2, a fund may give any or all of the following:

A retirement pension This is normally expressed as: for each completed year of reckonable service, one-sixtieth or one-eightieth of the final wage/salary or average earnings over the last three years before retirement. (Some schemes restrict membership to the age of 18 plus, but this limit is not an Inland Revenue restriction.)

Thus, for an employee with 20 years' reckonable service, a final salary of £10,000 p.a. and a fund based on sixtieths, the pension would be: £10,000 × 1/60 × 20 = £3333 p.a. (Only benefits up to 40/60ths, i.e. two-thirds (or equivalent) will count.)

Cash-plus-pension mix Alternatively, a tax-approved company scheme may allow a lump sum equal to 3/80ths (or equivalent) for each year of service up to 120/80ths (or equivalent), or a lump sum based on 2.25 times the annuity to be paid to the individual in the first year after retirement.

Note: **Earnings Cap** The Finance Act 1989 introduced an earnings cap for determining maximum benefits in an approved scheme. It was £60,000 p.a. in 1989/90, £64,800 p.a. in 1990/91, £71,400 in 1991/92, is £75,000 in 1992/93, and will be indexed annually. Employees who entered a scheme before 1 June 1989, where that scheme operated before 14 March 1989, are exempt from the earnings cap while remaining in that scheme.

Life assurance This consists of a lump-sum death benefit, for death in service, equal to n times the final year's earnings or average over the last three years prior to death. The Inland Revenue restricts the value of n in an approved scheme (usually to four times the final remuneration). This benefit ceases if the employee leaves the fund.

Disability pension If an employee is disabled, he or she may receive a disability pension equal to, say, half final earnings, or the average over the last three years before disability. Normally, an employee must be off work for six months before he or she qualifies for this benefit.

Widows' pension Provision for a pension for the widow of a married man should he die while in service (or in some cases, after retirement). There has been some inequality here, in that there is *no* facility for a widower's pension for the husband of a woman who dies in service or in retirement—though changing attitudes may bring changes in practice. There is no provision, either, for an unmarried co-habiting 'partner' should death occur in any circumstances.

Note: There is no inequality in IR rules, widows and widowers are treated identically and co-habitants can be provided for if they qualify as dependants. Recent EC Directives and judgments would make it unlawful to offer a widow's pension but not one for widowers.

Early leavers Upon leaving a fund early, the benefit accrued is held in credit or may be transferable to another scheme operated by the next employer or to a private pension scheme. Employees who leave an employer and, therefore, the pension fund may (depending upon circumstances which will vary widely):

- take a refund of contributions, less tax (not now widely available, but see below); or
- leave their contributions as a 'frozen' or 'paid-up' pension; or
- transfer the value of their pension to another scheme—called 'transferability'.

Note: A refund of contributions is only payable under restricted circumstances, i.e. when the individual has completed less than two years' services. A refund is *not* available to someone who opts out of the scheme but remains in the same employment. (Please see also Chapter 10—Retirement.)

'Top-up' schemes Unapproved top-up schemes introduced in the 1989 budget do not have tax-approved status and are not limited by Inland Revenue restrictions. A top-up scheme may run alongside one or more approved pension schemes.

'Appropriate' schemes No distinction is made between appropriate (contracted-out) and non-appropriate (those held by contracted-out individuals) personal pension contracts.

The 'Barber Judgment'

There have traditionally been differences between men and women in benefits from occupational pension schemes, including payment for women from age 60 years and for men from age 65 years, plus differences in actuarial rates because of sex differences and differences in life expectancy. Numerous objections to this have been not least that men pay into schemes for five 'extra' years up to the age of 65 years to receive the same benefits as women who pay only up to the age of 60.

The EC Court of Justice, in the *Barber v. Guardian Royal Exchange* case on 17 May 1990, ruled that such practices contravene the Sex Discrimination Act 1986. The EC Court ruled that every pensions scheme should calculate pensions benefits on the basis of equal pensions to both men and women. This ruling has far-reaching effects on equality in occupational pension scheme benefits (not private schemes) and thus, e.g. from 17 May 1990 occupational pensions scheme benefits accruing as a result of service must be calculated on equal bases for men and women.

There are several cases laid before the EC Court arising out of the Barber Judgment and taking into account the 'full retrospective interpretation' of article 119 of the EC Charter. Cases due to be heard from April 1992 onwards include such matters as deferred pensions for those who 'retired early' before the 17 May 1990 ruling, pensions which commenced payment before 17 May 1990, widowers' pension rights (non-existent in most current occupational pensions schemes), and redundancy effects. Other cases in the pipeline include the *Heath* v. *Steeper* case and the *Coloroll* case. It is considered that the additional costs of 'level pensions' could be between £40 and £50 billion.

Private Retirement Pension Arrangements

Additional voluntary contributions (AVCs)

Since 6 April 1988 employees have been able to elect voluntarily to pay additional contributions (AVCs) into their employers' occupational pension schemes. They can pay in AVCs to top up their normal contributions with a combined maximum up to 15 per cent of their earnings. They can contribute any amount desired beyond the 15 per cent limit without attracting income-tax relief with the specific authority of the Inland Revneue.

'Free-standing' additional voluntary contributions (FSAVCs)

As an alternative to AVCs, employees have also become able to elect to pay into a pension fund outside their employers' schemes. The same basic rules on income-tax relief for AVCs also apply to FSAVCs.

Whereas fund contributions and AVCs attract income-tax relief by the 'netting out' system against earnings at source (see Contributions, above), employees pay FSAVCs net of tax and the FSAVC fund administrators claim the income-tax relief from the Inland Revenue (up to the maximum of the income tax paid in PAYE).

Limitations

Should the funds accrued by FSAVCs provide benefits in excess of those permitted by occupational schemes, then the excess FSAVCs must be returned to the employee on effecting the pension at retirement, *less* a tax deduction of 35 per cent.

There are also further limitations on in-house AVCs and on FSAVCs above £22,400 p.a. in that these AVCs/FSAVCs cannot be paid if they would provide benefits which, when aggregated with benefits from all other sources, exceed Inland Revenue limits.

Note: The arrangements for funding excess of in-house AVCS or private FSAVCs are the same. Although FSAVCs are described as 'an alternative' to in-house AVCs, it is possible to pay into both at the same time provided that, when aggregated, the 15 per cent limit is not exceeded.

Personal pensions

Since 1 July 1988, employees have the *right* to completely opt out of SERPS and their employer's occupational pensions fund and to make their own private arrangements through approved contracted-out personal pension funds, mostly referred to as a personal pension plan. (No one can opt out of the basic state pension scheme.) Of course, no one with a personal pension plan is compelled to contract-out of SERPS.

Contributions to a personal pension plan will *not* normally be deducted through your payroll (although you could offer this facility), as individuals will normally arrange payments via direct debit or banker's standing order to the insurance company or broker.

The employee pays into his or her personal pension fund net of tax at the standard rate (25 per cent in 1992/93). He or she can:

- pay a regular monthly, quarterly or annual sum of any amount (usually with a minimum, normally £15);
- 'lump in' at any time with single larger payments, cease regular payments and retain reduced benefits, and by negotiation, re-start payments.

When regular contributions are maintained the employee's contracted-out personal pension fund will automatically be credited by the DSS, annually at the end of each tax year, *IN ARREARS*, with the following:

1 The contracted-out National Insurance Contributions (NIC) rebate, which is the difference between the normal contracted-*in* and contracted-*out* NICs. It is fixed for five years from 6 April 1988 until 5 April 1993 and is 5.8 per cent of the income in the 'middle earnings band' (ie. between £2704 and £20,280 p.a.). From 6 April 1993, a revised fixed rate will apply.
2 Subject to certain conditions, the special incentive payment (where payable), being 2 per cent of income in the 'middle earnings band' and again fixed until 5 April 1993. (The retrospective special incentive payment back-dated from 6 April 1987 expired after 5 April 1990.)
3 Income-tax relief at the standard rate (25 per cent in 1992/93) up to the maximum of the employee's share of the NIC rebate (i.e. 2 per cent of the 5.8 per cent rebate). (*Note*: There is *no* higher rate relief

Table 4.3 Maximum personal pension fund contributions

Ages	Percentages of relevant earnings
up to 35 years	17.5
36–45 years	20.0
46–50 years	25.0
51–55 years	30.0
56–60 years	35.0
61 and over	40.0

available and in 1992/93 the *lower* rate of 20 per cent PAYE on the first £2000 of taxable income is ignored for relief purposes.)

It must be noted that there are MAXIMUMS which a person can contribute to a personal pension fund (see Table 4.3) and claim income-tax relief—called an 'earnings cap'. The maximums are according to age, are a percentage of the 'relevant earnings' up to the maximum of the 'earnings cap' of £75,000. The ages and maximums are given in Table 4.3.

'(Net) relevant earnings' is a term used by the IR for those *gross* earnings which are taken into account for taxation purposes and are different for employed and self-employed. They are:

- *Employed*: gross earnings including benefits with monetary value, but excluding expenses.
- *Self-employed*: amount of PROFITS, *less* capital allowances, according to Schedule 'D' assessment.

The 'earnings cap' can be changed by Treasury Order, annually. Before 6 April 1989 it was 'unlimited', in 1989/90 it was £60,000, £64,800 in 1990/91, £71,400 in 1991/92 and is £75,000 in 1992/93. This information is necessary for calculating unused relief. The contribution figures are also different when calculating unused relief for years prior to 1989/90.

Self-employed The same rules on personal pension funds apply to self-employed persons. However, although the same rules apply to the self-employed they cannot get relief through the 'relief at source' arrangements, nor can they contract-out of any part of their Class 2 NI contributions.

Benefits

Personal pension schemes afford various benefits, the main ones are the following:

1 Contributions to the scheme normally end in the month in which the 65th birthday occurs, although one of the attractions of a

personal pension is that vesting is flexible and not necessarily tied to retirement.
2 Participants in a personal pension scheme may select a 'retirement' date at any time from their 55th birthday or later up to a maximum age of 75 years.

However, the contracted-out portion of the pension may not be taken before the age of 65 for males and 60 for females, though an EC ruling in 1990 may bring these ages into alignment with males and females both able to retire and take SERPS at 60 years of age, or at least at the same age (e.g. 65 years).
3 Income-tax relief is granted on investment growth WITHIN the fund, giving a tax-free build-up of fund value.
4 Normally, at the chosen retirement age, the pension fund realizes a 'fund value' with which the holder can purchase an 'annuity'. An annuity is the life pension which is purchased from the fund. The holder may then either:
   (a) purchase a pension, funded by the whole of the fund value, or
   (b) take a 'lump sum' (tax free) up to one-quarter of the fund value *plus* the purchase of a pension funded by the balance of the fund value.

The member may purchase a pension (annuity) from his or her own pension fund or an alternative pension fund, according to preference. This is commonly known as the open market option (OMO); some personal pension providers (banks, building societies) cannot provide an annuity 'in-house' and *must* use the OMO route.
5 A pension for a widow (or widower) or dependant, usually at half the rate of that normally payable under the scheme or more up to the maximum allowed by the Inland Revenue.
6 Carry-forward/carry-back provision. Simplistically, it means carrying the entitlement to income-tax relief backward or forward to preceding or succeeding years. These provisions are too complex for us to deal with in detail in this volume but are a popular selling point of personal pension schemes.
7 Personal pension schemes also have an element of flexibility and portability. Members can vary their contributions to their fund and can transport their fund value from one fund to another (whether employer or private).

Notes:
1 Through a rebate-only personal pension (i.e. one only capable of receiving minimum contributions from the DSS), it is possible to be in a personal pension and a company occupational pension scheme simultaneously.

2 Pensions are taxable as earned income, having attracted income-tax relief on contributions.
3 Contributions, once made, cannot be withdrawn but are 'locked in' until the chosen retirement date.

The Social Security Act 1990 provides for minimum annual increases in annual pension payments from occupational and personal schemes, greater protection of members and limits on self-investment.

Savings and investments with life assurance

An alternative means of provision for retirement is to pay into a good life assurance policy with provision for savings and/or investment. The disadvantage of this is that *no* income-tax relief is available on premiums for policies effected after 13 March 1984. The *advantage* is flexibility as to where the saver/investor places his or her funds, the ability to withdraw before retirement age and lump-sum benefits (maturity value) are often tax-free.

Savings and investment life assurance policies are a useful form of provision for retirement especially when a person has only a limited number of years left until retirement, but it must be remembered that the minimum period of a life assurance policy is 10 years and the return usually improves as the policy runs for a longer period.

Save as you earn (SAYE)

There are also arrangements with banks and building societies whereby employees may pay regular weekly or monthly sums into a savings account by deduction from their wages/salary. Payment is made by the employer direct to the bank or building society of their choice by credit transfer and employees simply present their account book to their bank or building society to be 'made up' with payment and/or interest, or for withdrawal.

Advice

The foregoing is a summary description of the pensions arrangements and alternatives available to employees and self-employed, and is not intended as detailed authoritative advice.

Note: Readers (and their employees) should seek independent financial advice, from an independent financial adviser licensed under FIMBRA or LAUTRO, on the kinds of pensions and/or investments which are suitable for them. This is particularly important when making arrangements through an intermediary and not, e.g. via one's own company occupational scheme.

Health checklist — payments and deductions

1 Have you decided on your methods of payment: salary/wage? Pay day? How to pay? Fringe benefits/perks (if any)?
2 Do you have itemized pay statements? Are they legal?
3 Did you (will you be able to) correctly take action on recruiting your first employee (if applicable)? Have you obtained your PAYE system (P.8, etc.) and IR 'Starter Pack'?
4 Are you making correct deductions from pay (avoiding illegal ones)?
5 Do you understand PAYE and NIC? And the methods of calculation?
   Are you deducting/contributing PAYE/NIC and paying to the IR?
   Have you acquired all the IR and DSS literature (see page 61, 71 and 78)?
6 Have you decided on pension arrangements (in-house or private)?
7 Do you have a SSP system in place?
   Do you understand the system (QDs, PIWs, linking, UEL/LELs)?
   What is *your* policy on notification and evidence of sickness?
   Have you decided on 'qualifying days' (QDs)?
   Remember to deduct PAYE/NIC and reclaim 80 per cent (or 100 per cent) of SSP.
8 Do you understand the SMP scheme?
   Are you clear on PAYE/NIC deductions and reclaims of SMP?

5 Health and safety

Health and safety is a very extensive and complex subject with considerable recent and planned UK and EC legislation which cannot be adequately covered in this volume. Thus, an appreciation of the essential principles only, as they directly affect employees, is given in this volume.

The reader who wishes to make a more comprehensive study of all aspects of health and safety is referred to the companion volume, The Health and Safety Survival Guide by the same author, also published by McGraw-Hill Book Company Europe.

Introduction

A safe workplace is an efficient workplace. Employees are your most valuable asset and they need to be protected. Managers have a vested interest and a legal duty to protect them.

The lack of safety awareness in workplaces has wrought much havoc in human lives. We cannot adequately describe trauma, e.g. the grief of the widow at the graveside, but we can see some of the effects outlined in the following paragraphs.

5.1 Why health and safety?

'Health and safety is just common sense!'

If it is 'just common sense', why are there so many accidents?

There is always the feeling of 'it won't happen to me', 'It'll only be for a minute', or 'we haven't had an accident—yet'.

In asking 'why health and safety', our answer should be 'because we want to protect our "most valued asset"', 'we want to ensure they are protected from ill health and injury'. But the sad fact is that industry all too often fails, as statistics show, and so the terrible toll of deaths and appalling injuries is motivation after the event.

The size of the problem

Statistics over time vary because of differing and incomplete methods of reporting, but in UK industry in the 1960s and early 1970s over 700 were killed and over 180,000* seriously injured every year.

* 'Reportable' accidents, i.e. those resulting in absence from work for four or more days.

Health and safety

Table 5.1 Accident statistics†

Year	Killed	Major injuries	Serious injuries
1970	700	180,000†	(New legislation
1977	412	268,288†	introduced in 1975)
1982	468	12,001	375,530
1987/88	361	20,057	159,852
1988/89‡	362	19,994	163,119
1989/90	362	20,396	165,244
1990/91	326	19,607	156,604

* 'Reportable' accidents, i.e. those resulting in absence from work of four days or more. If non-reportable accidents statistics were available, they would probably at least double these figures. Estimate of 'non-serious', non-reportable injuries is 1.25 million p.a.!
† Figures for major injuries and serious injuries combined.
‡ Does not include 167 killed in Piper Alpha disaster 6 July 1988.

In the 1980s, improved reporting procedures produced more accurate and meaningful figures.

Table 5.1 gives extracts from HSC Annual Reports.

We can see that after the introduction of new legislation the numbers killed dropped while serious injuries have risen dramatically.

The nature of the problem

If we look at those statistics in another way, we can see 'what people were doing' when they were injured.

The figures in Table 5.2, expressed as percentages of all death and injuries, may surprise you.

Notice in Table 5.2 that the highest and increasing accident-causes are handling goods and the high incidence of persons falling.

Table 5.2 Causes of accidents

Activity	Percentages					
	1974*	1984*	1988†	1989†	1990†	1991†
Operating machinery	16	16	5.4	5.6	5.3	5.3
Driving firms' transport	8	7	2.4	2.7	2.7	2.5
Persons falling	16	16	29.7	29.5	30.3	31.4
Striking against objects	9	8	6.4	6.5	6.3	6.2
Struck by falling objects	7	6	15.6	15.4	15.4	14.4
Handling goods	27	30	30.5	30.6	30.7	30.8
Using hand-tools	7	6	‡	‡	‡	‡
Using oils/chemicals	4	4	2.7	2.7	2.8	3.0
Not specified	6	7	7.2	7.0	6.8	6.4

* *Source*: MSC Safety Training manuals and statistics.
† *Source*: HSC/HSE Annual Reports for 1989, 1990 and 1991.
‡ Included in 'not specified'.

Statistics have a habit of proving themselves accurate and are often extrapolated into future events. The 'law of averages' is tough to beat. We want to ensure that neither your company nor your employees become part of those statistics; so we shall guide you through the basic essentials that you will need to know and do, both to help you keep 'safe' and to stay on the right side of the law.

Further, more detailed statistical data will be found in the companion volume *The Health and Safety Survival Guide*.

5.2 The costs of health and safety

In every aspect of business there are costs. When a health and safety item is required the question is invariably, 'how much will it cost?' We need to assess whether costs are reasonable and practicable, but with health and safety there are two ways to view costs.

The costs of providing for health and safety

Personal The first cost is a personal one of commitment. When the lives and limbs of your employees and yourself are at stake, leadership from the top is vital. A *safe* workforce is a happy workforce. You need to demonstrate and encourage two things:

1 *Safety consciousness*: the attitude of mind to *think safety* about everything that is done, to assess (*before* a hazard is created) the consequences of what we do or fail to do.
2 *Safety awareness*: the ability and keenness to *look for* health and safety problems in the workplace, to recognize hazards and take action to prevent them turning into accidents.

Time It will take *time* to organize safety, but time taken at the outset to ensure the health, safety and welfare of your employees (and yourself) will more than pay dividends later. Employees who see that *their boss* is interested enough to take the time to attend to health and safety matters will be happier and better motivated. Time given to health and safety matters at meetings or discussions will always pay benefits later. The old proverb 'a stitch in time saves nine' is never more true than in health and safety.

Money Health and safety always costs something in financial terms. Time costs money, and there are costs of protective wear, modification of plant and machinery (guards, fencing or mechanical), time devoted to safety and safety training. There may be professional advice needed from a specialist in health and safety. These costs will be well worth while both in efficiency and in preventing costly accidents. 'But what if it is too costly and unreasonable?' You have to weigh up the risk of injury against the cost–benefits and if the cost is out of proportion to the benefit perhaps the best advice is not to do that job at all.

The costs of avoiding health and safety

Experience and statistics have proven that the costs of not being healthy or safe are greater in the long run than of being made safe.

Personal A lack of safety consciousness and awareness will reflect upon your image or prestige with your employees, customers and the public—even without accidents occurring. When an accident occurs, especially one with serious consequences, employees have become unsettled and concerned for their welfare, firms lose the confidence of their customers and lose their good reputation with the public (or gain a bad one). The embarrassment and pressures upon managers personally will certainly take their toll.

Time There is a well-known advertisement which exhorts you to use a certain brand of product in your car or your car will wreak its revenge. Health and safety is a bit like that. For every hour not given to it there is a penalty to be paid many times over later.

Much more expensive time is lost because of accidents and accident investigation than is invested in accident prevention. How much time is lost, by everyone, as a result of accidental injury? For example, time lost by the victim; time taken by first-aid attendants, doctors, nurses, hospital staff; time taken to investigate the incident, write a detailed report and console grieving loved ones; time spent dealing with safety inspectors, police and inquisitive bad-news reporters; and time taken to restore the *status quo*.

There are also hidden costs: how much time (and money) is lost by those who work inefficiently in unsafe conditions, who feel insecure in their jobs, who have low morale and lack motivation because of a lack of management concern and who take time-off 'sick' regularly?

Money Time lost is money lost. Add to that the costs of damaged machinery and equipment and their reinstatement, damaged or lost materials, lost production, lost orders due to lost customer confidence (it does happen), payment of company sick pay and SSP, increased insurance premiums, costs of defending prosecutions (on the increase) and of paying fines, recruiting and training a replacement employee, costs of high labour turnover, *ad infinitum*.

Of course, another 'cost' of *not* taking care of health and safety needs is becoming one of those terrible accident statistics.

5.3 The Health and Safety at Work, etc., Act 1974

The Health and Safety at Work, etc., Act 1974 (HASWA) came into force on 1 April 1975, after the normal 'honeymoon period'. There are significant differences in this Act compared to previous safety laws. Several important sections of the Act are examined in detail later in this chapter.

The title of the Act itself was a revolution in safety law, with each word having significance.

'Health'

For the first time, health was specifically legislated for in the 1974 Act. Many diseases such as mesothelioma, dermatitis, cancers, silicosis, pneumoconiosis, *et al.*, had gone unchecked by regulation—often due to ignorance of the health effects of certain substances or processes until it was too late. The health aspects also incorporate emissions into the atmosphere which could poison the local population.

More recent legislation has been passed on specific matters affecting health, including lead, asbestos, noise, food preparation and hygiene and environmental pollution. Some are regulations issued under HASWA, while others are Acts in their own right.

'Safety'

This Act brought all the safety laws together under one all-embracing statute. The old Factories Acts, Offices, Shops and Railway Premises Act, Mines and Quarries Act, Agricultural Acts *et al.*, were not repealed but are all enforced by the new Act. Thus, a company can be prosecuted under HASWA for failing to guard a machine in contravention of s.14 of the Factories Act 1961.

'at Work'

This was a new concept in safety law. Until HASWA, only approximately one in twelve of the workforce in Britain enjoyed any protection in matters of safety, which left up to eight million people without protective legislation. There was no law to protect such workers as teachers and barristers, traffic wardens and policemen, bakers and milkmen or bus and taxi drivers (except by the Road Traffic Act). Nor was the army of self-employed either protected or made responsible (except under common law). And what of the travelling salespersons, protected while on company premises but not once they drove off in their company car? Now, anyone who is 'at work' in any situation or location is covered by this law—except domestic servants.

'etc.'

An enabling legislation, all-embracing and providing for every aspect of health, safety and welfare. It provides for regulations—to be enacted without recourse to Parliament.

Philosophy of the Act

Certain key points permeate the Act. They are:

- 'It shall be the duty': this is a recurring phrase in every section. It is an absolute *duty* on every employer and employee to fulfil every aspect of this law with no excuses. It is not a question of 'I will do it when I get round to it' nor 'No one has been killed, yet' nor even 'We cannot afford it.'
- 'So far as is reasonably practicable': this is not a 'get out' as many at first thought. If it is reasonable and practicable then it must be done. If an item of safety engineering is unreasonable because of 'cost' or is impractical due to genuine technical and/or engineering difficulties, then either personal protection must be provided or the job should not be undertaken.
- 'Who decides' what is reasonable and practicable? The onus is on the employer (or owner of the premises) to prove that something in the interests of health and safety is *not* reasonable or practicable. It is not for the factory inspectorate to prove that it *is* practicable. In normal circumstances, the professional opinion of a factory inspector carries considerable weight in a court of law.
- 'Guilty or innocent'? The normal principle of British justice is 'innocent until proven guilty'. However, in matters pursued under HASWA one is in essence 'guilty until proven innocent' and it is for the defendant to prove innocence, i.e. that they did their duty, so far as is reasonable and practicable. In many court cases under HASWA the pleas that we 'were about to do it' or 'have operated for 20 years without trouble' have held little sway in mitigation.

The Health and Safety at Work, etc., Act 1974 was designed never to need another Act to replace it. It is all-embracing, bringing every statute and regulation concerning health and safety which has not been repealed within its scope. It also provides for regulations to be made under the Act, of which there have been many.

Throughout the following sections of this chapter, we refer to various sections of the Health and Safety at Work, etc., Act (HASWA). This is done by use of the letter 's'; thus 'section 2' is shown as 's.2', and its subsections as, e.g. 's.2 (2) (c)'.

5.4 Duties of employers

The duties of employers are detailed in ss.2, 3, 5 and 6. These include:
s.2 – duties to employees;
s.3 – duties to non-employees (including duties of self-employed);
s.5 – duty to control emissions into the atmosphere;
s.6 – duties of designers, manufacturers, importers and suppliers of substances.

Two key phrases begin each section: 'It shall be the duty*', and 'so far as is reasonably practicable'.*

Duties to employees

Plant and equipment This must be *safe* and without risks to health and must be regularly maintained—s.2 (2) (a). The implication here is of planned preventative maintenance and not waiting until it goes 'bang'. This includes having all necessary guards on machines and protective devices such as 'fail-safe' machines.

Systems of work It is not just the machine or the process which is important but the 'system of work', i.e. the method of doing the job which must be safe and without risks to health—s.2 (2) (a). So you need to look not only at what is done (e.g. operate a machine) but how it is done. This includes the provision of protective equipment and clothing, fire-fighting equipment and safety signs (see below).

Handling goods Remember those terrible statistics of injuries caused by handling goods? There must be *safe* systems of handling, storage and transportation of substances used or produced at work—s.2 (2) (b). 'Substance' is defined in s.53 as 'any natural or artificial substance, whether solid or in liquid form or in the form of a gas or vapour'. Literally anything from handling a drum of chemicals or the office typewriter to moving a three-ton power-press is included here.

Information, training and instruction Every employee *must* be given all necessary information about the job, the nature and hazards of substances used at work and the method of doing the job—s.2 (2) (c). The HSE have declared that 'a key theme for (1991/92) is the importance of training . . . Time and again, accidents have been traced to poor training . . .' It is a requirement that only 'competent' persons are employed in positions. Also, all employees *must* be adequately supervised, trained and given information and instruction in:

- *their jobs*: especially the health and safety aspects, the job itself, its methods (not accepting anything as 'common sense'), the hazards of the job and health and safety precautions to be taken.
- *'fire!'*: what to do if a fire occurs. Do you have regular fire drills? Did you know that *not* having fire drills mitigates against you in the event of a fire where death or injury occurs?
- *safety signs*: do you have the correct signs? Are they understood? Red—prohibition; yellow on black—warning; green—safe condition; and blue—mandatory (*must* do).
- *first aid*: the arrangements provided for first aid and procedures to be followed when an accident and injury occurs, especially in particular situations where hazardous substances are used.

Supervision Companies must ensure that employees *comply* with health and safety rules—s.2 (2) (c). Saying 'I have issued protective gear and told them to wear it' is not enough; it is your duty to ensure compliance with the law and your company rules. If an inspector observed an employee not wearing safety helmet or goggles when the policy/rules say they should, the inspector would enforce those rules.

It is an offence *not* to provide supervision in the job as it is to fail to give information, training and instruction and for this reason, many firms do not allow 'lone worker' operations.

Drug abuse 1990 Regulations place the responsibility for 'knowingly permitting' drug abuse in the workplace on the employer. What the employees do off duty off employers' premises is their own affair, but you now have a clear duty to prevent ill-health effects of drug abuse—and, of course, the effects upon employees' safety performance.

A safe place to work in The building or grounds in which your employees work must be safe and without risks to health—s.2 (2) (d). The Act specifically mentions maintenance of buildings but also such things as fire escape routes, routine access to and egress from the place of work. One of the most needy areas for training is 'housekeeping', i.e. maintaining a safe place of work, ensuring employees keep their workplace and the area around their workbench clear of obstructions, with no clutter in gangways; floors in restaurants, hotels, residential and nursing homes must be kept clear; but also those cables for the office typewriter, computer, photocopier and (most lethal of all) the office kettle.

Environment
You must provide a safe and healthy work environment—s.2 (2) (e). This refers to adequate lighting, heating and ventilation but also to

decor (when was the office or factory last painted?), dispersal of gases, fumes and dust from the atmosphere. (There are instances of people killed by exploding dust in the atmosphere—two come to mind; one in which two died in a flour mill and another when six died in an ammunition plant.) Good housekeeping is, therefore, important to the working environment.

Concerning heating The *minimum* temperature which you *must* achieve in workplaces where a substantial proportion of the work is sedentary or with no serious physical effort is 16 °C (or 60.8 °F) within one hour of commencing work (s.3 of Factories Act 1961 and s.6 of Offices, Shops and Railway Premises Act 1963). There is *no* maximum temperature, but conditions must still be 'reasonable', and you must not use energy to create a temperature above 19 °C (66.2 °F) (Fuel and Electricity (Heating) (Control) Order 1980).

Welfare The Act reiterates the phrase 'Health, Safety and *Welfare*' throughout. Welfare is important for employees. In addition to environmental matters the law requires a minimum provision of sanitary conveniences (WCs, etc.) in a ratio to males and females. Do note that it is unlawful to have *no* provision for female employees; if a female is refused (or declines) a job because there are no toilets, she can sue for sex discrimination at an industrial tribunal and be awarded compensation (£4600 in the case of *Anderson* v. *Alexander Pollock Ltd*, August 1990).

Also, there must be adequate facilities for eating food away from the work bench and factory floor and not adjacent to toilets. In kitchens, there must be separate hand washbasins away from those for washing dishes and utensils and facilities for outdoor clothing/footwear away from kitchens.

HASWA information poster Requirements to display the Factories Act and/or Offices, Shops and Railway Premises Acts were repealed on 18th October 1989. The Health and Safety Information for Employees Regulations 1989 require you to display the laminated-plastic HSE poster 'Health and Safety Law—what you should know', available from HMSO, ISBN 0 11 701424 9 (£3.20 + VAT in 1992).

Health and safety policy Every firm employing five or more persons (including the owners/directors and ET/YT trainees) *must* have a written statement of their policy on health, safety and welfare—s.2 (3). If you have four or fewer, including the boss, you are not required to write one—but we would suggest it is still a good idea. There is no set format for health and safety policies, but a policy must contain the following:

- *What* you will do.
- *How* it will be done.
- *Who* will be involved.
- *Who* is responsible.

Really, for the first part, all you need to do is look at the headings in this chapter and say 'that is what we are going to do'. Your policy is already well under way.

Responsibility for health and safety must be with a senior person, and the policy document must be signed by the senior executive (yourself?).

Beware: Your policy should be realistic. Whatever you state in your policy becomes law, in effect, and as indicated above, employees are required by HASWA to obey it. Thus if, e.g. you decide that all employees must wear safety helmets and you put notices up to that effect even though there is in reality no need for helmets, a HSE inspector would enforce the wearing of helmets because your policy and the signs say 'helmets must be worn'.

A brief outline of a typical health and safety policy, which you may use as a guide, is given in Appendix G. The HSE have produced a useful booklet which enables you to write your own policy, called *Our Health and Safety Policy Statement* (ISBN 0 11 885510 7; price £2.00 from HMSO) which you can use as a guide or just fill in the blank spaces for *your* organization.

Safety representatives   If you have a 'recognized' trade union, they are permitted to nominate their own appointed safety representatives (HASWA s.2 (4) and regulations). They have certain rights including:

- Carrying out workplace inspections, but not more than once every three months with written notice one week prior to each occasion.
- New machinery or major changes can be inspected as they occur.
- Independently investigate any accident or serious incident in their own workplace, make reports and recommendations to management; receive copies of all relevant documents relating to occurrences.
- Represent the workforce (including non-members) to management in matters of health, safety and welfare.

The Act also provides for the appointment of safety representatives by non-union employees—s.2 (5); but this has not been backed by any regulation. Even if you do not have a 'recognized' trade union, we suggest that it would be a good policy to permit the appointment of representatives. Many 'non-union' companies have representatives who do a valuable job, but that is a matter for you.

Whether appointed by trade unions or by non-union employees, management has no legal right of influence in selecting representatives. It is the duty of employers to consult with safety representatives and involve them in the health and safety process—s.2 (6).

Safety committees If two or more safety representatives request that a safety committee be established then you must set one up—s.2 (7). If no formal request is made, there is no statutory obligation. Membership of the committee should be by election from the employees and appointment from management, with equal representation. Safety representatives may also serve on the committee, but not necessarily so. The function of the safety committee should be similar to that of safety representatives, but more inclined to the 'management' of health, safety and welfare than with 'policing'. It should, e.g.:

- examine accident, injury and diseases statistics and trends, conditions and practices;
- discuss and analyse health and safety audit or investigation reports and recommendations;
- advise management on safety policy/rules and safe systems of work;
- assess the effectiveness of safety training and of health and safety communication in the workplace.

Always ensure that a committee has an *agenda* and that it is adhered to. Avoid 'any other business', ensuring that *only* health and safety matters are discussed. Experience has found that where these principles are not followed, the committee develops into a broad forum for complaints.

If you have no statutory obligation, a committee is nevertheless a very useful instrument. Very small firms probably cannot afford time for health and safety committees, but perhaps items on the production meeting agenda or a small informal 'working party' would prove valuable.

Safety supervisor Various regulations require that a safety supervisor be appointed in certain sensitive industries. These industries are: construction, cinematograph film (manufacture and stripping), potteries, shipbuilding and repair, diving and ionizing. This person need not be a safety officer but must be a 'competent' person, suitably qualified and experienced in the particular industry or process being conducted. Indeed, a qualified safety officer, *per se*, may not be a 'competent' person in these particular situations.

The safety supervisor should check that regulations relating to the industry are being complied with and promote health and safety in the systems of work. He or she would also provide advice to the employer.

First aid There are three requirements upon an employer with regard to first aid, they are:

1 To provide adequate first aid. This should be to a scale determined by:
   (a) the numbers employed, the nature of the undertaking;
   (b) the physical size of the establishment and how the employees are deployed within it;
   (c) the location of the premises and of employees (e.g. 'on site').
2 To inform employees of the arrangements and procedures for first aid (see Information, training and instruction).
3 Where a first-aid room is provided, to conform with the standards set out in the 1990 Approved Code of Practice (ACOP).

The Health and Safety (First-Aid) Regulations 1981 and 1990 ACOP apply to all employers, employees and self-employed persons alike. The revised 1990 ACOP (available from HMSO) sets out detailed requirements under the 1981 Regulations.

First-Aiders With regard to the training and appointment of first-aiders, no rigid equation is laid down as to numbers of first-aiders to employees but the suggested ratio is 1:200 in non-hazardous situations (offices, schools) and 1:50 or more in hazardous situations (construction, factories). There is no specified ratio for very small firms.

First-aid boxes These should be of a 'suitable material', able to protect the contents. On the front, clearly visible, should be a white cross on a green background, with perhaps similarly the words 'first aid'. They should contain the minimum of materials suitable for the working environment, as laid down in the Regulations and ACOP. The *minimum* contents of boxes should be as follows:

- Static workplace boxes:
  - general guidance card (see below)
  - twenty individually wrapped sterile assorted dressings ('detectable' dressings for catering)
  - two sterile eye-pads with attachments
  - six individually wrapped triangular bandages
  - six safety pins
  - six medium-sized individually wrapped sterile unmedicated wound dressings (approx. 10 cm × 8 cm)

- two large sterile individually wrapped unmedicated wound dressings (approx 13 cm × 9 cm)
- three extra-large sterile individually wrapped unmedicated dressings (approx 28 cm × 17.5 cm)
- if no running water available: sterile water or saline solution (0.9 per cent) in sealed disposable containers.
• Portable, travelling first-aid boxes:
  - general guidance card (see below)
  - six individually wrapped sterile adhesive dressings
  - one large sterile unmedicated dressing
  - two triangular bandages
  - two safety pins
  - individually wrapped moist cleaning wipes.

Standard first-aid boxes are readily available. The contents of first-aid boxes *must* be kept up to the minimum levels listed above; a regular weekly or monthly check by an appointed person is recommended.

No other items such as safety helmets, office keys, flask and sandwiches or any item not on the prescribed list should be in the box. If you want to keep such items as eye lotion, Dettol or ointments, they should be kept in a separate container. *Never* keep or administer pills or tablets of any kind to anyone but refer the patient to a doctor.

You may also consider keeping adjacent to (but not *in*) the first-aid box such items as plastic gloves, aprons, blankets, blunt-ended stainless steel scissors and disposal bags. A 'General Guidance Card' to be kept *in* the first-aid cabinet is contained in the Regulations and government copyright is waived so that you may reproduce it.

First-aid room There is no legal obligation to provide a first-aid room, but where provided it must conform to the ACOP and should have the following: sink with hot and cold water; drinking water and disposable cups; soap; paper towels; smooth-topped working surfaces; suitable store equipped as for first-aid boxes; refuse containers and plastic bags; couch with waterproof surface and clean pillow/blankets; clean protective first-aiders' garments; chair; bowl; records; plus first-aider available at all times.

Incident or accident
An incident and an accident have different meanings. An *incident* is an occurrence which, although potentially dangerous and with possible health and/or safety consequences, does not result in injury, ill-health effects or damage. An *accident* is an occurrence which does result in injury, ill-health or damage, no matter how slight.

Under the Reporting of Injuries, Diseases and Dangerous Occurrences Regulations (RIDDOR) 1985, all incidents which are 'major' are called 'dangerous occurrences' and must be reported to the HSE within seven days of occurrence on Report Form F.2508 (available, in pads, from HMSO). They include such things as explosions, major collapses, fires. The list of 'dangerous occurrences' is quite extensive and is found in RIDDOR.

All injuries, however trivial, *must* be reported to management by the victim or, if unable, other responsible person within 24 hours. Details of first aid and/or medical treatment must be recorded in a 'first-aid register', which can be of your own design or using Register DSS Form BI.510.

Under RIDDOR, *all* injuries which result in absence from work of four days or more or which are fatal *must* be reported to HSE. This should be by the quickest possible means, normally telephone, and followed up by a completed Report Form F.2508 within seven days of the occurrence.

Also under RIDDOR, *all* notifiable diseases must be reported to the HSE or local environmental health officer (EHO) on HSE Form F.2508A.

Protective wear In addition to the duty to provide protective equipment and clothing as part of the 'safe system of work' (above), it is also unlawful to levy any charge for any protective device, clothing or equipment which is a *requirement* either by company policy or safety law. The test is: do you insist that they *must* wear or use an item in the interests of health and/or safety? If so, you must provide it *free*. But if you only 'recommend' the use, e.g. of safety shoes, then you may seek payment but you cannot compel employees to wear or use them.

Duties to *non*-employees
Both you and your employees have a duty to people who are not your employees. This duty is applied in two ways.

Directly to others To ensure that every task which is undertaken by you and your employees in your undertakings (on or off your premises) is safe and without risks to the health and safety of: visitors, customers, suppliers, and the general public—s.3 (1). Self-employed have the same duty under s.3 (2). Employers and self-employed must provide information to those who are not their employees about things they do or supply which may affect them—s.3 (3). In mid-1991, a firm of consulting engineers whose design and advice led to hazards to the public when a building facia collapsed was fined £20,000 plus £75,000 costs.

Trainees and students on work experience and sub-contractors are to be regarded as employees while on employers' premises. They must be given all the protection under s.2 as detailed in Duties to employees above.

Indirectly, through the environment To ensure that there are no harmful emissions into the atmosphere—s.5. This means not emitting noxious and offensive substances and rendering harmless and ineffective any substance which may be emitted. It would appear from s.5 (3) that what is 'noxious or offensive' is not confined to the description on a label but what is perceived by a user or third person as noxious or offensive, including noise. S.5 (4) attributes responsibility to the person in control of the process of manufacture and not only the owner.

There have been instances of employers doing their sincere best to expel fumes, dust and gases from inside their workplace (obeying s.2 (2) (e)), only to find themselves in trouble for polluting the external environment (s.5). Hence the duty of 'rendering harmless', above.

Footnote
There are other specific duties which employers have to their employees. These duties will depend upon your particular produce or service and are so significant and extensive as to warrant separate in-depth explanation. For example 'control of substances hazardous to health', 'noise', 'abestos', 'food preparation and hygiene', 'environmental pollution', 'electricity at work', 'stress management' and 'manual and mechanical handling'. These are given detailed explanation in the companion volume: *The Health and Safety Survival Guide*.

Also, there are other statutes and regulations, too numerous and complex to include in this volume, which apply to employers. We have included here only those which are essential and of common application in part or in whole to *all* employers regardless of operation, produce or service.

5.5 Duties of employees

Very clear duties are placed on employees, towards themselves and others, for protection from their own acts or omissions. This does not absolve management from their responsibility for what employees do or fail to do. It must be remembered, too, that in an incorporated company the director/manager is also an employee and has the same duty of care.

Philosophy

The same philosophy applies to employees as to the employer concerning 'duty', what is 'reasonable and practicable' and the 'burden of proof' (see previous section). Also, under civil law the manager is responsible for the actions of his or her servants and can be sued for compensation, but under HASWA, as criminal law, the employee is responsible for his or her own actions.

Duty to himself or herself

The employee has a duty to *himself* or *herself* to take reasonable care that his or her acts or omissions do not endanger personal health and safety—s.7 (1). The strong emphasis here is on personal accountability and, by inference, any employee who causes serious consequences to himself or herself is liable to prosecution. Numerous prosecutions of individual employees have followed even without accident or injury occurring.

Duty to others

By the same statute there is a *duty* to safeguard the health and safety of other employees and of those who are not employees (visitors, customers, suppliers, the public) by unsafe acts and omissions—s.7 (1).

Duty to the employer

It is the *duty* of all employees to cooperate with their employer, to obey all the health and safety rules of the company and comply with the requirements of HASWA. They must also use all necessary protective wear and equipment provided by their employer in the interests of health and safety—s.7 (2).

The employee must *not* misuse or abuse any equipment provided in the interests of health and safety—s.8. Such high-spirited pranks as setting off fire extinguishers or the misuse of compressed-air lines are both highly dangerous and criminal.

5.6 Sanctions and penalties

There are sanctions and penalties under HASWA which affect both employee and employer equally. These include: Enforcement Notices (either improvement or prohibition), fines of up to £5000 for each offence (£20,000 to £25,000 under certain other statutes), unlimited fines for very serious offences, and imprisonment for up to two years.

Help

There are some sources of help which you may find valuable:

1 Your local HSE office, where a duty inspector will be pleased to advise you on any problem. You may be anonymous if you wish, but you will need to indicate which industry you are in so that the appropriate inspector can speak with you. Consult your local directory for the local office address and telephone number.
2 An extremely useful A.4 booklet entitled *Essentials of Health and Safety at Work* is produced by the HSE. It is of particular interest to small businesses and is available from HMSO at £2.95.
3 HSE booklet *Our Health and Safety Policy Statement*, available from HMSO.
4 *Health and Safety Monitor* (subscription) from Monitor Press, Rectory Road, Great Waldingfield, Sudbury, Suffolk, CO10 0TL.
5 Croner's *Health and Safety at Work* (subscription) from Croner Publications Ltd, Croner House, 173 Kingston Road, New Malden, Surrey KT3 3SS.
6 Tolley's *Health and Safety at Work Handbook* published jointly with RoSPA and available from Tolley Publishing Company Ltd, Tolley House, 17 Scarbrook Road, Croydon, Surrey CR0 1SQ.

Health and safety checklist

1. Are you familiar with the Health and Safety at Work Act?
2. Are you providing:
   Safe systems of work, including maintenance?
   Protective equipment and/or wear as appropriate? Do you ensure that it is used/worn?
   Safe systems for handling, storage and transportation?
   Information, training, instruction and supervision?
   A safe place of work, with safe access and egress?
   A healthy environment and adequate welfare facilities?
3. Have you displayed the HSE notice 'Health and Safety Law—what you should know'?
4. (If you employ five or more people) Have you prepared a *written* statement of your health and safety policy, including your arrangements for COSHH and noise assessments? Is it signed?
5. Are you familiar with your duties to: employees (s.2); the public and other non-employees (s.3); customers (s.6).
6. Have you made all your employees aware of their duties: to themselves; other employees; non-employees; customers?
7. Is a senior person appointed responsible for health and safety?
8. Do you keep a register of *all* first-aid treatments, no matter how trivial?
9. Do you keep an accident register (DSS Form BI.510) and reports Forms F.2508 and F.2508A (even if you have had *no* accidents, injuries or diseases)?
10. Do you have an employer's liability insurance certificate? Is it in-date and displayed?
11. (If you employ fewer than 21 at ground level, or fewer than 11 on upper floors) Do you comply with the Fire Precautions Act?
12. (If you employ more than 10 above ground level) Do you have, or have you applied for, a fire certificate? Are you complying with the requirements of the fire certificate?
13. (If you employ more than 20 at ground level) Do you have, or have you applied for, a fire certificate? Are you complying with the requirements of the fire certificate?
14. Have you appointed a 'competent' safety supervisor in those areas where required?

We hope that this health and safety checklist will help *you* to keep your most valuable asset—your employees—*healthy* and *safe*.

6 Training and development

Training?—Not for me!
Would you permit a person with no driving experience, or whose only tuition was to 'sit by' an untrained teacher for an hour, to take your car out on the road? Of course not! Yet, in many work situations, that is exactly what happens. Untrained staff are told 'here is your job' or are placed by an 'experienced' worker for a while and then expected to 'get on with the job'. (Not all firms are like that—there are notable exceptions.)

In this chapter, we look at what training is really all about and is not about. We give some hints on developing your staff, their jobs, and your business. We give some hints on how to go about training and staff development in the most beneficial, least costly, most cost effective and **profitable** *manner.*

6.1 Why train?

Every business (large, small or sole trader) has five basic resources within it. Called 'The 5-Ms', these resources are:

Manpower, Money, Materials, Machinery and Minutes.

All businesses are in business for one single purpose: to make profit. Business resources need to be managed efficiently and utilized cost effectively to bring **profit** *to your organization. The first and most important of those resources is 'manpower', i.e. your* employees.

Firms may have ample financial resources, voluminous high-quality raw materials, expensive 'high-tech' computers, machinery and equipment, and give all their time to the business—but unless that most valuable (but often least valued) resource, i.e. *people,* is utilized effectively, all those other very expensive resources become ineffective and wasted.

To *increase profits,* you have only three options:

1 increase your *price;* or
2 reduce your *costs;* or
3 increase your turnover.

In today's highly competitive market the first is difficult, so becoming cost effective is preferable. That means utilizing those resources cost effectively. Manpower is probably your most expensive resource, costing you by the hour—why waste it? Scrapped or recycled materials cost money—why waste them? Machinery damaged or under-utilized costs money—why not maximize it? Time costs money—why not use time effectively? In other words, when inefficiently and ineffectively used, those resources are a *cost* and diminish profits. Utilized efficiently, effectively and at minimum cost, they *increase* profits.

The *only* way to accomplish this is through your workforce. What better motivation could there be for good training, than to boost and maintain company *profits*?

What is training and development?

Good training and development is the equipping of your workforce with all the necessary knowledge, skills and motivation to enable them to do their jobs with proficiency to the benefit of both employer and employee. It is also the identification and development of employees' potential to their own future job improvement and your organization's growth and profit.

To be effective, the training and development must have four elements:

1 It must be *valid*, i.e. pertinent to the job;
2 It should resolve identified *problems*;
3 It must be aimed towards *objectives* (individual and company);
4 It must give assessable or measureable *results*.

Training can be an individual matter (as with job training, college education, courses or seminars) or it may be a group matter (as with team or management development programmes).

Your company will have a business plan—and your training and development will need to be directed towards fulfilling those plans and achieving your business objectives, i.e. it should be objective based. Every business has problems; training and development needs to be aimed at overcoming those problems, i.e. it should be problem centred.

In climates of recurring economic constraints and continuing inflation, these principles hold very true. Industry and commerce are required to become more efficient with a trimmed workforce. Sadly, one of the first casualties in times of constraint is training and development, with health and safety a close second; but training and development can greatly help a company in such difficult times, especially when costs have to be minimized and the same number of jobs (ever more complex) have to be done by fewer people.

Rather than expecting an employee automatically to take on all or part of additional tasks without extra help or saying 'You will have to become more economical and cost effective', expecting what is required to be accomplished, good training in the new job or those things required by economic constraints will pay dividends.

What training and development is *not*

Training is *not*, to cite some present-day approaches to training, 'send them on a course', nor is it 'we have a training budget to spend', nor 'here is a training seminar, can we send someone?', nor 'whose turn is it for a day out?', nor is it the 'annual company/sales seminar'. These are what we call 'horses for courses'—training for training's sake which benefits no one least of all the trainee, demotivates trainees, diminishes attitudes towards training and gives training a poor reputation.

Development is *not*, to cite some more common occurrences, 'Jimmy wants to learn cabinet making (in a non-ferrous metal company?) let's train him', nor is it 'Jane is under 18 years of age, send her to college' (for what purpose—Does that college course serve her job-development needs?), nor 'Debbie wants to learn to type' if Debbie is a shrink-wrap packer, unless you also want her to type the dispatch notes. Of course, some firms encourage employees to train for a non-work-related hobby as a morale maintenance strategy, but not staff development.

Management development is *not* 'run some in-company management seminars', unless those seminars are part of an overall strategy and serve the company's future development needs.

Why firms do *not* train

Attitudes to training and development vary widely across industry and commerce. To many, training is a *cost*, something for the very large firms but not for us, something we do if we have time or something for our high flyers but not for ordinary employees.

Many say that training is a thing they cannot do: 'because we are too busy', 'because we have too many problems to cope with', 'because we do not have sufficient staff to release anyone for training' or 'we cannot afford to train'. Some say that training is: 'something we do after a fashion—"They watch me and I tell them what their job is"'; what we call the 'sitting by Nellie' (see later comment). Others pay lip service by agreeing 'Yes, it is important' and having good training programmes, yet doing nothing with them.

Note: These are some of the many actual real-life reactions.

But let's be honest with ourselves, how can we expect to get the best out of our employees, for them to be happy or to do a good job of work for us unless they have been properly trained?

Results of *not* training

We thus end up in a vicious circle of the 'no training syndrome' (see Fig. 6.1). We don't train—because we don't have time—because we have too many problems to cope with—because our staff don't do their jobs properly—because we don't train—because we don't have time . . .

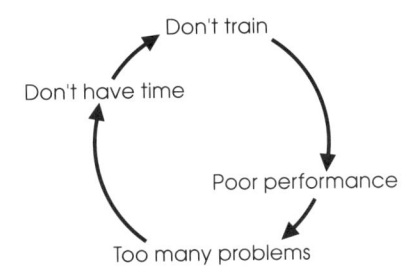

Figure 6.1 The no training syndrome

This syndrome causes those vital '5-Ms' to become wasted and a *cost*—with the further result of lost profits (bringing us back full-circle to our earlier comment). Added to that, we have staff who are demoralized because of dissatisfaction with their jobs or their own poor performance and the feeling that 'my job isn't important—my boss doesn't take time to tell me and show me'. So they leave and thus begins the labour turnover syndrome with its inevitable costs.

There is a psychological effect also. Employees who receive *no* training for their job feel that their role is unimportant, 'so why bother?' How often have we heard 'I am only the . . .' They may also lack confidence and seek to avoid areas where they lack knowledge or skill, as no one likes to appear foolish in the eyes of others, e.g. salespersons (field, telephone or shop) will sell those products about which they have greatest knowledge of the features and benefits, while avoiding those about which they know little.

Results of *poor* training

Poor training can be almost as bad as or worse than no training at all. If training is poorly designed, irrelevant to the job or badly delivered by a person with poor communication skills, the result is time and money wasted, and probably (even worse) a poor job done by the newly 'trained' worker.

'Sitting by Nellie' A popular, cheap and easy method of imparting knowledge or skill to a new employee is what is known as the 'sitting by Nellie' method. In this situation, the new worker sits (or stands) by another 'experienced' worker and watches what 'Nellie' does and listens to Nellie's explanations. The trainee may be told, after an hour or a day, 'you will soon get the hang of it'. 'Nellie' may be the company's best operator/clerk and the most likeable and willing person, but the problem is that she (or he) may be the world's worst communicator. Many people are excellent at their own jobs yet very poor at communicating their job to others; they may be extremely nervous or else will have bad habits which they pass on to the new trainee. Many a job has been embellished by 'Nellies' and still more have passed on short-cuts of which management are unaware and which may present safety hazards.

But let's again be honest with ourselves; how can we expect to get the best out of our employees, for them to be happy, for them to do a good job of work for us or be *sure* they are safe, unless they have been properly trained? It is also a matter of motivation (see Chapter 7—Motivation).

Overall negative effects
The overall negative effect of poor training or of no training at all is shoddy workmanship producing poor quality goods, so that competitiveness suffers, with resulting high imports of better quality alternatives and perhaps a negative effect on exports. A market which is flooded with foreign cars and electrical and household goods is testimony to a lack of investment in training and development with high manufacturing costs. We cannot adopt a lethargic 'we will get by' approach to training.

Investment or *cost?*
Training and development can be a 'cost', if it is viewed in the light of the reasons (dare we admit 'excuses'?) given above for *not* training. It can also be a most unnecessary cost if the training is simply in response to a seminar brochure, has no clear objective, is not designed to resolve identified problems or has not been properly thought through and designed correctly. It is reliably estimated that a seminar delegate will retain only 50 per cent of an average seminar content in the memory and that only 50 per cent of that retained will be relevant to the job, yielding a net benefit of only 25 per cent.

A business or a craftsperson buys a raw material, works on it, gives it added value and then sells it at a *profit*. Anyone who puts money into his or her company, a building society or stocks and shares expects to receive a return on capital (ROC) and/or a return on investment (ROI). Good training and development should also be an 'investment'.

The problem with training is that it is difficult to measure the return or 'profit'; yet it can be done. But *how*? There are a few simple conditions which we need to fulfil in order to make our training and development profitable, i.e. to assure a return on our investment. You may find any or all of these will apply to your situation:

1 Before the training and/or development:
   - *Need*: what need is there for training? Have you conducted an analysis of training needs (ATN) to discover what training is needed and why it is needed? Is this training course or seminar, or new trainee which you are considering really necessary (see later comment)?
   - *Objectives*: what do you intend to achieve? What are the objectives of your programme? Does your overall staff or management development programme have objectives in terms of your company's development? Does the individual seminar or college course have an objective? Does the job-training programme meet the needs of the job? If *not*, why are you doing it?
   - *Problems*: what specific problems does the programme seek to resolve? Is the training problem centred? Does it address itself to resolving problems. These problems may be:
     poor results, low sales, poor quality, customer complaints, high scrap and/or re-work, health and safety problems, accidents and injuries, damaged machinery and equipment, external audit findings, low machine utilization, high costs, low profits, high labour turnover, low morale, high absenteeism and sickness incidences *et al*.

   Which brings us again to the ATN. These questions form an important part of the ATN which is dealt with in full later.

2 During the training and development:
   - *Validation*: is the training valid? Does it relate to the job in terms of company, departmental and training objectives? Is it relevant to the tasks undertaken by the trainee?

3 After the training and/or development:
   - *Evaluation*: is there provision for evaluating the training (to assess its effectiveness) at these four stages?
     (a) at modular intervals during training (above);
     (b) at the end of each seminar or training programme;
     (c) one/three/six months after seminar/programme completion;
     (d) one year after completing the seminar/programme.

   This is most important, not only to assess the effectiveness of

previous/present training activities but also to determine whether the same seminars/programmes should be embarked upon again in the future and, if so, with what modifications. Much time and money can be wasted on repeats of seminars and training programmes which have not been truly profitable.
- *Measurable results*: can you measure performances before and after the training activity to assess true benefits? Some suggestions are given in the next section.

6.2 Benefits of training and development

The benefits of training should be the reversal of all those negative situations and resolution of all the problems outlined earlier, or at least as many of them as humanly possible.

We said that training should not be viewed as a *cost* in 'money terms' alone. Nevertheless, we should always view training in terms of *benefits* — in money terms, since everything (even intrinsic values like morale and motivation) comes back to us in monetary terms — *profit*.

In summary; reduced costs and increased profits through:

- greater efficiency in utilization of resources with improved output;
- greater proficiency;
- improved quality standards;
- reduced scrap and re-work of raw materials;
- improved machine and equipment utilization;
- improved time taken to do jobs;
- reduced time away from work-stations;
- better time management;
- more cost-effective operations with improved cost–benefit (more for less);
- reduced labour turnover;
- reduced accidents and down-time;
- reduced sickness, lateness and absenteeism.
  All of which are measurable items.

All these benefits either add to the attractiveness of your product to your customers or reduce your costs in producing them. Some items may be obvious 'financial' benefits; but let's look at some of the not so obvious ones:

- *Quality*: apart from saleability, poor quality produces customer complaints and costs in returns and replacements or credit notes.
- *Scrap*: this is not just the material value of the scrapped item, but the lost sales revenue. In an analysis of training needs in one small West Midlands company (1988), scrapped product was

discovered to cost them a staggering £108,000 per year in lost sales revenue, even though the 'scrap' value was only £14,000! This was only discovered when undertaking an ATN and shocked the directors who quickly instituted a training programme.

- *Re-work*: sometimes, as with some non-ferrous metals, there may be no actual material loss in re-working. However, there are the greater combined costs of labour, machine time, depreciation, unrecovered overheads and ancillary costs.
- *Machine/equipment utilization*: machines suffer wear and tear and the costs of depreciation cannot be covered if they are not properly utilized. Also, plant and machinery depreciate with time as much as usage and so maximum utilization in the time available is vital in order to improve profitability. This is the main reason for multiple-shift working, apart from possible demand push.
- *Time taken*: time is money. People are paid by the minute or hour and, therefore, the less time taken to produce a quality product accurately, the less will be the labour costs. Also, overheads will be reduced as they are often in direct proportion to production time.
- *Time away from work-station*: this is often a sign of boredom or lowered morale and costs time which costs money. Improved time spent at the work-station will improve productivity and contribute to the items mentioned above.
- *Labour turnover*: 'Why worry if people leave?—we can replace them!' But the *costs* of labour turnover are very considerable: costs of advertising, interviewing, induction and training, reduced output until required standards are reached, new sets of PAYE/NIC paperwork.
- *Accidents/injury*: These are very costly. An accident takes only seconds to occur, but can take many hours to investigate and report upon. Analyses of time-and-money costs in accident and injury cases prove to be frightening. Add to time the costs of materials and product lost, machine damage and down-time, company sick pay, compensation claims, insurance premiums, lost reputation (see Chapter 5, page 111).
- *Lateness and absenteeism*: it is most frustrating *not* to be able to rely on employees being at work when needed. Their lateness or absence can lead to machine down-time, other workers being idle waiting for replacement labour and wasted management time.

There is no claim or cast-iron guarantee that training *alone* gives all the above benefits. Other factors also affect these items. Labour turnover, for example, is also affected by economic, environmental and unemployment situations. But training and development

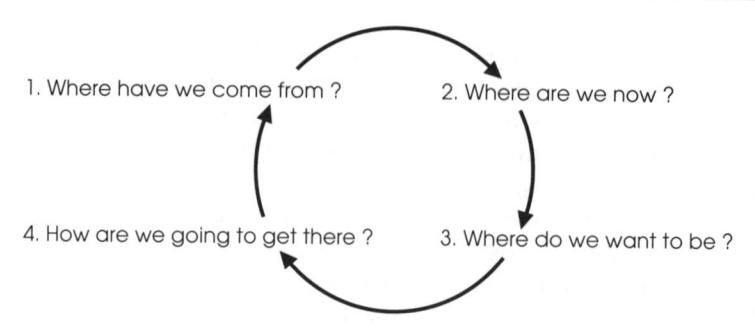

1. Where have we come from?
2. Where are we now?
3. Where do we want to be?
4. How are we going to get there?

Figure 6.2 Systematic training needs cycle

undoubtedly *does* contribute very much, *can* be measured and can show a 'profit' on training expenditure. For example, what was the sales volume of the field/telesales force before training and after training? What were the scrap levels or the customer complaint levels before and after training? These measurable differences indicate levels of benefit.

There are other non-measurable (some would say immeasurable) benefits of good training—it pays off in terms of staff morale and motivation. Employees who are properly trained feel that their job is important and, having confidence in their own knowledge and skill, will often speak to others about their jobs, tackle certain tasks with enthusiasm and may respond positively in a crisis situation (see Chapter 7—Motivation).

6.3 Determining your training needs

The difficulty in deciding 'what training' and 'how to train' is knowing how to go about it from the beginning. The easiest way is to have a system of determining what training you need right at the start, i.e. an analysis of training needs (ATN). Sounds a high-faluting complicated phrase but in reality it is quite valuable and a fairly easy process if done methodically. A cursory glance around the department will not yield results.

The difficult part of any project is knowing how to start. To commence your ATN, just ask four questions about your company in the systematic training needs cycle (Fig. 6.2), then repeat them for your product, service and department, your jobs and your employees (including the boss):

1 *Where have we come from? What is our history*? How and when did the business start? What were the products/services at the beginning, one year ago, six months ago? What was the competition

then? What jobs were done? How were they done? What machinery and equipment did we use? What were the levels of technology then? What were the skill, knowledge and educational levels of the employees then? What problems did we experience? You are looking for change.

2 *Where are we now?* What are our products/services now? How have they changed? What new products/services do we sell? What is the competition now? What jobs are done now and how have they changed (or should have changed)? What new or different machinery and equipment do we have? What are the new technologies, methods, legal (e.g. product, health and safety) requirements? What are the levels of employees' knowledge, skill and qualifications now? Are they keeping pace with new developments and demands of the marketplace? How do they fall short of what is required? What problems do we experience now? What are the costs of scrap, re-work, absence, labour turnover? Which are your most costly areas of operation? Which areas/jobs are least cost effective? With these last three items, the old 80:20 principle is very reliable, i.e. you will find that 80 per cent of your costly problems are in 20 per cent of your operation so that by resolving only 20 per cent of your most serious problems you can eliminate 80 per cent of unnecessary costs!

Comparing (1) with (2) what progress have we made? Have we improved or deteriorated or have we just stood still?

Answers to these questions will tell you much about your training needs.

3 *Where do we want to be?* Considering your future direction:
   (a) Where do we as a *company* want to be in one/three/five/ten years' time (whichever time scale is appropriate to your situation)? Think about technology, products and services, methods, expansion, EEC in 1993 and beyond, competitiveness, BS.5750, cost effectiveness, reduced costs, improved productivity, new legislation.
   (b) If your company has two or more *departments*, break down those same questions in (a) for each department or function.
   (c) In order to achieve (a) and (b), break these requirements down still further. Where do we want each *job* to be? What levels of skill, knowledge, aptitude, potential and/or educational qualification do we require?
   Also, what are the legal requirements? Some examples are:
      (i) all power truck drivers (i.e. of fork-lift, reach-truck, dumper-truck, etc) *newly* recruited/appointed after 1 April 1989 *must* be (or have been) carefully selected, receive training to Joint Committee of Industry Training Boards

(JCITB) approved standards by JCITB-approved training centres and be authorized/licensed. Permitting an 'experienced car driver' to operate is illegal. The Road Transport Industry Training Board (RTITB) will be pleased to advise about approved training centres (see your local directory for the regional office telephone number).
  (ii) *All* employees *must* receive adequate information, training and instruction in all matters of health and safety, including company policy, which affect their jobs (HASWA s.2 (2) (c)).
  (iii) All employees must receive fire-drill training at least according to the requirements of your fire certificate (if one is held) or to the Fire Precautions Act 1971.
  (iv) What are the legal implications for training in: COSHH, noise, lead, asbestos, environmental pollution, food safety and hygiene?
  (v) There may be others directly related to *your* industry.
4 *How are we going to get there*? What types of activity will you employ to achieve your long- and short-term objectives? Should you use training courses and seminars? On-job training/coaching? College education? Government initiative—BGT, ET, YT? Which source should you use—your own (there is expertise within your company), or an external provider (consultant, college, government agency)?
  (a) External v. internal: if possible, the preferred choice is *always* for internal training, providing you have sufficient staff to undergo the training. The advantage of internal training is that it can be 'tailored' and made relevant to *your* situation and may also be cheaper (but not always). It does not essentially have to be on company premises but can be an in-house seminar in, e.g. an hotel.
    Internal training will certainly be more cost effective and will boost your company's image in the eyes of employees (of your own and those of other firms). Many training providers now offer in-company services but, of course, certain types of training, such as college courses, may not be suited to in-company presentation, though some very large firms do run their own in-house college courses.
  (b) *Retention*: remember the 25 per cent retention benefit mentioned above? With *relevance* to jobs, this can be much improved.
  (c) *Cost*: fees vary widely (for both external and internal services) and high fees do not always indicate high quality. The advice

as always is 'shop around'. Internal training is not only more relevant but can be cheaper per trainee/delegate and yield cost-effective benefits also.

6.4 Designing your training programme

How successful your training programme is going to be depends very much on the design stage. Just as no one would begin to build a house with blueprints, so a good training seminar needs its blue print.

Job descriptions

Remember our section on job descriptions in Chapters 1 and 2? This is where that handy document comes into its own. It has served to tell you the type of person you want, it has guided you through advertising for applicants and selecting your new employee. Now it becomes the basis of your training programme. It may be that for a new employee the whole job description is reflected in the whole of an (extended) training programme; it may be that you select out one task at a time and design a programme of instruction in that task (see below).

The training course or seminar may be an external one and not be extracted directly from the job description, but it should nevertheless be carefully selected so as to be reflected in it. If the training being given does *not* fulfil some part of the job description, then either the training is irrelevant or, if it is pertinent to the job, the job description needs to be updated.

Structured training

Your training programme should be structured but not too sophisticated (Example 6.1). It should be appropriate to *your* company and situation, the job and the type of training undertaken. This applies whether it is an individual seminar or course, or a lengthy series of training activities. The types of programme are too many and varied to illustrate here, but we give a few simple examples.

Example 6.1   Seminar programme (1 day)

Telephone techniques

1. Introduction: Welcome and outline of the day's proceedings.
2. First impressions (a gentle lead-in topic).
3. Communications.
   Tea/coffee break.
4. The *role* of the receptionist/secretary/telephone user.

5. Preparation.
6. Telephone manner and personality.
   Questions on morning session
   Lunch break
7. Incoming calls—how to/how *not* to answer.
8. Customer interrogation.
9. Questioning techniques.
   Tea/coffee break
10. Outgoing calls—how to/how *not* to call customers.
11. Abusive/difficult customers.
12. Role play with closed-circuit telephone simulators.
    Questions on afternoon session
12. Review of day
13. Evaluation—delegates' opinions on day's proceedings (useful if senior manager sits in here).

In designing the training seminar illustrated in Example 6.1, the following principle has been built into the structure, as it will always be fruitful:

> Tell delegates what you are going to tell them; then tell them; question delegates (and invite questions from them) to clear understanding; tell them what you have told them (review); then evaluate.

While seminars are a well-known feature of training, much training takes place 'on the job' and, for this, training notes or programmes are just as important as the off-the-job seminar programme. On stage, every actor knows his lines but relies on a prompter from the wings to give the words or 'cues' when he forgets those lines so that embarrassment is avoided—no actor would go on stage without a prompter. Job training is no different.

A simple form of training schedule for on-the-job instruction is called a 'job breakdown'. You may view this job breakdown (and job analysis which we show later) as your 'prompt' to which you refer to ensure that you don't miss anything. This job breakdown is so-called because it 'breaks down' the job into suitable 'stages' small enough for the trainee to master.

The stages are then further broken down into 'key points', which are those important aspects you need to emphasize, such as health and safety, quality, specifications and important information. Experienced instructors will tell you that even though they are very very familiar with the job, it is easy to 'forget' small but very important details. So a job breakdown is most important. Example 6.2 details a simple assembly task, assembling imaginary 'widgets'.

You may apply this job breakdown technique of training to any manual/operator or administrative job.

Example 6.2 Job breakdown

JOB BREAKDOWN	
Job: Assembly of widgets	
STAGES Portions suitable for learner to master	KEY POINTS Quality, health and safety make the work easier.
1. Ensure all parts are present	Parts: A, B, C, D, E and F.
2. Check quality	Clean and bright, features OK, no cracks, no burrs, all moving parts OK
3. Locate A into B	Ensure correct fit
4. Locate C and D together and insert into B	Ensure parts move freely and fit tight into B
5. Attach E to D	By means of . . . Ensure tight grip
6. Insert all into case (F)	Ensure correct cushioning

More often, the job may be complex, involve more specific or technical information and may have important health and safety implications, requiring more detailed breakdown. In this situation, we simply extend the job breakdown format (Example 6.2) with further analysis into a 'job analysis' of the type shown in Example 6.3.

In Example 6.3, the stages of the job breakdown are divided into element and method, and the key points further divided into knowledge and skill, key points, health and safety and performance parameters (explanations of each are given in parentheses). The 'key points' in this analysis allow for important aspects not specifically included under the other headings.

6.5 Types of training

The types of training employed should be carefully chosen to make sure that your particular training needs are satisfied.

Induction training
The first important type of training is that of 'induction'. Induction means, simply, to 'put or introduce into' and is essential in order to introduce properly your new employee(s) to the company, to the department and into the job.

New employees often experience feelings of bewilderment if they

Example 6.3 Job analysis

JOB ANALYSIS					
Job: Two-crane operation (much simplified)					
ELEMENT	METHOD	KNOWLEDGE AND SKILL	KEY POINTS	HEALTH AND SAFETY	PERFORMANCE PARAMETERS
(*What* is done)	(How it is done)	(Abilities needed)	(Important factors)	(Dependency factors)	(Standards of assessment)
1. Cab crane and pendant crane joint oper	2 booms, 4 slings	Coordination of movement	Pendant operator controls actions	Trained and licensed staff *only*	Proficiency and safety in operation
2. Slinging	Nylon slings	Ensure know weight/nature of load	Position slings, load *balanced*	*Watch* for load swing and for people in area	No damage to loads; smooth hoistings
3. Convey load to benches	Cab/pendant operation	Press-button controls	Coordinated and smooth movement	Care in moving load. Warnings	Smooth conveying
etc.					

do not know anything about the organization, who people are, what the different departmental functions are, what the raw materials and products are or even where the canteen and lavatories are! They feel embarrassed when they are asked questions by, e.g. a telephone caller, visitor or potential customer and have to reply 'Don't know'. Health and safety is also an essential part of induction training and is required by law (HASWA s.2 (2) (c)—see page 114).

A checklist of induction training is given in Appendix H. Note the provision for the trainee's signature, which helps overcome problems of lapses in memory and provides proof for you that you have in fact given training in particular aspects. (This can be important where there are certain legal requirements or to protect interests in event of mishap.)

Health and safety training

As indicated in Chapter 5, there are legal requirements to provide 'information, training and instruction' under s.2 (2) (c) of HASWA. Apart from the legal aspects, nothing can be more important than the health and safety of your most valuable asset—*people*. Health and safety training must, therefore, be a vital part of management practice and needs to be regarded as such. Health and safety training must be included in the induction training programme and should be given throughout employment as requirements arise. If you have not given any health and safety training, the best way is to start with a general programme for *everybody*; then follow on with induction training and specific updating training in specialized skills. The health and safety programme can be designed in the manner described under Designing your training programme above, and should include the following important topics:

- The Health and Safety at Work Act 1974 (HASWA), what it says, the duties of management and employees to themselves, other employees, non-employees and the public (see Chapter 5, pages 112, 114 and 122).
- Company health and safety policy—what it says, its expectations, factory/office rules.
- Details of safety regulations that apply to your company, e.g. power press, food hygiene, abrasive wheels, electricity, COSHH, noise, asbestos, environmental pollution.
- Fire drills and emergency procedures; fire/emergency exits; importance of *clear* egress routes.
- Fire-fighting procedures/practices, equipment and their safe usage.
- Vehicle movements, especially on company premises and inside workshops and other buildings.
- Protective equipment and wear—types and uses—importance.
- Job safety: important aspects of the work methods/processes, machines, raw materials, hazards (e.g. moving parts, burrs, cutting edges, stairs and steps, office safety, paper, fire risks, chemicals, electrical), guards and fences must be used and not removed or interfered with.

Job training

Following induction and health and safety training, job training is the next most important need: to explain what the job is, what is done, why it is done (very important to employee motivation), other related operations or tasks (what comes before and follows after), what skill and knowledge are required for the job. Programmes, simple or extended, should be drawn up according to the nature and complexity of each task or group of tasks.

You might say 'it is too much trouble to write a programme for each job, it takes too much time'. But time taken to prepare instructional notes properly and use them pays back dividends many times over, you *know* that the job content has been covered and taught fully and, of course, you only need to write a job breakdown or analysis once but use it often.

A reasonable question is, 'shouldn't we assume knowledge, e.g. in the case of a qualified electrician, a skilled computerized numerical control (CNC) machining engineer or an experienced secretary?' 'No' is the short answer. Skilled and professional people will learn the central core of their trade in college or training centre, but they will have been trained to someone else's way and will not have learnt the peculiarities of *your* particular situation. Also, with the passage of time they will need refreshing and updating in skills and knowledge in a world of ever-changing methods and technology and the many changes in law affecting every aspect of working life (as above).

There is another danger in assuming knowledge: that workers may have picked up bad and lazy habits in former employments or become 'rusty' through unemployment or through lack of practice of certain skills not needed in their former employment—and in health and safety particularly. In the quality of *your* product or service or in safety, you cannot risk shortcomings.

'So, should we give *full* training to everyone?' Again, 'No'. A happy medium is the best; one where you find out new and present employees' existing knowledge and build on it. So, if you have designed a programme with ten items in it and the trainee is already skilled in items one to five, just give a quick refresher in those to ensure he or she is up-to-date and adapted to your methods, then add in detail those aspects which are new to the trainee.

Job training can be carried out in two situations:

1 *Off-the-job*: there will be introductory/theory training to give knowledge of the company and its products and services (including updating existing employees), the 'foundations' of their job, health and safety, pure 'knowledge' aspects of their job and certain things which cannot be taught 'on-the-job' because of impracticalities such as noise or certain hazards to which those new to the situation should not be exposed. These should be conducted in a lecture/training room or an office, away from the workplace and free of interruption if possible.

   Another form of off-the-job training is a college or training centre course or seminar which can be quite valuable, especially if you do not have the facilities or skill to impart the training yourself. But remember the criteria of relevance and validity, as college/centre programmes are essentially aimed at a broad spectrum of industry and commerce and not 'tailored' to your company.

2 *On-the-job*: once the important initial off-the-job aspects have been satisfactorily covered, you can then progress to training 'on-the-job' in which the trainee is shown and told about the job, in detailed, methodical fashion (as described above). It is important

to ensure that the trainer is a competent person, skilled in communications (often an innate quality, though it can be taught) who is trained to instruct, otherwise you end up with the problems which 'sitting by Nellie' can bring. If 'Nellie' happens to be your best option, OK; perhaps you can give 'Nellie' some training in communications and instructional techniques.

Instructional techniques

A very important aspect of job training is the programme of instruction in the job, in the on-the-job situation, called 'job instruction'. There is much mystique surrounding instructional techniques in job training, many fearing it to be an extremely difficult job. We shall dispel that myth: first, the only basic qualification needed is a communications ability combined with some confidence and, second, a methodical, step-by-step approach to instruction—just as the training programme itself needs to be structured, so also we need to assure the effectiveness of our job training through method.

As with any letter or lecture which has an introduction, a main body, and a conclusion, so we structure the presentation of our job instruction in a similar way. Example 6.4 is a simple guide to approaching instruction, called the 'four-step plan', which has been very widely and successfully used in industry for five decades.

Example 6.4 Four-step plan

Step 1: Prepare Having done your preparation (job breakdown):

Put at ease	Important, with new employees or old hands being re-trained in new skills. Precede instruction with informal chat, introduction, encouragement.
State the job or subject	Sounds obvious, but do 'tell them what you are going to tell them'.
Check existing knowledge	What does your trainee know already? Build on that knowledge, avoiding unnecessary repetition.
Create interest in learning	Your worker needs some motivation for the job; job value, job features or performance benefits.
Ensure correct position	It is important that your learner can *see* your demonstration and hear your explanantions.

Step 2: Present. Here, the instructor demonstrates the job to the trainee:

Tell and show or illustrate	Do the job yourself first, one stage at a time, with your trainee watching—using the job breakdown or job analysis which you designed earlier.

Stress the key points	The key points/columns in your job breakdown/analysis need to be stressed as you 'tell', and 'show'.
Be clear, complete and patient	Your trainee will need to understand completely the whole job, patience will assist greatly, especially if he or she is nervous.
Steady delivery	Give only *essential* information (avoid irrelevant and distracting 'chat'), at a suitable pace for the learner.

Step 3: Try out.   It is essential that you test the trainee's understanding and new skill, do not just ask 'do you understand?' or 'do you know how to do it now?'—the answer will always be 'yes', whether or not he or she can actually do the job:

Trainee does job and explains	Get the trainee to do the job, and explain to you what he or she is doing, and observe closely. You may feel need two or three 'tryouts' until sure.
Correct errors *as* they occur	Do not wait until the end, unless to stop the trainee mid-stream would be dangerous.
Check understanding	In second and subsequent 'try outs', ask trainee to explain the key points to check understanding, stressing importance and 'why' something is done. Repeat until satisfied they have 'efficient worker standard' (EWS).

Step 4: Put to work.   Here, we ensure your worker (no longer a trainee) is able to function confidently. Indicate personal responsibilities: what is expected of the worker, health and safety, quality standards, output.

Name person who will help	When the worker has a problem, to whom should he or she go for guidance or assistance?
Encourage questions	People are often afraid to ask questions for fear of appearing foolish. So really *encourage* them to ask questions (even apparently silly ones).
Follow-up	It is important that you check on progress, correcting any faults as necessary.

Applying the pattern in the four-step plan (Example 6.4) to teaching or lecturing notes will also be very helpful in an off-the-job seminar situation.

Coaching

The most effective form of training or instruction is that given personally and informally by the boss (supervisor or manager), at his or her desk with manuals, drawings, documents or computer, or maybe at a machine. This is especially useful in developing staff towards job enlargement or promotion. You can also use coaching to discuss a job being instructed/taught more informally, more directly and in a more relaxed setting. Coming from 'the boss', coaching gives greater impact and status to the training and development.

You would find the job instruction technique (Example 6.4) very useful in the coaching situation but it does not need to be so overtly presented (just hold your notes discreetly) and, of course, the job itself will present you with some 'prompts'.

Verbal communication

Some jobs require verbal explanation rather than practical instruction and visual aids (drawings, diagrams, examples) may not be possible. In situations where the job requires lengthy verbal explanation or direction, an employee receiving long, rapid, verbose directions is very likely to become confused and to lose you after the first sentence.

The job breakdown technique (Example 6.2) can be used in just the same way as a practical job instruction to very good effect. Do not forget to pause at the stages, perhaps checking understanding as you pause, as lack of 'visual' demonstration (being purely verbal) may be a hindrance to the learning process to some degree.

Delegation

An excellent form of training and developing your staff is delegation. Many bosses are afraid or reluctant to delegate. They fear the job may not be done correctly, think that only they can do it or fear that their own position may be threatened by their subordinate knowing as much as or more than they.

But one sign of a good manager is his or her ability to delegate—and to *trust* the employee to do a good job. If you are overloaded with work, which can lead to a stress situation, see what tasks you could easily give to an employee. Perhaps you can keep those proactive 'corporate tasks' on which your company's cash flow and profitability depend but delegate routine tasks which do not need your level of skill and knowledge. Of course, as the company grows and your employees become more deeply involved in its true corporate function, then some of your major corporate tasks can also be delegated.

Instruct the employee as necessary, as shown above, supervising

Example 6.5 Art of delegation

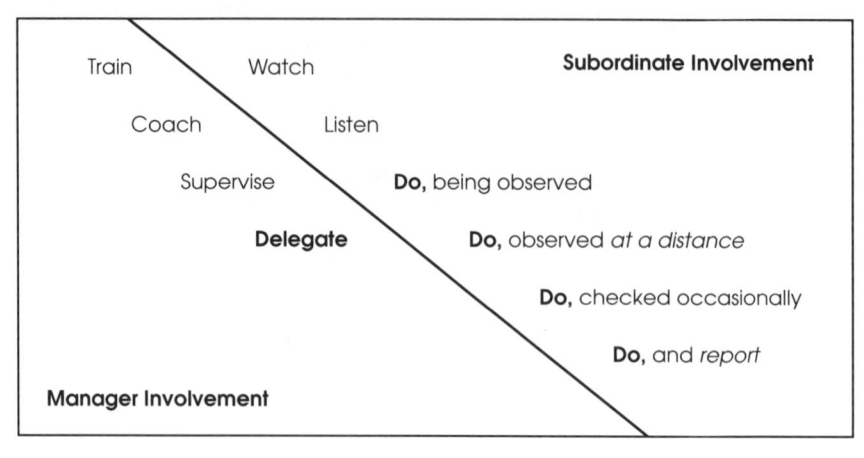

```
Train         Watch                Subordinate Involvement
   Coach         Listen
      Supervise     Do, being observed
         Delegate      Do, observed at a distance
                          Do, checked occasionally
                             Do, and report
Manager Involvement
```

Begin – – – – – – – – – – – – – – – – – (time span) – – – – – – – – – – – ➤

closely at first and then steadily withdrawing until he or she can work without close supervision; then finally give the job over to him or her. Gradually you can delegate more tasks and, as you do, you will find the employee's motivation and feelings of job satisfaction growing. Keen and ambitious employees who are denied opportunity to develop into more complex and responsible tasks invariably leave to find satisfaction elsewhere. Conversely, you will find they will stay with a boss who trusts them to do important tasks and you will have the spin-off of less stress upon you as manager.

A delegation chart of progress is shown in Example 6.5.

We hope that following this delegation guide will prove quite valuable to you in the development of your staff and of your business.

National Training Task Force (NTTF)

The NTTF consists of representatives from business, education and local authorities and was established in 1989 to advise the Secretary of State for Employment on training matters, particularly the work of TECs.

They assess the performance of TECs against policy objectives, encourage investment in the TECs by industry and oversee the Investment in People (IIP) initiative.

Training and Enterprise Councils (TECs)

The Training Agency (formerly known as the Manpower Services Commission and then as the Training Commission) has ceased to exist *per se* and its activities have mostly been absorbed into the TECs. The TECs have four basic functions:

1 To administer Youth Training (YT) (formerly YTS);
2 To administer Employment Training (ET) which replaced Community Programmes;
3 To liaise closely with enterprise agencies and the National Council for Vocational Qualifications (NCVQ) which administers National Vocational Qualifications to, e.g., YT and ET trainees;
4 To provide Business Enterprise Training (BET), formerly Business Growth Training (BGT), to industry.

There is no provision for training or development of companies' existing employees. There is only very limited involvement of TECs in small firms employing fewer than 20 people and no involvement in very small firms with fewer than 5 employees. TECs are concerned mainly with training and work experience for school-leavers and the unemployed through Training Agents (TAs).

Youth Training (YT)

YT is a scheme which takes school leavers aged 16 and 17 years to train them for a career in industry and commerce. It is valuable for training young people for future engineering requirements and for other skills. The method of operation is outlined in Chapter 3, pages 48 to 50.

A significant part of the YT scheme is the provision of national vocational qualifications (NVQs) through a combination of in-company 'sponsored' work experience, training agent based training and/or college courses. It is hoped that the NVQs will be relevant to industry's needs and trainees' aspirations alike.

Employment Training (ET)

ET is a scheme that is aimed exclusively at the employed. It is intended to provide training and work experience and is outlined on pages 50 and 51. For a variety of reasons, many of them associated with trainees themselves, ET has not been viewed as successful in many parts of industry and commerce. That the scheme is trainee-led, seeks to give participants training and experience in skills of their own choice and not necessarily in skills relevant to sponsoring companies' needs, and that it depends very much on trainee motivation, is also a disincentive to employers.

NVQs extend into ET, to make trainees more employable when they complete their training.

There are also plans to provide certificates of 'National Standards of Competence for Small-Business Start-ups' to ET trainees who wish to train to start up their own businesses. These can be an 'add on' to NVQs, but are not intended as substitutes for NVQs.

Training credits

A system of training credits (or vouchers) has been launched, with its pilot stage in 1990/91. The intention is that trainees (initially those on YT, but also possibly those on ET later) can carry a credit or voucher with them to a sponsoring company and 'purchase' their training. In theory, trainees have control over their training and if not satisfied can leave a sponsor, taking their credits/vouchers with them, and seek another more acceptable training provider.

Health and safety Remember that, whatever form of training you decide upon for YT or ET, the trainees have to be treated as any other employee for health and safety purposes (see Chapter 5).

Business Growth Training (BGT)

BGT is designed to provide consultancy and training to companies to assist them in developing their management, products and services and towards future growth.

Potential users of BGT have five 'options' from which to select:

- *Option 1*: kits for better business and training plans (designed for small businesses).
- *Option 2*: better business skills for owner-managers (series of business management seminars in the Private Enterprise Programme (PEP).
- *Option 3*: using consultants to manage change (subsidized consultancy to assist small and medium-sized companies to manage change for success).
- *Option 4*: tackling your skill needs jointly with other companies.
- *Option 5*: how to implement your own innovative training solution (developing companies' own ideas for innovations in training to meet their business-development needs).

Similarly to ET, it is planned to provide certificates of 'Standards of Competence for Owner-Managers of Small Businesses'. They can also be an 'add on', but not a substitute for NVQs.

BGT* and other similar business development and training activities are undertaken by the TECs and Enterprise Agencies (EAs). They are not widely 'marketed', *per se*, and not interventionist in approach, but rely very much on firms initiating contact with them.

Industry Training Boards (ITBs) All but three of the remaining ITBs were wound up by the end of 1991. Their activities were not absorbed into the TECs or EAs, there being no further 'interventionist' approach to industrial training or direct government involvement with companies in their training and development, as was the case

---

* BGT is also known as Business Enterprise Training (BET).

with the ITBs. The Government's objective (1990/91) was to encourage the establishment of standard-setting bodies, such as Industry Training Organizations (ITOs), which derive their income from subscriptions and charges and not levies.

The three remaining ITBs are: the Construction Industry Training Board (CITB), the Engineering Industry Training Board (EITB) and the Road Transport Industry Training Board (RTITB). The scope of the EITB has been reduced to cover only the construction part of the engineering industry and is now known as the Engineering Construction Industry Training Board (ECITB).

Computerized training
There are many training packages which are computer based and provide opportunity for individual or group instruction in the workplace, training centre or at home. The computer package is combined with a detailed manual which is well structured and gives immediate feedback as to whether the learner has understood, whether an error has been made and 'why', and directing the trainee to the correct answer or understanding before proceeding to the next phase in the learning.

Correspondence courses
There are a number of sources which provide training and education by correspondence courses. Training material similar to that provided by university or college is provided, questions/tests to assess understanding are included, and there is opportunity to communicate by letter or comments sheet and by telephone with a designated tutor.

Distance learning
Some higher education establishments now provide high-level education and training through a combination of correspondence courses and computer training, called distance learning. This may be obtained direct from a university, e.g. Open University, or via a management training agency.

6.6 How do people learn?

You want your training programmes to be successful. But why is it that some people sit in a lecture, listening attentively yet not learning, while others seem to absorb information easily? Or why do some learn by working in a practical situation while others flourish by watching videos and films?

Everyone learns in different ways. Lack of assimilation of training or teaching may not indicate a poor mentality but may suggest that the training methods used were not suited to personal 'learning styles'.

When designing a training programme, if it is to be effective, it is essential that two qualities are incorporated into it:

1 It should not consist solely of audio (speaking) or of visual (videos, films, slides) but should have a combination. People will retain and recall much more information if it is given both aurally and visually. It is estimated that most people can recall only 20 per cent of verbal input, 50 per cent of visual input, while an audio-visual combination can produce 80 per cent recall ability.
2 It should take account of the person's or group's dominant learning style and incorporate that in the programme as far as possible. This is, of course, more easily accomplished in individual programmes.

Learning styles

There are four basic learning styles of which one or two will be present in each individual. They are: Activist, Reflector, Theorist and Pragmatist.

Activists Activists will involve themselves fully, without bias, in new experiences. They enjoy the 'here-and-now' and are happy to be dominated by immediate experiences. They have open minds and tend to be enthusiastic about new things. Activists enjoy challenge and 'I'll try anything once' is usually their motto, sometimes rushing in 'where angels fear to tread'. Their days will be activity centred, enjoying the short-term crises and 'fire-fighting', and immediately one activity is completed they will look for another. Activists perform well in brain-storming sessions, but become bored with implementation and consolidation.

Activists learn best from activities which provide new experiences, challenges, engrossing short-term and immediate projects, excitement, crisis, change, prominence, opportunity to generate ideas without constraints, 'in at the deep end' challenge, involvement with people.

Reflectors Reflectors like to stand back, to ponder and observe from many different perspectives. While everyone else is busy discussing, the reflector will take a back seat in meetings and discussions, quietly considering while listening and observing before committing his or her own viewpoint. Reflectors collect detailed data, review it carefully and then reach conclusions.

They postpone definitive conclusions to problems, being methodical, cautious and leaving no stone unturned. 'Look before you leap' and 'sleep on it' are their mottoes, considering every aspect and implication before taking action. They will remain slightly distant but tolerant and unruffled; when they do act, it will be within an overall strategy which takes account of all considered factors including others' observations.

Reflectors learn best from activities where they can observe, consider, stand back, think before acting, assimilate, research, review, consider analyses and reports, make unhurried decisions.

Theorists Theorists respond well to complex but logically sound theories, preferring to think problems through in a logical, step-by-step manner. They are able to assimilate disparate facts into coherent theories and tend to be perfectionists, requiring theories to fit into their rational schemes. Theorists have analytical and synthesist minds, are keen on basic assumptions, principles, theories, models and systems. 'If it is logical, it is good' is their motto, asking questions like 'does it make sense?' and 'how does A fit into B?' or 'how does X compare with Y?' Theorists tend towards logical approaches to problems with objective rather than subjective judgements and do not like ambiguity or flippancy.

Theorists learn best from activities which are systematic, conceptual, methodical, questioning, probing, intellectually stretching, structured, purposeful, analytical, complex, with ideas or concepts and listening or reading.

Pragmatists Pragmatists are keen to try out new ideas, theories and techniques and to assess practicability—'will it work?' Leading with experimentation is central to their activities, always keen to try out new ideas. They emerge from management seminars with new ideas which they are keen to get on with, acting swiftly, confidently and decisively on those ideas which are attractive to them. They will not 'beat about the bush or waffle', are impatient with open-ended discussions where no practical, down-to-earth decision making has resulted. Problem solving, in a practical way, is their forte as they enjoy challenges and new opportunities. 'Always a better way' and 'if it *works*, it is good' are their mottoes.

Pragmatists learn best from activities where there are linked subject matters, practical advantages, try-outs and practice, role-models which can be emulated, current and relevant techniques, immediate implementation, valid 'real' situations.

By assessing your own learning styles and those of your employees, and by building those styles into your training programmes as much as possible, the benefits of training can be considerably enhanced.

6.7 Management development

Whatever style your management development programme takes, it should always be subordinated to and lead towards achievement of company objectives. Training, as discussed so far, has been geared to the individual but individuals are part of a team or a department within a company. Even the self-employed or owner-managers of very small businesses are themselves part of a company—their own.

Management development is not concerned solely with individual needs but with the group needs and their performance as a team.

What management development is *not*

There are some popular misconceptions of what management development is about, so let us first of all dispel the myths. Management development is *not* about training seminars for managers and sending people on courses. So what is it about?

What management development *is*

Briefly, management development is an activity directed towards the development of a group of people in an organization, beginning with the whole company and then breaking the whole down to the departments or sections of that company. Its purpose is to enhance the skills and knowledge of people towards achieving corporate objectives, resolving company problems and achieving job and department objectives. It is about developing the whole group towards improvement, growth and cohesion as a team more than as individuals.

Whatever development strategy your company selects for its management development programme, whatever training and development activities are adopted, they should always be subordinated to and lead towards the achievement of *corporate objectives*, i.e. what the company is all about and where it intends to go in the future. Management development is thus an activity directed at projecting the management team in their respective departments towards clearly defined departmental goals, and then the management team in a company towards staged corporate goals. It looks towards future change, growth and development—not only of people, but of markets, products, technologies, systems and organization. It is 'evolutionary', proceeding towards eventual (but ever-moving, ever-changing) targets.

Management development consists of three basic ingredients, leading to an eventual fourth (dealt with later):

1 The development (not just training) of management collectively as a group (e.g. the management team).

2 The development (not just training) of individual managers.
3 Performance appraisal.

Training seminars for managers will, of course, be required but as means to ends, not as ends in themselves. It should be 'selecting seminars for managers', not selecting managers for seminars—what is commonly called 'horses for courses'.

Development process You will recall the four-step systematic training needs cycle discussed earlier in this chapter. To determine development needs we simply adapt those same questions to the management development cycle, in relation to group and individual needs (Fig. 6.3).

1. Where have we come from? (as a company/group)
2. Where are we now? (management inventory)
3. Where do we want to be? (as a corporate body)
4. How are we going to get there? (what group/individual activities)

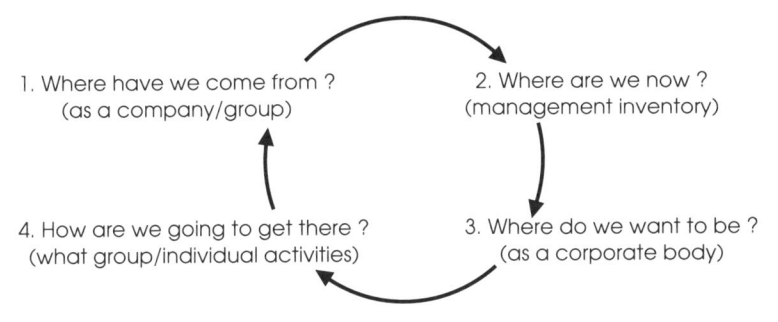

Figure 6.3 Management development cycle

Group development

To develop the managers as a group, ask the four questions in Fig. 6.3, not by taking the job descriptions as the standard but by determining the company and group development needs in terms of the requirements of the company's corporate business plan with its objectives. This business plan should contain within it:

- The company's future corporate objectives (one, five and ten years ahead or whatever intervals are appropriate to your particular industry).
- The levels of skills and knowledge required to meet those objectives—usually contained in a manpower plan. This manpower plan can be extended into a management inventory.

You will note the term 'management inventory' under Step 2 in Fig. 6.3. Making an inventory is an excellent method of determining the strengths and weaknesses of the group and then their development and training needs. It may sound complicated, but in reality is quite simple: list all the managers, their personal details, age, length of service, qualifications and experience; then compare the levels of those qualifications and experience against those required for the company's future needs. The gap is your development and training needs and will form the nucleus of your management development programme.

Incidentally, a management inventory such as this can give advance warning to the company of future retirements and the need to commence developing and training for succession. Many firms have been 'caught out' by a sudden unanticipated series of retirements for which no replacements had been groomed.

Organization of group development activities should be in group settings, otherwise they become individual and unique. In-company group management seminars, for example, have an excellent value in addressing the company's particular systems, method of organization, future projection, products and services and company policies. Management skills which are either lacking or need to be enhanced for future growth can be addressed. BGT (outlined earlier) can be useful for development into new business activities, including product development.

Individual development

To develop the individual, adapt those same four basic questions:

1 'Where have you come from?' What was their level of knowledge, skill, experience on joining the company or one year ago?
2 'Where are you now?' What is their level of knowledge, skill or experience now? What is the gap between that and the levels required by the job description?
3 'Where do we want you to be?' What are to be the individual job objectives in relation to the organization as a whole? What level of skill, knowledge or experience do we need you to have in relation to the job description, the company's future direction and how the individual fits into that? 'Skill' in this context may include personal skills such as interpersonal relations or some other trait which is lacking and is needed for development.
4 'How are we going to get you there?'

The answer to number four may not be a training course or seminar, *per se*. It may be additional work experience, personal coaching by the boss, on-the-job training, secondment to another department or company, engaging in 'brain-storming', quality-circle type meetings, joining in management discussion groups or seminars or any of those activities outlined earlier in this chapter. Sometimes, individual ambitions and aspirations may be at variance with organizational objectives, a problem which can be anticipated and resolved in a group development setting.

Development and motivation

Management development is not only about objectives, systems, products and services; it is also about 'people' in the organization. It is about individuals with differing sets of attitudes, aspirations and belief systems. The morale of the group will be influenced very much by the interactive nature of the systems or organizations (see the next section—Organizational development)—how it successfully integrates individuals into the systems and organization, how it takes into account and endeavours to fully utilize human resources, in other words *motivation*. A vital part of motivation of people within the development programme will be their acceptance of their personal objectives. It will be essential to *involve* them in setting targets and to obtain their *agreement* (see Chapter 7—Motivation).

Performance appraisal

As staff and management development activities progress, controls are essential to ensure that objectives are being achieved. If training and development is allowed to continue without checks, it can end up being completely off course, missing objectives, contributing nothing to company direction and growth and being a very expensive waste of time and money. So it is important to institute a system of checks along the way. This is best accomplished by performance appraisal.

It must be stressed that performance appraisal is of limited value or effect and will not achieve its purpose as a tool of management if it is restricted to only one part or few parts of the organization.

The pivotal element of a performance appraisal system is the job description. In this, the job holder finds direction in his or her function set out under headings such as: duties and responsibilities, accountability, job relationships (quantitative and qualitative), agreed job objectives and key result areas (see Chapter 1 pages 3 and 4).

It is important that each employee, but especially each manager, has a job description and that it has been drawn up in direct consultation with him or her—perhaps even by the job holder. The most important parts of the job description in relation to performance appraisal are the agreed *objectives* and the *key results areas* (KRAs). If these are absent there is nothing against which to appraise; the appraisal form and interview become quite subjective, influenced by personalities and personal opinion and not by objective requirements.

Appraisal forms There is no set pattern or design of appraisal forms and there are many types in use. It is important that the document should be pertinent to the company's particular needs. It should contain objective data by which to measure performance as well as subjective judgements on job skills and should contain at least the following:

- Personal details, list of key tasks or duties and responsibilities, list of key results areas (those results expected from the duties and responsibilities), a space against each for comment on whether objectives or KRAs have been achieved. There should also be sections for comment on strengths, weaknesses, development and training needs and recommendation for future advancement and/or job enlargement. In addition to the boss's comments and signature there should be space for the appraised manager to record his or her own comments and signature.

Appraisal interview Again, there are no hard and fast rules but the following will be a general guide. First, determine who will carry out the appraisal—the immediate boss or the next senior manager? If the appraisal is by the immediate boss, then opportunity should be given for the appraisee to have recourse to the next senior manager, if need be.

It is essential that the appraisal be conducted in such a relaxed and informal manner as to facilitate a happy and constructive discussion. You will find the recruitment interviewing process outlined in Chapter 2 very useful here, as the same principles apply. It will be important, more for the appraisee than for the manager conducting the appraisal, that the interview be private and without interruption.

Do remember to be *objective* throughout; indeed, have an objective in mind, 'what are we, boss and subordinate, aiming to achieve in this discussion?' In this latter respect, a memo to the appraisee outlining the purpose of the appraisal and the form it will take will be most helpful; if possible, give a few hints of the kinds of points to be raised so that the appraisee can have some answers prepared, together with a few questions of his or her own.

Do allow the appraisee freedom to express views, air criticisms and make suggestions. It may be, for example, that poor performance is due to lack of skill or knowledge—but there could also be problems due to failures by the boss or someone else, or to problems in the computer systems, communications or work methods. Perhaps they may suggest some useful changes and improvements of help to the company.

Finally, at the close of the appraisal discussion do make sure that agreement is reached as to future action, with the full understanding of the appraisee. Also, arrange a follow-up meeting during which progress can be assessed and any action to assure a correct course is taken.

How often do we appraise?

There is no hard and fast rule about frequency of appraisals. The simplest answer is 'all the time', on a continuous basis. But there should be at least one formal appraisal interview per year, with interim appraisal to check on progress at three- or six-month intervals in between.

What about salary?

Ideally, performance appraisal should *never* be used for the purpose of determining salary increases; nor should salary reviews be undertaken in the guise of performance appraisal. If this happens, the appraisal loses its objectivity, becomes a 'how much are you worth' session instead of an 'objectives and how we can help you meet them' session. So, the suggestion is, hold appraisals several months before or, better, after the salary review; that way the incumbent has opportunity to put advice and direction into action before any separate salary review.

Staff development

Other people in the organization need the benefit of performance appraisal also, such as sales, clerical, engineering, technical and other employees. The procedure for a staff development programme would be no different from that of management development, subject only to modification to adapt it to the appropriate level. For example, your performance appraisal form may not need to be so detailed for shopfloor engineers or secretarial staff as for management.

6.8 Organizational development

In the last section, it was mentioned that there is a fourth element in the process. It is that the development and appraisal systems should ultimately be concerned with the development of the company as an organization. Hence the advance from development to organizational development.

In management development, we are concerned with setting and achieving corporate, departmental and job objectives and we carry out appraisals to assure that we are 'on target'. If the processes are conducted efficiently and objectively, they should highlight matters concerning not only plans and objectives but also the company structure, organization and systems. These can arise from observations or suggestions raised in performance appraisal discussions, as mentioned above, which infuence changes in the organization and system.

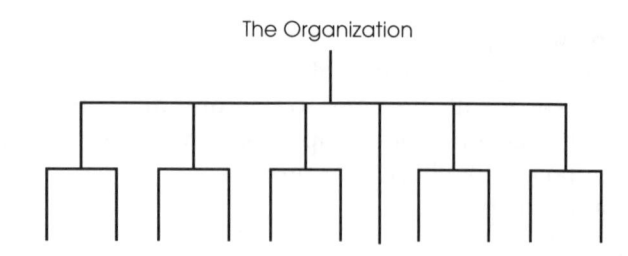

Figure 6.4 The management structure and family tree

As your development programme progresses to higher, fully objective activities, it takes on an organizational development flavour. You then see a system which enables the company—the body corporate and not just management and staff teams—to develop, to grow, to change, in order to meet and adapt to societal, industrial, market and technological advancement. One can also see that, instead of a traditional hierarchical 'family tree' structure with separated functional lines of authority (Fig. 6.4), the system evolves into a totally integrative structure whereby individuals and teams retain their identities but become (by processes of development, education and socialization) objectively integrated into the whole organism, not just organization (Fig. 6.5).

As companies develop their organization, as they expand and

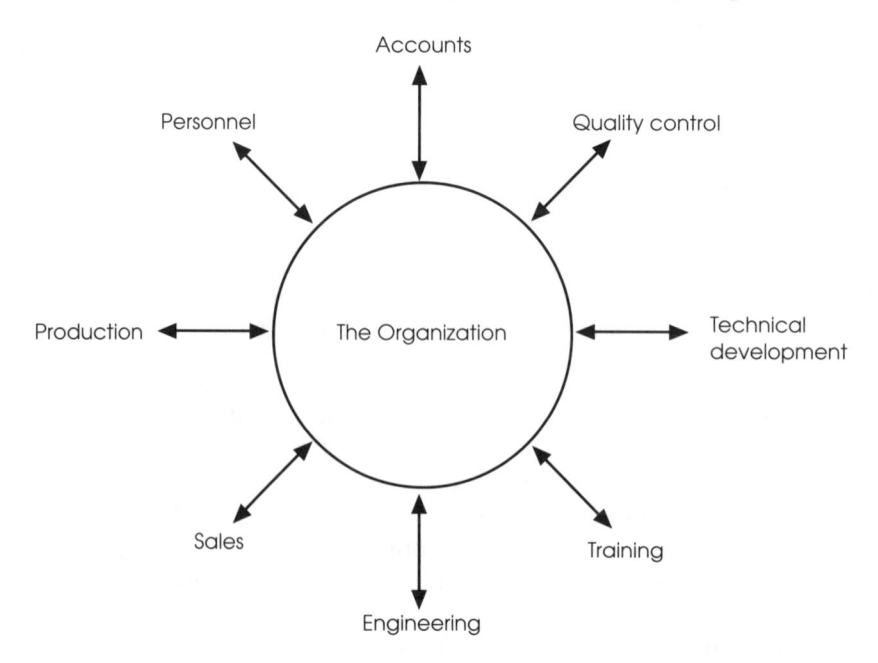

Figure 6.5 Integrative structure of the organization

Example 6.6 Phases of organizational growth (after L. E. Greiner, Harvard 1972)

Phase 1 →	Phase 2 →	Phase 3 →	Phase 4 →	Phase 5
(Young) (Small)				(Mature) (Large)
Growth through creativity	Growth through direction	Growth through delegation	Growth through coordination	Growth through collaboration

(These growth phases bring with them the various crises in management:)

| Crisis of leadership | →Crisis of dependence | →Crisis of control | →Crisis of bureaucracy | →Crisis of ????? |

develop new systems and technologies, they pass through several phases of organizational growth (Example 6.6).

Greiner states that every organization which is growing passes through a series of periods of stability followed by shorter periods of turmoil as each next phase approaches. A corporate system of organizational development, following from objective-based management/staff development and systems of performance appraisal can help a company to adapt and pass through these growth phases successfully.

6.9 Cost–benefit evaluation

We mentioned earlier in this chapter under Investment or cost?, the need for evaluation to determine whether our training and development is proving worth while. There, we looked mostly at physical things such as performance levels, scrap and re-work, and problem solving. We look at those same items here, adding to them aspects of efficiency, effectiveness, reduced labour turnover, raised morale, reduced absence and sickness, and progress in the organizational and growth aspects of the business.

The real evaluation, as hinted earlier, comes in the assessment of financial cost–benefit and profit. This is never more true than with management and organizational development. It will be a necessary and most fruitful exercise, therefore, to assess the *profit* of your development programme, by looking at the 'before and after' financial costs and benefits:

- How much did that department, product, system, management team cost you (or waste!) *before* the development programme commenced?
- How much do they cost (or waste) *after* a period of six months, one year or as appropriate to your situation? Have costs been reduced?
- Against these costs, what has happened to productivity, sales, gross profit and net profit in those same areas and over that same period? Have your profits increased? Or, even if your gross profit has not increased (because of external market forces), have your overhead costs reduced and thus your *net* profit increased?
- If the answer to these questions is 'Yes', then we can reasonably assume that your development programme has been cost effective and has contributed to your profitability.

National Vocational Training and Tax Relief

From 1st April 1992 (but effectively from the academic year beginning September 1992), employed or unemployed persons may undertake National Vocational Qualifications (NVQs) or Scottish Vocational Qualifications (SVQs) training, at levels 1 to 4, via approved training providers and pay their course fees net of income tax at the standard rate of 25 per cent (*not* the lower 20 per cent rate). This scheme operates in similar fashion to the Mortgage Interest Relief At Source (MIRAS) scheme and the training providers affected include local authority and independent colleges, commercial training organizations and awarding and examining bodies.

How does it work?

Any UK training organization offering training towards NVQ or SVQ is affected. The training provider accepts the fees less tax at 25 per cent and then claims the tax element back from the Inland Revenue (IR). To reclaim the tax, the training provider must complete an IR form VTR.1 (ensuring that the trainee signs it) and submits the claim to the IR. Repayment can take up to eight weeks. Training providers with a total PAYE and NIC bill of £450 *or more* per month will claim quarterly, while those with a total PAYE and NIC bill of *less than* £450 per month may claim monthly. Providers can submit claims in advance, i.e. upon registration, to assist in cash flow and overdraft reduction, for example where trainees book well in advance for future college sessions.

That concludes our discussions on training and development. Before proceeding to our next important subject—motivation—on the next page is a health checklist to assess how your organization shapes up.

Health checklist — training and development

1. Have you carried out an analysis of training needs (ATN)?
2. Do you understand, fully, *why* you are training?
3. Do you have a training *plan*?
4. Is your training valid, problem centred, with training *objectives*, and measurable in terms of 'results'?
5. Do you have job descriptions? Are your training programmes/courses based on them (and not just 'horses for courses')?
6. Do you evaluate your training, in terms of *benefits*?
7. Do you provide job training for your employees?
8. Are your instructors trained? Do they use written training notes?
9. Do you provide induction training to *all* new employees?
10. Do you provide health and safety training to *all* employees as required by s.2 (2) (c) of HASWA?
11. Have you considered what types of training are appropriate to *your* situation—coaching, verbal, delegation, YT, ET, BGT, computer, correspondence, distance learning, seminars *et al.*?
12. In deciding on the training mode, have you identified group and individual learning styles and selected accordingly?
13. Do you have a management and/or organizational development programme for your company?
14. Is it *objective* based? Does it help the development of your management team and organization?
15. Do you have a performance appraisal system at each level in the company? Does it facilitate individual development?
16. Do you have a method of analysing the cost–benefit and the contribution to profits of your training and development programmes?

7 Motivation

What motivates you? What reasons do you have for working or for launching into action on a project? Everyone has reasons. In other words: motivation.

In Chapter 6, we said that industry invests in the '5 Ms'—manpower, money, materials, machines and minutes—with the objective of making profits. But industry is not only about producing goods and services for profit; it is also about 'people'. It is about employing individuals with differing attitudes, aspirations and belief systems. The success of a business depends on the morale of its employees which in turn is influenced by how successfully that company endeavours to utilize fully its human resources through motivation.

The most valuable asset in which a company can invest is its people. Therefore, the most essential skill managers need is getting the best out of their team of people—to motivate them. In this chapter we look at some well-tried principles of motivation at work.

One of the most important skills of 'people management' in industry is the ability to consider why their most valued asset should want to do a job beyond pure 'money' reasons. While money is very important and is a prime reason for going to work, in many people it is not necessarily the only motivating factor nor even the first in a list of motivators for doing a particular kind of work.

What is motivation?

A dictionary definition of 'motive' is:

> An emotion, desire, physiological need, or similar impulse acting as an incitement to action.

Similarly, a definition of 'motivation' is:

1. An incentive, inducement or motive, especially for an act.
2. The mental process, function, or instinct that produces and sustains incentive or drive in human . . . behaviour.

Motivation

We could thus reasonably define the management skill of motivation as:

> creating an incentive or drive in employees, based on their motives (their emotions and desires) to get the best out of them for the company's benefit and the employee's satisfaction.

Some well-tried principles

For the student of personnel management or of psychology, there have been a number of eminent industrial psychologists who have attempted to define motivation and advise managements on how to go about motivating their staff. Among the most prominent are Maslow, Herzberg, McGregor, Lickert and McClelland. We take a simplified overview of them here. (If you find what follows a bit 'heavy', just skip to Application on page 168.)

Maslow Maslow (1965) considered what he calls the 'Hierarchy of Needs'. Everyone has basic needs in life which become the motivating factors which energize them into action. To motivate employees, look at their individual needs to discover their particular incentive, starting at the basic level and rising to the pinnacle of the true self. The principle here is that once a lower-level motivational need has been satisfied, to motivate further you have to move up the scale to the next-higher level and so on until reaching the person's *altar ego* (see Fig. 7.1).

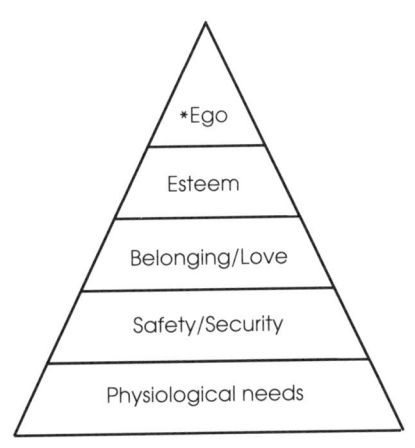

Figure 7.1 Maslow's hierarchy of needs
* Self-actualization, achievement of *altar ego*, the true inner self.

Porter (1961) replicated Maslow's findings in a study of 64 foremen and 75 managers in a company and found a close correlation to those five levels and the ways in which these 'needs' were satisfied, as follows:

Expressed need	Satisfied by:
Self-actualization	growth, personal development.
Autonomy	authority, independent thought and action.
Esteem	self-esteem in position, prestige of job.
Social	opportunity to help others and develop self.
Security in employment	feeling secure in position.

Concerning salary/wage as a motivator (at the 'safety/security' level), Maslow speaks of the 'escalating zero' ('0') in which the initial impact of an increase in pay is to motivate, but only for a while. It is likened to a pendulum, which is swung to one side, but then swings to the opposite extreme. Eventually, as inflation takes its toll or personal aspirations are raised, the value of that salary/wage decreases and so loses its motivational power.

Herzberg After a joint study in industry, Flanagan (1959) wrote:

> There are few problems of more basic importance to our culture than an understanding of the motivations to work. The authors (Herzberg *et al.*) state findings and conclusions that are contrary to popular belief and at the same time highly critical of the attempts at worker motivation being made by the industrial relations departments of . . . industry.

Herzberg (1959) published his thesis, *The Motivation to Work*, arising from his studies in industry, which correlated somewhat with Maslow. Herzberg takes Maslow's principles a step further and says that it is not just that basic physiological and psychological needs are motivators, reaching higher levels of motivation as we move up the 'hierarchy triangle'. It is *absence* of certain conditions which is a disincentive to work and is a form of negative demotivator.

Herzberg splits these physiological and psychological needs into what he calls 'hygiene factors' and 'motivators'. The presence of the hygiene factors does not motivate; rather they are a foundation on which to build motivation and it is their absence which demotivates. Herzberg calls them 'hygiene' factors because they need cleaning up. The presence of 'motivators', on the other hand, is what motivates.

Herzberg placed these hygiene factors and motivators in order of priority, with those which motivate on the right-hand side of a line '0' and those which are hygiene factors on the left (Fig. 7.2).

Motivation 165

| Hygiene factors (Dissatisfiers) | Motivators (Satisfiers) |

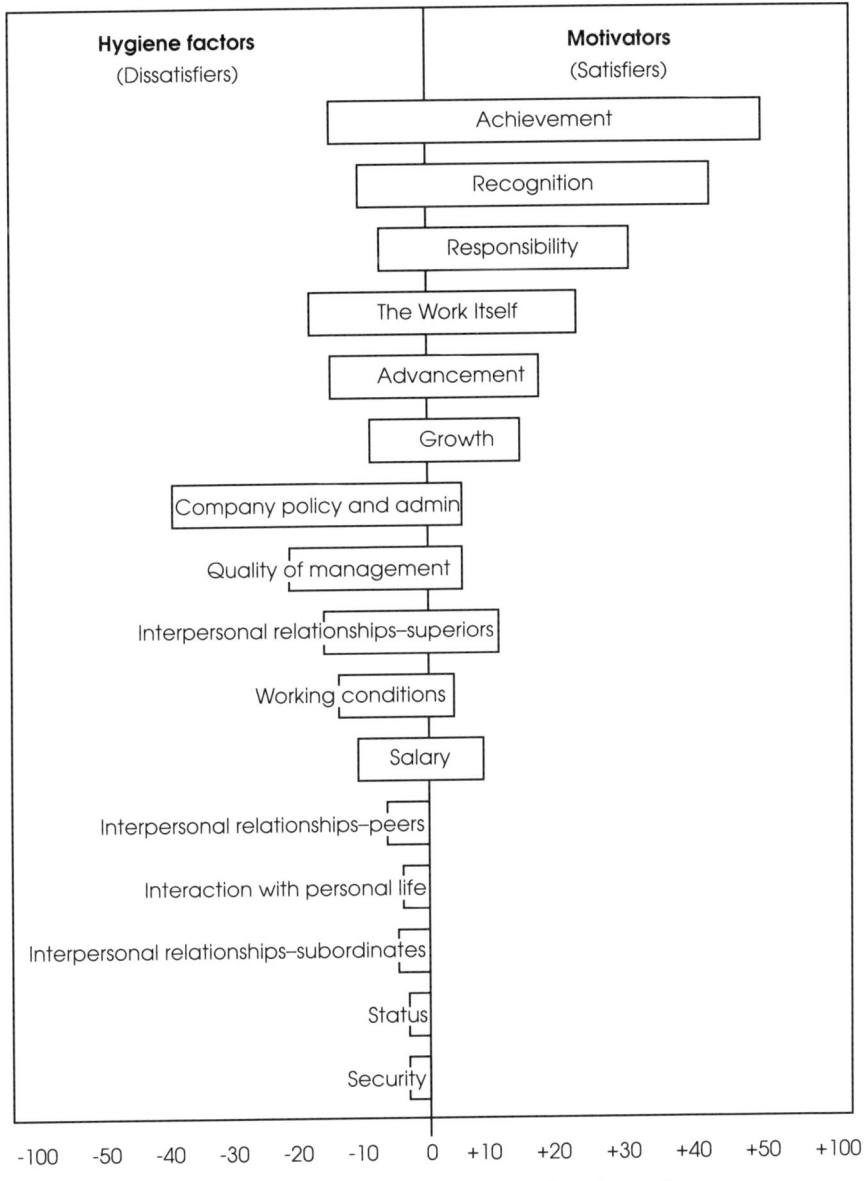

Achievement
Recognition
Responsibility
The Work Itself
Advancement
Growth
Company policy and admin
Quality of management
Interpersonal relationships–superiors
Working conditions
Salary
Interpersonal relationships–peers
Interaction with personal life
Interpersonal relationships–subordinates
Status
Security

-100 -50 -40 -30 -20 -10 0 +10 +20 +30 +40 +50 +100

Figure 7.2 Herzberg's motivation–hygiene theory

The boxed strips indicate the average degrees of satisfaction or dissatisfaction in a group of managers on a scale -100 through '0' to $+100$.

Herzberg found that motivation in industry consisted of attempts to pacify employees by satisfying those hygiene factors, i.e. the basic physiological and material needs of workers. Things such as working conditions (lighting, heating, ventilation, decoration), toilets/wash facilities, restaurants, pension schemes, social and sports facilities are all used as a means of 'motivation'. He calls this approach 'KITA' management, i.e. 'kick in the (pants)' and describes it as 'negative physical' and 'negative psychological'. He also states that it is

> inelegant, contradictory to the precious image of industry's benevolence, and (when seen as a physical attack) directly stimulates the autonomous nervous system which often results in negative feedback. [Further] a psychological attack is not visible, affects higher cortical centres of the brain thus precluding physical backlash, having so many psychological pathways, is multiplied in direction and target, offers ego-satisfaction to the initiator, and finally (with no tangible evidence of attack, being psychological) it labels complaining employees 'paranoid'.
>
> KITA Management, says Herzberg, accomplishes one thing—'if I kick you in the rear (physically or psychologically), I am motivated, YOU move!' Negative KITA does not lead to movitation, but to movement.

Herzberg then considers 'Positive KITA', i.e. a forward pull rather than a rearward push. He is frankly astounded that many managements agree that negative KITA is not motivational yet believe that positive KITA *is* motivational. He then goes on to state that negative KITA is 'rape', while positive KITA is 'seduction'—both are dishonest and neither leads to true motivation. He uses the anology of a dog: it is one thing to kick or push the dog along (negative KITA), another to pull it along by its lead (positive KITA), but the secret is to have the dog walk at your side off the lead without pushing or pulling, which is motivation. Motivation is *not* about 'moving' other people (stimulus–response) but about other people moving themselves with their built-in generator, the *want* to move.

An example of negative KITA would be a threat or emotional blackmail, 'if you don't'; while a positive KITA would be a salary increase as a means of motivation.

During research by your author (for a thesis in 1978/79), Herzberg's theories were tested in the management team of a large group in Greater Manchester. A fairly close correlation was found in the desire for achievement, recognition, responsibility, the work itself, advancement and growth as a means of motivation—as per Herzberg; there was also a close correlation in the dissatisfiers of company policy and administration, quality of management, working conditions and salary; but there was greater satisfaction than Herzberg suggested in the other factors of interpersonal relationships (all three), interaction with personal life, status and job security. It must be said that these latter differences may have been due to the launch of an extensive management development programme at the time of the research (and perhaps would have become subject to Maslow's escalating zero).

Styles of management

McGregor McGregor (1961) suggested that there are two basic types of manager, what he calls 'Theory X' and 'Theory Y' manager.

1 Theory 'X' managers' attitudes are that employees are basically lazy and will avoid work if at all possible. Therefore, they must be coerced, controlled, directed and threatened in order to achieve results. They believe that most people actually like this approach, avoid responsibility and have little ambition, seeking only safety and security in employment.
2 Theory 'Y' managers, on the other hand, believe that employees find expending physical and mental energy stimulating, with intellects not fully utilized in industry. They are self-motivated, increase commitment to objectives as rewards increase, seek responsibility, are imaginative, ingenious and creative in solving problems.

The problem with McGregor's theory is that it is polarized, with managers classed as one extreme or the other, i.e. either X *or* Y. However most managers are not so clearly defined in character but are a combination of X and Y, with probably more of one and less of the other.

Lickert To balance McGregor, Lickert (1967) suggests four management systems which can be equated with Theory X and Y, called the Autocratic/Democratic scale. The four systems are:

System 1 Exploitive–authoritative (or autocratic)
System 2 Benevolent–authoritative (or selling)
System 3 Consultative (or involving)
System 4 Participative group (or democratic)

McClelland McClelland (1961) suggests there are six basic styles of management:

Management style	Predominant feature
Coercive	direction, control, standards, crisis.
Authoritative	efficiency, targets, performance, feedback.
Democratic	participation, team spirit, concensus.
Affiliative	personal relationships, belonging, trust, liking, one-to-one.
Pace-setting	example, standard, performance, feedback.
Coaching	development, growth, support, encouragement.

These six styles correspond fairly well across the four styles of management as given by Lickert and the polarized 'X' and 'Y' styles of McGregor. We could compare them approximately side-by-side as follows:

McClelland	Lickert	McGregor	
Coercive	System 1	Theory 'X'	(all 'X')
Authoritative	System 2		(Mostly 'X', some 'Y')
Democratic			('XXY')
Affiliative			('YYX')
Pace-setting	System 3		(Mostly 'Y', some 'X')
Coaching	System 4	Theory 'Y'	(all 'Y')

It is stressed that this is not a precise matching of management styles, but an approximation only.

Application

Research and the experience of many have proven the importance of motivation. So how can we apply these principles? Both Maslow and Herzberg start from the same basic premise: that people have certain physiological and psychological needs which need to be met and which can be used as motivators at work. If we relate Maslow's Hierarchy of Needs to working situations, the various levels of need are satisfied, generally, as follows:

Need	Satisfied by
Physiological	provision of warm and dry conditions, lighting, toilets/washrooms, canteen, etc.
Safety/security	secure employment, support by management.
Belonging/love	group cohesion, friendship, social club, good interpersonal relationships, welfare system.
Esteem	recognition, appreciation, praise, importance.
Self-actualization	goal-achievement, growth, personal development.

Thus, applying **Maslow**, depending on individual levels of motivation, you can motivate by satisfying that need, at whatever level. But one must not assume that everyone is motivated by the one same thing, say, security which we can satisfy by giving a minimum term contract and paying high wages. You may provide excellent pay and conditions and a social club; but if there is no recognition or goal-achievement your staff may still not be motivated. Many good employees have left excellent employers who provide excellent working conditions and salary for reasons of 'advancement' or 'opportunity' because they lack the satisfaction of the type of work or challenge which they really enjoy.

To apply **Herzberg**, it must be remembered that 'hygiene' factors are not effective as motivators, and that those 'positive motivators' (or satisfiers) should be engaged as a means of motivation.

Are we suggesting that hygiene factors should not be used—that good working conditions and management policies are of no value? No! They are essential and you cannot motivate without them; but they should be used as a foundation on which to build motivation through the positive satisfiers, not as motivators in themselves. Employees will feel dissatisfied if working conditions and benefits are inadequate but they will respond to recognition of a job well done, to praise, to encouragement and a simple but sincere 'thank you'. Job enlargement is another quite strong motivator—recognizing the person's ability and delegating higher level or wider scope work to them as they are able (not always with the inducement of additional payments).

To apply **McGregor** and **Lickert** to motivate your most valued asset it is more productive to tend toward the Theory 'Y'/System 4 level, with full involvement, recognition of the qualities and abilities in your people.

To apply **McClelland**, it may not be productive to adopt just one management style—we need a balance across his six-point scale. A suggested balance is 1 with 6, 2 with 5, and 3 with 4, but perhaps with a tendency towards pace-setting/coaching (remembering that in pace-setting, the boss runs with the employee at first!).

'Where should *I* be on this scale?' Well, if you are all 'Coercive/System 1/Theory X', you will place yourself in a stress situation, with an overload of work on yourself and the constant pressure of 'chasing' people. On the other hand if you are all 'Coaching/System 4/Theory Y', you are likely to lose control and be equally unproductive. Perhaps the answer is to be somewhere in the middle, with a tendency towards 'Coaching/System 4/Theory Y'—not abdicating responsibility, but involving your staff in decision making and practising good delegation.

Management by walking around

A common dissatisfier in employees is the absence of senior management, especially the chief executive, from the factory floor and offices. Executives who practise 'management by walking around' (MBWA) can keep themselves in touch with the workplace and boost employees' morale just by 'being seen'. MBWA, i.e. senior management showing that they are interested, being seen, and speaking to employees, gives recognition to employees and is a great motivator.

Training and motivation

Although not specifically addressed by any of the eminent psychologists above, training and development is an excellent motivator (see Chapter 6). If no training is given to employees but they are told 'there is your desk (or bench)—get on with it', they will regard the job and themselves as unimportant. Lack of training and information will do nothing to boost their confidence in themselves to master the job or to deal with others about their work. Errors will occur, problems will arise for which the employee is 'blamed', and they either end up being dismissed as 'unsuitable' or leave in disillusionment.

A boss who takes time and effort to arrange training and development programmes for employees gives them the feeling of recognition: both that they are worth while and that their job is worth while. When they have completed the training and have attained efficient standards, they feel a sense of achievement.

Information imparted to employees about their company, its organizations, products and services will also give them an affinity with the product, a pride in their work and confidence in communications with others.

Health and safety and motivation

'Well, the bosses don't care, so why should I?' is a comment often heard during health and safety audits. But bosses who show that health and safety is important, who take time to train their employees in health and safety and keep them informed of essential matters of law, who inspect (or ensure inspections are carried out) and take remedial action, will demonstrate to employees that it *is* important, that they care and (most important of all) that their employees are important. It is also a form of recognition, especially when employees' observations and suggestions are listened to and acted upon by management.

References

Flanagan, J. C. (1959) In Herzberg (ed.) *The Motivation to Work*. New York: Wiley.

Herzberg, F. et al. (1959). *The Motivation to Work*. New York: Wiley.

Likert, R. (1967). *The Human Organization—its Management and Values*. Also explained in Glen, F. (1975). *The Social Psychology of Organizations*. Methuen.

McClelland, D. C. (1961). *The Achieving Society*. New York: Van Nostrand.

McGregor, D. (1960). *The Human Side of Enterprise*. New York: McGraw-Hill.

Maslow, A. H. (1965). *Motivation and Personality*. New York: Harper.
Porter, L. W. (1961). 'A Study of perceived need satisfaction in bottom and middle management jobs.' *Journal of Applied Psychology*, vol. 45, pp. 1–10.

We have now come to the end of our discussion on motivation. Before proceeding to our next subject—discipline and grievance—on the next page is a health checklist to help you keep your staff motivated.

Health checklist — motivation

There is a need for application of good principles in movitation and for a commitment to the morale of employees. So how do you shape up?

1 Which is *your* company's most valued asset?
2 Do you understand the principles of motivation?
3 Are you applying the principles of good motivation?
4 What is the level of morale in your company?
5 Have you considered what motivates *your* employees?
6 Which of the tried principles/theories appeal to you?
7 Are you using 'hygiene' factors in an endeavour to motivate?
8 Are you employing motivators/satisfiers to motivate?
9 What are your styles of management?
   (a) Autocratic/Theory 'X'/Authoritative/Coercive?
   or
   (b) Democratic/Theory 'Y'/Participative/Coaching?
   or perhaps a middle-course with combinations of several?
10 Should you modify any of your styles of management?
11 Do you provide training and development?
12 Is a commitment to health and safety shown from management?

If you or your company fulfils all or most of this motivation checklist, then you will be successful in the staff motivation process.

8 Discipline and grievance

Everyone likes to be treated fairly and to be given opportunity to speak up for himself or herself if accused of a misdemeanour or if he or she feels aggrieved about something. The fair operation of disciplinary and grievance procedures is an essential part of good management practice and aids good employee morale. If employees are dealt summary justice without a hearing, they will feel dissatisfaction, morale will suffer and any motivation the person may have had will be negated. A good company name could also be adversely affected by claims of unfair treatment.

We have combined discipline and grievance procedures together in this chapter because, although they have different connotations, their operation and purpose is the same—to give fair hearing to employees and ensure they are treated fairly. Even where the only recourse open to a company is dismissal or where a grievance remains unresolved, an employer will retain its good reputation if its procedures are fair and seen to be fair.

We want you to maintain good morale and motivation, to continue the good name of your company and to avoid being sued for unfair dismissal in an industrial tribunal.

Disciplinary procedures

In Chapter 3—Employing, we outlined the essential ingredients of terms and conditions of employment which must be issued to employees, subject to qualification, within 13 weeks of commencing employment. Those terms and conditions are the ground rules which are necessary in order that orderly and uniform standards of operation and discipline are able to be maintained in a company. Disciplinary procedures are the means by which an employer deals with any breaches of those ground rules, in a fair and equitable manner.

There is a requirement under s.57 of the Employment Protection (Consolidation) Act 1978, as amended, that any employee who is dismissed must be treated with fairness. Many an employer's good case for dismissal has been lost because of shoddy treatment, unfair procedures or just the absence of any properly designed disciplinary code. (We deal specifically with dismissal in Chapter 11.)

Remember that every employee *must* be issued with a contract of employment, as outlined in Chapter 3. In every company which employs 20 people or more, the disciplinary procedure must be written down and *must* be included in the terms and conditions of employment, as part of the contract of employment issued to employees. But even though not compulsory for small firms employing fewer than 20 people, it is suggested that it would be a valuable thing to have included in the terms and conditions of employment.

As at 1992/93, an employee who has been employed for less than two years has no recourse to an industrial tribunal, unless dismissed for trade union activities or because of sex or race discrimination (see Chapter 13—Industrial Tribunals), but that should not preclude treating employees fairly in the event of a disciplinary matter arising. The company's good name and employees' morale and motivation still have to be considered. Also, what happens if, after a long history extending for more than two years, an employee is dismissed and sues in an industrial tribunal? The absence of any fair procedure during a period of disqualification will not help an employer's case.

What about poor performance? It is reasonably argued that poor performance, unless wilful, is not a disciplinary offence in itself and to imply 'discipline' may be seen as a reflection on the person's character. The employee may not have the aptitude or knowledge for a task, he or she may be suffering from ill-health or may have personal problems which affect concentration. Also, after two years' employment, a tribunal may judge that you knew the employee well at this point.

The procedure for dealing with poor performance, except through performance appraisal (see Chapter 6), is basically the same as in disciplinary matters, but with the emphasis on fairness it would be better to adapt the procedure to incorporate work standards, to be seen as a non-disciplinary matter. Thus, a suggested title may be: Disciplinary and unsatisfactory performance procedure.

Structure

The Advisory, Conciliation and Arbitration Service (ACAS) has produced an Approved Code of Practice (ACOP) Number 1— Disciplinary Practice and Procedures in Employment. This is contained in a helpful booklet entitled *Discipline at Work* which covers both the structure of procedures and conduct of disciplinary interviews (see below). Every disciplinary (and unsatisfactory performance) procedure *must* be written down to ensure that employees know what is required of them and so that there is consistency between managers in applying the system. In the event of a claim of unfair dismissal, an industrial tribunal would ask for the disciplinary procedure and if none exists in writing, this would mitigate against the company.

Paragraph 10 of the ACAS-ACOP states that the disciplinary procedure should have some important features. It should:

- Specify to whom the procedures apply.
- Provide for matters to be dealt with quickly.
- Indicate what disciplinary actions may be taken (see below).
- Specify the levels of management which may have authority to take the various forms of disciplinary action, ensuring that immediate superiors do not have the powers of dismissal without reference to senior management.
- Provide for individuals to be informed of the complaints against them and to be given an opportunity to state their case before decisions are reached.
- Ensure that, except for gross misconduct, no employee is dismissed for a first breach of the rules of conduct.
- Ensure that disciplinary action is not taken until the case has been carefully investigated.
- Ensure that individuals are given an explanation for any penalty imposed.
- Provide a right of appeal and specify the procedure for appeals.

The ACAS-ACOP states that the procedure should also contain information on the standards required in time-keeping, absence, health and safety, use of company facilities and sex or race discrimination. We have already suggested that you include these items under terms and conditions of employment in the contract of employment (see Chapter 3), but you may either include them in that document or in this disciplinary procedure, the choice is yours. The important thing is that they are clearly defined, as where no *written* documentation is provided the conditions will still be taken as 'implied' orally or by custom and practice.

In addition to stating the disciplinary rules of conduct, the procedure itself *must* contain at least the following *minimum* disciplinary actions in order to afford an employee fairness if accused of an infringement of the rules of conduct (or deemed to have produced substandard work). These steps are:

1   *Verbal warning*: if discipline or performance is not up to standard, a verbal warning should be given first. This should inform the employee of the reason for the warning, that it is the first stage of the disciplinary (or unsatisfactory performance) pro-

cedure. It would be helpful to the employee to be advised on how to avoid repetitions of this and more serious warnings.

Notes: A written record of this verbal warning *must* be made and maintained in the employee's personal file. The absence of written records will prejudice a company's case in a tribunal.

1(a) *Further verbal warnings*: the legal minimum is *one* verbal warning, though there is nothing to preclude giving further verbal warnings. But beware, the more verbal warnings that are given, the greater the contempt which the procedure will attract with the result that management is seen as weak and the procedure becomes abused and ineffective. Do not forget to record the date and content of *all* verbal warnings.

2 *Written warning*: if the offence is more serious or the cause of the earlier warning is repeated, a written warning should be issued. This should state the nature of the complaint against the employee—referring to verbal warnings where given, the standard of conduct or performance required in order to prevent any further action and give a time scale (e.g. one month, three months) as appropriate within which satisfactory standards must be achieved.

When the warning letter is given to the employee, its contents should be explained and the employee should have an opportunity to respond to the contents.

Notes: Include on the warning letter a place for the employee to sign as having received and understood the written warning. This provides important proof should such be needed later.

You *must* ensure that a copy of this warning letter, with the employee's signature, is maintained in the employee's personal file for possible future use.

2(a) *Further written warning*: as with verbal warnings, the legal minimum is one. The same caution concerning further written warnings applies as for further verbal warnings. Don't forget to obtain a signature on any further warning letters beyond the first and to maintain them on the employee's personal file.

3 *Final written warning*: if there continues to be a failure to improve standards of conduct or performance, if the offence is sufficiently grave or if the act or omission causes very serious loss to the company, a final written warning may be issued. This letter should contain full details of the offence, the previous warnings, the standard required, the time scale within which satisfactory standards must be achieved and the consequences of further infringements (e.g. suspension or dismissal). As in the earlier written warning(s), it should allow space for a signature and acknowledgement and a copy should be kept on the personal file.

Notes: This stage of a *final* written warning is not essential for small firms employing fewer than 20 people; it is optional.

There should only ever be ONE final written warning! If further infringement occurs, further 'final' warnings will subject the disciplinary procedure to contempt and derision.

4   *Suspension*: if verbal, written and final written warnings prove to be unfruitful, suspension without pay for a period up to a maximum of five days may be considered appropriate. This may also apply in instances of 'gross misconduct' (see below). This should be accompanied by a written explanation, set out as for the final written warning, with the provision that any further infringement will automatically result in dismissal.

Notes: The letter should be acknowledged by the employee and a copy *must* be maintained in the personal file.

This stage in the procedure is optional.

5   *Dismissal*: if verbal, written and final written warnings or suspension are unfruitful in bringing about the desired standards of conduct or performance or if gross misconduct occurs, the final option is dismissal.

Notes: If the employee has been employed for two years or more (including any period of notice), a letter setting out the reasons for dismissal should be given. If written reasons for dismissal are not given, they may be sued for in an industrial tribunal and compensation (equal to two weeks' pay, as at 1992) may be awarded if still not provided after an Order is obtained.

The issue of written reasons for dismissal is not a legal requirement if the employee has been employed for less than two years including any notice period.

Examples of offences/unsatisfactory performances

As a guide, the following are suggestions of the types of offence and unsatisfactory performance which may be regarded against each stage in the procedure:

- *Stage 1*. Lateness or unauthorized absence, general poor conduct, minor errors in one's work through carelessness, failure to wear or use safety protection.
- *Stage 2*. Persistent lateness or absence over a period of four weeks, continued poor conduct, serious or continued error in one's work, continued failure to wear safety protection.

Table 8.1 Stages if commencement of procedure

Complaint	Stages				
	1	2	3	4	5
Poor conduct or performance	Verbal warning	Written warning	Final written warning	Suspension	Dismissal
Continued or serious poor conduct or performance	—	Written warning	Final written warning	Suspension	Dismissal
Continued or very serious poor conduct or performance	—	—	Final written warning	Suspension	Dismissal
Gross misconduct or	—	—	—	Suspension	Dismissal
Gross misconduct	—	—	—	—	Dismissal

* Column 4, suspension, optional at management discretion.

- *Stage 3.* Continued unresolved problems as Stages 1 and 2, serious breach of company rules or of health and safety regulations.
- *Stage 4 and/or 5.* Gross misconduct.

Gross misconduct The following are examples of offences which are normally regarded as gross misconduct:

- Theft, fraud, deliberate falsification of records.
- Fighting, assault on another person.
- Deliberate damage to company property.
- Serious incapability through alcohol or being under the influence of illegal drugs (see Chapter 5).
- Serious negligence causing unacceptable loss, damage or injury.
- Serious act of insubordination.

Does action always start with a verbal warning? The appropriate stage in the procedure at which action commences would be at the discretion of management and depend on the nature and severity of the offence. As a guide, we can summarize the disciplinary procedure outlined above in graphic form as shown in Table 8.1.

Action on discovering an offence

Disciplinary action should not be automatic but a last resort. People have many and varied reasons (e.g. personal problems) for committing breaches of disciplinary rules or for poor conduct. It is important for employees' morale and motivation and to protect the company's good reputation that the procedure affords fairness and equity. The immediate manager of the offending employee should first investigate the facts of the case. Following this, one of four courses of action will be appropriate:

1 *Drop the case*: the matter may be so trivial as not to warrant action, an immediate admission and an apology may be offered by the employee or evidence may not support the accusation.
2 *Offer counselling*: part of the art of counselling is to *listen*. The employee may have genuine personal problems—a domestic situation may be causing distraction and apparent (but unintended) breaking of rules, he or she may lack skill or understanding in an area of work and need further training. For example, why is an employee persistently 15 minutes late, despite warnings? Perhaps he or she may have illness in the family which prevents them leaving for work on time and the solution may be to change temporarily his or her working hours while the crisis lasts, so avoiding the pressure and the offence. Do remember to maintain written records of any counselling in the employee's personal file—you may need it.
3 *Initial disciplinary action*: after investigation, verbal warning may be appropriate and the matter taken no further. But do remember that written records must be maintained.
4 *Disciplinary interview*: if after initial investigation it is considered that a verbal warning is inappropriate, any further action should follow from a disciplinary interview as outlined below.

The disciplinary interview
The most critical aspect of the disciplinary procedure is the disciplinary interview. So the following 'interview plan' is suggested as a disciplinary interview.

Before the interview The immediate manager should gather together all the facts of the case before memories fade, including anything the employee may have to say, any mitigating circumstances, physical evidence (damaged equipment, erroneous documents, customer complaints) and details of any previous offences. In serious cases, witnesses' statements should be taken at the earliest possible opportunity. The employee must be told of the complaint, that he or she is required to attend an interview and of the procedure which will be followed, remembering to inform him or her of employees' rights to be represented by a person of their choice from within the company (or their trade union, if they are a member).

The disciplinary interview is a formal occasion, but it should be conducted in as polite and as informal a manner as circumstances permit.

There should be a minimum number of four persons present at a hearing, with the following persons attending:

- the senior manager hearing the complaint; the employee against whom the complaint is raised; the employee's representative; any witnesses for or against the case; a management representative to take notes and to act as a witness. This will permit equity.

The manager hearing the case should impose a 'no interruptions' rule and instruct the switchboard and/or secretary that no telephone calls are to be routed through. This is important, as permitting intrusions could result in counter claims about how the interview was handled.

Procedure Interviews will vary widely in order of stages, but the following is a guide:

1 The manager conducting the interview should: introduce those present to the employee and explain their role; explain the purpose of the interview, that it is in accordance with the company's disciplinary procedure; explain how the interview will be conducted; and explain that the proceedings will be recorded in some way (a copy to be provided to all parties in due course).
2 Briefly outline the complaint against the employee and the evidence in support of it.
3 Establish whether the employee accepts that he or she has done something wrong and record any agreement or disagreement.
4 Call upon the person raising the complaint and the witnesses to state their case. If witnesses are not present, consider whether their presence is important to the case or whether the case can proceed without their evidence, without prejudice to the employee.
5 Ask the employee if he or she has any explanation for the alleged conduct.
6 Give the accused employee ample opportunity to state his or her case, ask questions and present personal witnesses (if any).
7 *Listen* to the evidence and particularly what the employee has to say and ensure fairness throughout the hearing.
8 Decide whether further investigation is necessary or whether the case can continue based on the evidence and replies given.
9 Develop a good questioning technique, using open-ended questions and 'tell me about' questions, avoiding closed questions which attract only 'Yes/No' answers (see pages 28 and 29).
10 Avoid becoming involved in arguments or making personal or humiliating comments. Physical contact and gestures must be avoided, as these might be regarded as threatening.

Summing up After all the evidence and responses have been heard, the senior manager conducting the interview should summarize all the main points of the case, for and against, together with any mitigating circumstances. After summing up, he should ask if anything has been missed and whether the employee considers he or she has been given a fair hearing.

Adjournment Before any final decision on disciplinary action is taken, it is good practice to adjourn the hearing to allow full and proper consideration of all the matters raised. If the facts are in dispute or there is conflicting evidence, decide which version is most probable. Seek fresh information if necessary, and then decide whether the case against the employee is proven.

Deciding disciplinary action In deciding what disciplinary action is appropriate, if any, take account of the following:

- What likely penalty the disciplinary procedure indicates.
- What penalties have been imposed in similar cases in the past.
- Any special circumstances which may mitigate and make a lesser penalty appropriate.
- The employee's disciplinary record, age, position, length of service.
- Whether the proposed penalty is reasonable in the circumstances.

Taking action After considering all available information and circumstances, take action at the appropriate stage of the disciplinary and unsatisfactory performance procedure, outlined on pages 176 and 177.

Appeals procedure

There should be an appeals procedure which permits an accused employee the right of appeal against action at any stage in the procedure, if he or she disagrees with the decision and/or disciplinary action taken, or wishes to seek leniency. The appeals procedure should state the time limit within which appeals should be lodged, e.g. three clear working days, and indicate to whom the employee should appeal, e.g. the next higher manager.

Any appeal hearing should follow broadly the same procedure as for the disciplinary interview, ensuring that fairness is observed throughout.

Grievance procedures

It is not required in law for grievance procedures to be included in terms and conditions of employment but, in order to assure fairness and protect the good reputation of a company, a written grievance procedure is most necessary. It should state the name and/or appointment of the person to whom the employee can apply for redress of any grievance and the procedure by which redress of grievance is obtained.

The airing of a grievance is in many ways similar to that of a disciplinary matter, except that it is the employee who raises the complaint and he or she is not under threat. The procedure for hearing a grievance should broadly follow the pattern of the disciplinary interview with the same provisions for fairness and equity.

When a grievance is raised, the objective should be to resolve the matter as quickly and fairly as possible and at as low a level as possible in the organization. The first attempt should be to air the grievance verbally with the aggrieved employee's immediate boss and to resolve it in an informal manner, if at all possible. However, if this is not possible then it should be referred up the chain of command to higher management *in writing*.

The way in which a grievance is dealt with is primarily a matter of discretion, there being no set format, but the broad procedure should be as follows:

1 The employee should raise the grievance with his or her immediate manager/supervisor and that person should endeavour to resolve the matter verbally and informally at first. If the grievance is against the immediate manager/supervisor, an impartial member of management e.g., personnel or other manager, should handle the case.
2 If unsuccessful in resolving the matter to the satisfaction of the aggrieved employee, the manager concerned should then set out *in writing* a report of what he or she understands the grievance to be and what action was taken and forward their report to the next-senior manager. At the same time, the aggrieved employee must now put the complaint *in writing* also, to accompany the manager's report.
3 The next-senior manager should hear the grievance fully and impartially, giving careful attention to all points of view. This manager should do all in his or her power to resolve the matter but, if unsuccessful, should then pass the matter to the next-senior manager. If still unresolved, then the matter continues to be passed up the line of management, theoretically up to managing director or owner-manager status. (We hope it should never be necessary to reach this stage of exhaustion. Every person should endeavour to resolve the problem at his or her own level and avoid passing it up the line.)

Grievance hearing

The hearing of a grievance, at whatever level in the organization, should be conducted in exactly the same manner as suggested for disciplinary interviews. Every attention must be paid to fairness and equity—both to the person airing the grievance and to the one against whom the complaint is raised.

The final decision should be an impartial one, based on a thoroughly unbiased and objective assessment of the facts in an impartial review. If a manager is unable to be impartial, because of his or her position, relationships or personal interests, then the matter should be passed to another suitably independent manager or other person suitably qualified to act for the business.

Help

The Advisory, Conciliation and Arbitration Service (ACAS) is available to assist in resolving any difficult cases. The telephone number and address of your local office can be found in the telephone directory. ACAS's recommendations for dealing with disciplinary matters are in their booklet *Discipline at Work*, available *free* from local ACAS and Employment Department offices. ACAS has also issued a helpful advisory booklet Number 5 titled simply *Absence*.

Guidance about grievance procedures is given in paragraphs 120 to 123 of the Code of Practice issued under the Industrial Relations Act 1971.

A useful reference is a pocket-book *Guide to Discipline*, by Croner Publications—ISBN 0 90 031926 7.

That concludes our discussions on discipline and grievance. However, failure to follow procedures or comply with legal requirements could result in your company losing a case at an industrial tribunal. So before continuing to our next subject—redundancy—here is a health checklist to assess compliance and fairness within your organization.

Health checklist — discipline and grievance

1. Do you have a disciplinary (and unsatisfactory performance) procedure?
2. Is it written down?
3. Does it conform to ACAS Code of Practice Number 1?
4. Does it have at least those features set out in paragraph 10 of the Code?
5. (If you have 20 or more employees) Is the procedure included in the contracts/terms and conditions of employment?
6. Is it fair and equitable?
7. Does it have a structure, with clear stages?
8. Are the various kinds of offence and their penalties clearly defined in the procedure?
9. Do you have a clear procedure for investigating offences?
10. Do you offer advice and counsel as a preference to discipline?
11. Do you keep the numbers of verbal and written warnings to the minimum possible (preferably one), according to circumstances?
12. Do you have a disciplinary interview procedure clearly set out?
13. Is it fair and equitable? Does it give the accused employee full opportunity to state his or her case?
14. Do you make and retain *written* records of all warnings?
15. Do you have an appeals procedure?
16. If you dismissed someone, would it be fair (see also Chapter 11)?
17. Do you have a grievance procedure?
18. Is it written down? Is it communicated to employees?
19. Is it fair and equitable?
20. Are employees told to whom they can take their grievances?
21. Does it give full opportunity to air problems in confidence?
22. Do you have a grievance hearing procedure?
23. Is it fair and equitable?

9 Redundancy

Times of economic restraint weigh heavily on many firms when facing recession or the need to become more cost effective.

There are only two ways to increase or maintain profit levels (as discussed in Chapter 6), i.e. to increase prices or reduce costs. When the market will not stand increased prices, the only option to a company is to reduce costs. This initially means applying strict controls on expenditure, calling a halt to non-essential items and seeking reduced prices or seeking deferred payments for other purchases.

When cost reduction does not produce the required savings to protect the business then, in many instances, the shedding of labour becomes the only option. There are also instances in which firms transfer their operation to a different location and the labour force which cannot move with them have to be dismissed, or more sadly firms close down and the entire workforce is dismissed. In all these situations, the dismissal is known as redundancy.

The human aspect

Being made redundant can be an extremely emotional experience for the individual concerned. There will be concerns for the welfare and financial security of the employee's family, worries about a possible threat to their home and possessions. There may also be feelings of loss of status with family and friends, of worthlessness to society or of lingering resentment, especially if they continue in unemployment for some time afterward.

The experience of making someone redundant can also be harrowing for the directors or owner-managers who reach the decision and for the particular manager who administers the process. It is thus important for all concerned that redundancies be effected in as fair and equitable a manner as possible, and with minimal ill-feeling. Following the advice in this chapter will assist.

The legal aspect

Redundancy is, *de facto,* the breaking of a contract of employment through dismissal and is covered by the Employment Protection

(Consolidation) Act 1978, as amended by the Employment Acts of 1980 and 1982.

It is important that when dismissal takes place it is fair and seen to be fair. Because it is the breaking of a contract, three legal criteria for redundancy are therefore important: definition of redundancy, fairness in selection for redundancy; and mitigation.

1 *Definition*: a person shall be regarded as fairly dismissed due to redundancy, in accordance with s.81 (2) of the Act, if the dismissal is 'wholly or mainly' due to any of the three following situations:
   (a) The employing company has ceased trading or intends to cease trading, e.g. closure of a factory or office
   (b) The employing company has ceased or intends to cease trading for the particular purpose for which the employee was engaged (e.g. has ceased the machine-toolmaking part of a business, or has changed from making machine-tools to making chocolates).
   (c) The employing company has ceased to trade in the place where the employee was engaged to work. i.e. has moved to another area.
   (d) The requirements for the particular work for which the employee was engaged no longer exist or are diminished, e.g. because the business has diminished, there have been new advanced machinery purchases or the work is now carried out by a different method.

2 *Fairness*: for redundancy to be fair and equitable, certain criteria must exist:
   (a) The job must genuinely be no longer available. If, after an employee is made redundant, another person is given the job, then the selection for redundancy would be deemed to be unfair as the work clearly still exists.

   An exception to this would be if, for genuine financial reasons or diminished work requirements, several jobs had to be combined into a smaller number of jobs e.g. three jobs into two.
   (b) The offer of an alternative suitable position of equal skill, status and pay must be offered, if available. If an employee was made redundant and a new employee was recruited into another vacant position for which the redundant employee was qualified but it was not offered to him or her, the redundant employee could sue for unfair dismissal at an industrial tribunal.
   (c) In selection for redundancy, the particular employee made redundant must be selected for genuine reasons and given fair

treatment in comparison with others in similar positions. They must not be selected for redundancy because of reasons unconnected with the work or the workplace, e.g. personal dislike, race, sex, pregnancy or personality.

Firms faced with difficulty in giving equitable treatment among a group of employees of equal status may call upon a number of employees to accept voluntary redundancy, so selecting themselves.

(d) The dismissal due to redundancy must be in accordance with an agreed procedure or established customary arrangement, there being no valid reason for departing from that agreement or arrangement.

If the above criteria are *not* seen to be applied, then the employee may be able to sue at an industrial tribunal for unfair dismissal due to unfair selection for redundancy.

3 *Mitigation*: in accordance with the Industrial Relations Code of Practice, an employing company faced with the prospect of redundancies must take the following action to try to mitigate redundancies:
 (a) Consult with employees or their representatives.
 (b) Devise a policy for dealing with reductions in the workforce, should they become necessary, well in advance.
 (c) Seek to avoid redundancies by the following means:
   (i) Restrict recruitment.
   (ii) Retire employees who are beyond normal retirement age (being careful to treat males and females equally).
   (iii) Reduce overtime working.
   (iv) Introduce short-time working during temporary reductions in demand for work.
   (v) Re-train redundant workers for alternative jobs.
   (vi) Transfer redundant workers to alternative positions.

Easing the situation

If, after all possible alternatives have been investigated, redundancies are still unavoidable, the following action should be taken to minimize the effects of redundancy on employees and on the company:

1 Give advance warning to the Department of Employment as early as possible before any redundancies take effect.
2 Investigate the possibility of voluntary redundancies, retirements or early retirements, or transfer to other undertakings within the employing company.
3 If large numbers of redundancies are inevitable, plan a phased redundancy programme.

4 Do the utmost to place employees in alternative employment by:
   (a) liaison with the Department of Employment (Jobcentre);
   (b) giving affected employees reasonable time off for job-seeking and employment interviews;
   (c) establishing contact with other companies in the area with the offer of details of redundant employees, including their skills, knowledge, experience and particular capabilities;
   (d) ensure that the employees are informed of redundancies before any public announcement is made to the media.

If an employer fails to comply with these requirements, this would not automatically render the redundancies 'unfair'. But in the event of any claim for unfair dismissal due to redundancy at an Industrial Tribunal, the fact of failure would weigh against the company's defence.

So, should redundancies unfortunately occur—follow the procedure.

Counselling Sudden redundancy can have a devastating effect upon people, even if warning is given. When it finally occurs the reality can still bring shock and dismay. Redundancy can result in *stress*, either directly or indirectly, because of other problems brought on by the redundancy some of which were mentioned earlier. It will be most helpful, therefore, if a counselling service can be provided by internal sources, such as the personnel manager or welfare officer or by external and independent sources such as professional stress counsellors.

Large numbers

The foregoing applies particularly to individuals or to small groups, but it also applies to larger groups who are made redundant. However, when a company makes larger numbers redundant, there are certain obligations placed on the employing company. They are:

- *Ten or more*: if 10 or more employees are to be dismissed, 30 days' notice of dismissal must be given to the Secretary of State for Employment.
- *One hundred or more*: if 100 or more employees are to be dismissed, 90 days' notice of dismissal must be given to the Secretary of State for Employment.
- If notice of redundancies has been given and later further dismissals are necessary, additional notice will be required of the aggregate numbers, including those already notified. This can create problems if, for example 50 redundancies are given 30 days' notice and then a further 50 redundancies become necessary, the total

would become 100 with the notice period of 90 days for the balance.
- In all the above cases, contact the Redundancy Payments Office of the local Employment Department office who will advise on action and provide necessary documentation.
- *Recognized trade union*: consult with any recognized trade union in accordance with existing agreements (see below).

Consultation with trade union

An employing company intending to dismiss employees because of redundancy has a duty to comply with s.99 of the Employment Protection Act 1975, as amended, as follows:

Recognized Where trade union membership exists, in order to be entitled to consultation about forthcoming redundancies, that union *must* be a 'recognized' trade union. A recognized trade union is one with which the management have entered into a formal agreement to 'recognize' them for collective bargaining on behalf of their members for the purpose of negotiation on pay and conditions in that company. Recognition may be given to a single trade union or to several trade unions.

Although individual employees have a legal right to trade union membership, unless a trade union is 'recognized' it has no rights in this respect, even if (theoretically) 100 per cent of employees are in membership.

Notice 30 days' and 90 days' notice of 10 and 100 dismissals, respectively, must be given to the recognized trade union, as above. In addition to these, 28 days' notice must be given of fewer than 10 dismissals (of recognized trade union members). In cases of successive redundancies, aggregate numbers dictate notice periods, as above.

Information When giving notice of dismissals due to redundancy to a recognized trade union, the employing company must include in its notice the following information:

1 The reasons for the proposed redundancies.
2 The number of employees and their occupations or skills.
3 The total numbers of each category employed in the company.
4 The method by which employees will be selected for dismissal.
5 The method by which redundant employees will be dismissed, with reference to existing procedures and including planned time scales.

Consultation The employing company must consult with the appointed representatives of the trade union members. That consultation must:

- take account of the views and representations of members conveyed by their representatives;
- give response to those views and representations, stating reasons for rejection of any of those points raised.

Note: If you delay consultation with a recognized trade union, this may result in a claim for unfair dismissal at an industrial tribunal. One such case was upheld by the Employment Appeals Tribunal (EAT) in 1991 (1991.IRLR.194).

Transfer of undertakings You will recall the section on transfer of undertakings in Chapter 1. Regulations require employers to consult with recognized trade unions in a transfer of undertakings situation (see Chapter 12—Industrial relations).

Protective awards See Chapter 13—Industrial Tribunals.

Do remember that trade union members, albeit included in collective bargaining, are individuals and entitled to the rights of individuals as outlined earlier in this chapter.

Notice periods

Minimum periods of notice of dismissals of individuals must be given to each employee, in addition to any redundancy pay which may be due. There is, of course, nothing to prevent an agreement with the employing company that notice to individuals shall be served via their elected representatives.

Pay in lieu of notice If employees are dismissed wholly or mainly because of redundancy and such dismissal is without notice, then pay in lieu of notice must be given. Whether this is taxed is outlined in Chapter 3.

Note: Beware of giving pay in lieu of notice as a means of effectively reducing employees' total continuous service and so preventing them from qualifying for redundancy pay. An employee so dismissed can claim at a county court for 'loss of rights' to redundancy payments and/or unfair dismissal compensation (1981.IRLR.437).

Details of notice periods are given in Chapter 11—Dismissals.

Redundancy payments

Qualifications To be entitled to redundancy payments, an employee must have been employed *continuously* for a minimum of two completed years, including notice if any, up to the date on which employment is terminated. This is the 'relevant date', which differs according to whether notice is given. Thus:

1 If an employee has worked for 9 years and 11 months at the time of being given notice of dismissal and proceeds to work through the notice period, the notice period brings the employee's continuous employment to ten completed years (see Chapter 11).
2 If an employee has worked for 9 years and 11 months at the time of being made redundant and is dismissed without notice, then his or her continuous employment is counted as nine years. (But remember to give pay in lieu of notice as per Chapter 11.)

If there are breaks in the employment contract (not breaks due to illness, etc.), then continuous employment counts from the latest date of re-engagement.

Payments Redundancy payments are covered by Schedule 4 of the Employment Protection (Consolidation) Act 1978 and are calculated on a scale according to length of service in *completed* years, and age, as follows: Working backward from the 'relevant date', i.e. the effective date of dismissal:

- For each completed year during which the employee was aged 41 years or over—one-and-a-half week's pay for each year.
- For each completed year during which the employee was aged 22 years or over (but not including the year in which he or she was 41 years old; see above)—one week's pay for each year.
- For each completed year during which the employee was aged 18 years or over but under 22 years, one-half a week's pay for each year.

However, there are two restrictions:

1 A 'week's pay' for the purpose of redundancy pay calculations shall be up to a *maximum* of £205.00 (as at 1992/3—likely to be increased from 1 April 1993).
2 The *maximum* number of years which can count for redundancy pay calculations is 20.

Thus, the theoretical maximum which any individual redundancy payment can amount to is 20 years × 1½ × £198.00 (in 1991/92), i.e. £6150. Croner Publications include an excellent 'ready reckoner' in their *Reference Book for Employers*.

Over 64 Where an employee who is redundant has passed his or her 64th birthday, the amount of redundancy payment is reduced by one-twelfth for each *complete* month's service beyond the 64th birthday.

To determine entitlement, first calculate redundancy pay as in the foregoing, then *reduce* it by what is called 'the appropriate fraction'. This is arrived at by taking the number of completed months since the 64th birthday and then dividing by 12, e.g. a person aged 64 on 1 August whose 'relevant date' is 15 November has three complete months' service: 3/12 = 1/4. Reduce the redundancy pay by one-quarter. Or, if the appropriate fraction is 2/3, reduce the redundancy pay by two-thirds, leaving an entitlement of one-third of the total redundancy pay.

No employee is entitled to redundancy if he or she has reached the normal retirement age for the company (whether 60 or 65, or in between). In any event, *no* entitlement exists beyond the age of 65 years. No entitlement can be claimed later than 6 months after the relevant date.

Additional terminal payments The above are minimum legal requirements but if companies wish to pay more than these amounts, they are free to do so. You may be able to pay additional terminal lump-sum payments, e.g. 'golden handshakes'—tax free—of up to a maximum of up to £30,000. Amounts over £30,000 are subject to PAYE in the normal way.

Alternative appointment
An employer has a duty to try to place the employee in an alternative position of equal status, pay and conditions to the redundant position. If the employee accepts the new position, no redundancy pay is payable. If the employee refuses it without good reason, and an industrial tribunal finds that it was reasonable for the employee to accept the new position, then no redundancy pay would be due.

Effect of employee resignation
If the employee resigns (in writing) from employment before the period of notice given by the employer has expired, he or she shall still be entitled to redundancy pay *unless* the employer gives notice (in writing) that the employee is required to complete the notice period and the employee refuses. In the event of an industrial tribunal hearing in which an employee complains of being refused redundancy pay in these circumstances, the tribunal may make an award of (part or all of the) redundancy pay—depending upon the reasons for the resignation.

Disqualification from redundancy pay
The following circumstances will disqualify an employee from entitlement to redundancy pay:

- Employment outside Great Britain, unless under the contract of employment he or she normally worked in Britain.

- Employment on a fixed-term contract of more than two years in which it was agreed before the term expires that redundancy pay would not be payable.
- The employee unreasonably refuses a suitable alternative position of similar status, pay and conditions, or resigns during a trial period for the alternative position without having given the new position reasonable opportunity to be tried out.
- Resignation by the employee during the period of notice when the employer had given written notice that he or she wished the employee to work the full period of notice, *unless* the circumstances were considered reasonable (as above).

Rebates The scheme whereby firms could reclaim a rebate of 35 per cent of redundancy payments made to employees ceased in February 1990.

That concludes our discussion on redundancy. Do remember to refer to associated information on dismissals (Chapter 11) and industrial relations (Chapter 12).

Overleaf is your health checklist to help assure that you are on the right tracks.

Health checklist — Redundancy

1 Do you take into account the human aspects of redundancy?
2 Have you drawn up a redundancy plan or programme?
3 Does your redundancy plan include all the legal aspects, including:
    Definition—ensuring that the dismissals really are redundancies?
    Fairness—ensuring that your programme is fair and equitable?
    Mitigation—ensure that you will do everything possible to avoid redundancies or reduce the effect of them?
4 Does your programme allow for:
    – advance warning of redundancies?
    – possible voluntary redundancies?
    – phased dismissals?
    – endeavours to place employees in alternative employment?
5 Will you provide redundancy counselling?
6 Do you know the minimum notice periods for redundancies? And who must be notified?
7 Do you have 'recognized' trade unions? If so have you drawn up a collective agreement, including consultation with them on future redundancies? Will you provide all the information required by law?
8 Do you know the minimum notice periods required to individuals?
9 Do you know how to calculate redundancy payments?
10 Remember to reduce redundancy payments to employees over 64 years.
11 Are you able to pay terminal gratuities, e.g. 'golden handshakes'?

Following the guidance in this chapter and keeping a check on the checklist will ensure that any redundancies you may have to administer are done so fairly and equitably.

10 Retirement

Retirement can be a devastating experience, more damaging than the shock of redundancy, even though being made redundant is often a sudden event while retirement is anticipated well in advance. Redundancy produces more emotional reponses, as discussed in the previous chapter, while retirement brings on a 'shock to the system'. Suddenly, there is an awakening to the reality of 'no longer having to get up and go to work each day', but additionally the body's system, having become accustomed to a working routine, is upset. Human beings are creatures of habit and to adjust to changes in routine is often very difficult—unless prepared for well in advance.

Post-retirement life expectancy in men is less than in women, partly because traditional domestic roles mean that women are able to continue working in the home while most (not all) men suddenly find themselves with nothing to do. But it is mostly because of under-stimulation of the brain; people who become inactive usually deteriorate more rapidly than active people.

The key is preparation. *In this chapter we give some hints on when and how you can prepare your employees to look forward to and enjoy retirement.*

The legal aspects
It has been traditional in Britain for many years for men to retire at the age of 65 years and women at 60. These are also the ages at which state pensions still automatically become payable—though this may change. While the law on state pensions remains unaltered, a 1986 Economic Community (EC) ruling has changed the position in relation to retirement from working and EC Directives have been backed by several recent Court of Appeal rulings which give equality to men and women.

In determining its employment policy, a company can set whatever age it wishes for the retirement of its employees; there being no legal stipulation whether that should be 75, 65, 60, 50, or any other age. If the company has no formal written policy, then the general custom (backed by labour turnover statistics) will be taken as the rule in any claim at an Industrial Tribunal. If no policy exists and no clear custom and practice can be identified, then the upper state retirement age of 65 years will be deemed to be the company's normal retiring age.

What is clear is that whatever retirement age an employer chooses, it *must* apply equally to all employees, both male and female. Remember also that if the directors of an incorporated company (plc or Ltd) set a retirement age at, say, 60 years for employees, then that same rule applies to directors also. In this situation, retired directors are often retained as 'consultants' to their firm.

Thus, if the age for retiring for women is set at 60 years, then men must also retire at 60. If men are permitted to remain at work until 70, then women must be given the same right. If the retirement age for men is 65 years and a woman is compelled to retire at 62, she will be entitled to claim unfair dismissal due to sex discrimination at an Industrial Tribunal, albeit that she is over state retirement pension age. By the same rule, if a woman is able to receive an occupational pension from the age of 60 years, men must also have the same privilege.

It should be noticed that a European Court of Justice (ECJ) ruling on 17 May 1990 states that the benefits under occupational pension schemes for both men and women should be the same, in line with the ruling on equal pay for equal work. This has yet to be incorporated into UK law, but there may be several cases of inequitable treatment *since* the date of the ruling which may also come to the ECJ for hearing.

Note: The ECJ will not accept claims arising from retirement prior to 17 May 1990.

Employing retirees If a company has a policy of 'not offering employment to persons in receipt of an occupational pension' and so refuses work to a man in receipt of an occupational pension, that is sex discrimination. The reasoning behind this ruling is that statistically 99.4 per cent of women can satisfy the company's policy while only 95.3 per cent of men can—more men being on occupational pensions than women. Thus men are disadvantaged and discriminated against (1990.LRLR.372).

So, considering all the foregoing legalities, the advice is: have a strict, common employment and retirement policy which applies to all employees and both sexes, including directors.

Succession planning

In Chapter 6—Training and development, we mentioned that a management inventory (as part of a management development programme) will indicate future retirements. It will be most important to keep a check on who is due for retirement so that succession planning can be implemented.

Succession planning consists of a number of things:

1 Manpower plan of what future skills will be needed and whether to replace employees who retire.
2 A recruitment plan to bring in replacements for retirees in ample time to prepare them for the position becoming vacant.
3 Succession training and development.

Succession training Most skilled and professional people are proud of their work and like to show it to others. When a new employee, or someone transferred from another department, is brought in to learn the job of the retiring person, who better to instruct the new employee in that job than the retiree themself. If the skills transfer will take a number of months and if the retiree is not trained to instruct, why not upgrade the retiree to a competent instructor by training him or her well in advance? It will be well worth the investment! (See Chapter 6.)

Having dealt with the legal and succession aspects, we come to other matters affecting retirement. For many, preparation for retirement is left until the last few months of working life and many firms' retirement programmes commence just six months before the final working day. Nothing could be more damaging to retirement itself. Preparation and planning are essential to a long, happy and successful senior citizenship.

Below are the chronological stages at which points action should commence in order effectively to prepare employees for retirement.

Fifteen years

Financial

It is no use leaving financial planning until six months before retirement. It takes a minimum of ten years for any effective savings policy to build up a worthwhile capital sum, and many more years than that for a pension to produce a sizeable annuity with which to buy a pension. Thus, planning should begin as early as possible.

Pension Planning for a pension should begin as early in working life as possible. To build up a pension equal to one-half of final salary, based on '60ths' it takes 30 years or based on '80ths' it takes 40 years. Most employers who have occupational pension schemes commence membership at the age of 18 years. However, where no company scheme exists or a person is self-employed, the earlier in working life one begins contributions into a personal pension scheme the better. Even a delay of one year can cause considerable losses of potential benefits.

Savings and investments   There are many savings and investment schemes which have life assurance attached and give good returns either after ten years or after longer terms or upon retirement. But it should be remembered that the minimum term during which premiums should be paid-in in order to reap real results is ten years—one can 'cash in' one's policy, but usually at a loss or little more than break-even.

Two to five years

It is important to avoid the 'shock to the system' mentioned earlier. So the following advice from suitably qualified persons would be very helpful.

Health   Should any health problems exist close to retirement age they would not necessarily be assisted by retiring, unless a 'rest cure' was the prescription. Under the NHS contracts, Doctors now provide regular health screening to patients on their lists who are over the age of 18 years, with special attention to those over 50 years of age. These 'health screens' include the following:

- First screen: age, occupation, relevant family history, height and weight, smoking?, alcohol intake, blood pressure, cholesterol level, last smear (females), tetanus immunization, 'urinalysis'.
- Subsequent screens: blood pressure, weight (band), smoking?, cholesterol level, alcohol intake, subsequent action.

So medical checks, if none has been undertaken, would be a valuable thing and would point the person in the right direction should any remedial steps be necessary.

Exercise   Regular exercise is an important factor in continuing good health, and so advice on taking non-stressful exercise would be useful. This can help with many health problems, but a medical check for any intending to take up exercise for the first time would be advisable.

Diet   'You are what you eat' is a well-known phrase in healthy-eating advice leaflets. Without advocating expensive diets or 'crash diet' weight-loss programmes, some helpful advice from a dietician would assist in correcting excesses or deficiencies in diets.

While a local doctor, fitness adviser or dietician would be a valuable *ex officio* person in the company; if none is available, the local office of the Health Education Council has some excellent leaflets and booklets on all aspects of health and fitness which are available free of charge. Their address and telephone number are in the local directory.

Finances How are those financial investments getting along? Is the pension fund or savings policy going to yield enough or will it need more money put into it? What outstanding debts will there be (including credit cards) and will they be cleared or will there be a continuing commitment?

One year

A year is a short time and not much in which to make final preparations.

Pre-retirement training At least one year but not less than six months before retirement, all employees due for retirement should attend pre-retirement training. If your company has its own training manager training can be provided in-house, otherwise there are excellent pre-retirement courses which can be provided cheaply or in some cases free of charge. Most consist of six or more one-day or half-day seminars at which every important aspect of retirement is addressed, including the following:

- *Adjustment*: how to adjust to life in retirement and make the most of it.
- *Health and exercise* (as above): how to maintain health and fitness.
- *Finance*: pensions and savings (above), State benefits and grants.
- *Leisure interests*: hobbies, pastimes, creative art, light sports?
    In the home, in the community, service to the community?
    Using the skills gained in industry to others' benefit?
- *Home*: whether the present home is suitable for retirement, and weighing up that dream 'retirement home' at the seaside before rushing off.
- *Travel*: visiting those places one has always wanted to visit.
- *The future*: what it holds for self and one's spouse and kin.
- *Relationships*: making new friends. Putting the best into and getting the best out of friends and relationships.
- *Working*: will continuing in a 'consultancy' capacity or starting a second career be an attractive proposition? Will the retiree take up other full-time or part-time work? What will be the financial implications (tax, pensions, State benefits, etc.)?

Three months

Countdown to retirement day

By far the greatest 'shock' is to have been working 40 hours per week regularly for 40 to 50 years and then suddenly not have to work at all. The feeling of loss and disorientation in the first mornings after retirement when one routinely wakes up, then remembers that one doesn't have to go to work can be stressful. Retirement is a known stressor.

These effects can be minimized, or even eliminated, by a scaling-down work schedule in which the retiring employee gradually reduces working hours until on the final day he or she is 'eased' into retirement with no work commitment. A suggested programme could be as follows:

- *Three months before retirement*: reduce from five days per week to four days per week (beginning preparation for non-working).
- *Two months before retirement*: reduce hours from eight (or seven) hours per day to seven (or six) hours per day by starting work one hour later each day (beginning preparation for late rises in the mornings).
- *Six weeks before retirement*: reduce hours further from seven (or six) hours to six (or five) hours per day by finishing work one hour earlier each day (beginning preparation for leisure hours).
- *One month before retirement*: reduce from four days per week to three days per week, still at six (or five) hours per day (continuing preparation for non-working).
- *Three weeks before retirement*: reduce working hours to five (or four) hours per day by finishing work one more hour earlier (continuing preparation for leisure hours).
- *Two weeks before retirement*: reduce from three days per week to two days per week.
- *One week before retirement*: reduce to one day per week.

By this reduction programme the retirement date is reached without the sudden shock of no longer working. Following the suggestions in this chapter will both help your employees to be 'eased into retirement' and enhance your company's image with employees and society.

Finally, do encourage your retired employees to maintain contact with the company and to call in to see colleagues from time to time.

Help

There are various sources available for advice and for retirement training. Some training consultancies offer training for retirement, and an excellent training manual *The RETIREMENT Pack* is published by Leisure Magazines Ltd, 26 Queensway, London W2 3RX.

Other useful contacts are:
Advisory Council for Adult and Continuing Education
Age Concern
Health Education Council
Help the Aged
National Institute of Adult Education
Retirement Fellowship

That concludes Retirement. Before continuing with our next subject—dismissals—a brief health checklist to help you plan your employees' retirement and training for retirement is given on the next page.

Health checklist — retirement

1. Do you have a retirement policy?
2. Have you determined a retirement age for all employees?
3. Is it the same for both male and female employees?
4. Do you have a succession planning and training programme?
5. Do you use the skills of your senior workers to train younger ones who will replace them?
6. Do you provide financial, health and diet information for your future retirees at appropriate stages?
7. Do you provide pre-retirement training one year before retirement?
8. Does it include advice on all those aspects outlined in this chapter?
9. Do you have a countdown work schedule for retiring employees during their final three months of working?
10. Will your employees look forward to retirement or dread it?
11. Will your employees plan for a long, happy and successful life as senior citizens?

11 Dismissals

Every employer faces the prospect of dismissing an employee at some time, for a variety of reasons. When dismissal of an employee occurs, it is important that it is conducted in a manner which is fair *and* equitable, *for the employee's and the employer's benefit.*

When an employee considers the termination of his or her contract of employment to have been carried out unfairly, this may result in a claim of 'unfair dismissal' at an Industrial Tribunal.

To keep you on the right tracks and avoid the unpleasant and very costly experience of a dispute arising out of dismissal we give some guidelines on how to follow correct procedure.

The legal aspect
Dismissal in law is, *de facto*, the termination of a contract of employment by action of the employer and occurs when one of four situations exists:

1 When the employee is dismissed by the employer with or without notice being given.
2 When the employee terminates the contract due to circumstances in which the employer's conduct makes the employee so entitled.
3 If the contract has been frustrated (see below).
4 When a fixed-term contract expires without being renewed under the same contract.

A contract of employment can be 'frustrated' in common law where the contract is brought to an end by an act independent of either party. If, for reasons not necessarily in the control of either party, the operation of the contract has become impossible or if the future operation will only become possible in a radically different set of conditions than had been foreseen by either party, then that contract may, in the view of the courts, be deemed to be at an end. An example may be an employee who is imprisoned for some time or on very long-term sickness and prevented from returning to duties.

The human-relations aspect
Dismissal, for whatever reason, can have unpleasant and long-lasting effects on employees. Even where dismissal is unavoidable

as with redundancy, or justified as with serious disciplinary problems, feelings can nevertheless run high and there can still be emotional reactions, as discussed in Chapter 9 on redundancy. So the key will once again be fairness and equity in relation to *all* employees and the law.

The protection and maintenance of a firm's good name (with employees and with the public), and the outcome of an industrial tribunal hearing, will depend more on how a dismissal is handled than on the fact of the dismissal itself.

Notice

Both parties to a contract of employment have a legal duty to give notice if either wishes to terminate the contract, unless there are good grounds for not so doing.

By the employee   In the case of an employee it is either:

- for employees who have been employed continuously for at least one month: the legal minimum required by the Employment Protection (Consolidation) Act 1978 (EP(C)A), as amended, i.e. one week (no notice is stipulated if employment has lasted less than one month) or;
- the minimum required by the contract of employment, if greater than one week, e.g. one month's notice, three months' notice, three months' notice from the first of a calendar month, etc.

Whether notice is given in writing is a matter for the employer to decide and should be included in the contract of employment. It is suggested that it is always a good idea to ask for notice in writing.

Do bear in mind the caution given in Chapter 3, page 40, about the difficulty in enforcement through the civil courts of conditions in the contract which are in excess of the minimum laid down by the EP(C)CA.

By the employer   The minimum period of notice which an employer must give to an employee who has been continuously employed for at least one month but less than two years is one week. Beyond this, a scale of one week's notice for each *completed* year of service up to a maximum of 12 weeks' notice applies (see Tables 11.1 and 11.2).

Pay in lieu of notice   If a person is dismissed without notice, whether because of redundancy, poor performance or disciplinary action or by mutual consent (except for gross misconduct) then payment of one week's pay for each week of legal notice requirement must be given. Whether this pay is taxed is outlined in Chapter 3.

Table 11.1 Scale of notice required to be given by employer

Minimum continuous service	Minimum notice by employer
Less than two years	One week
Two completed years	Two weeks
Three completed years up to 12 completed years	One week for each year up to 12
More than 12 years	Maximum 12 weeks

Fair dismissal

An employee will usually be deemed to be fairly dismissed in the following circumstances:

- Genuine redundancy (see Chapter 9).
- Retirement at the company's stated retirement age, or the retirement age by custom and practice (see Chapter 10).
- Following the exhaustion of the company's disciplinary (and unsatisfactory performance) procedure (see Chapter 8).
- By mutal agreement that the employment should end.
- Being involved in unofficial industrial action (EA 90).
- At the end of a fixed-term contract of employment.

In the last case in the bulleted list there is no legal requirement for notice; but it is suggested that notice should normally be given (except in cases of gross misconduct), as to fail to give notice may result in the fixed-term employment being unintentionally extended and the contract deemed to have continued and been renewed.

No notice is required for retirement; though, of course, if you follow the advice given in Chapter 10, notice is effectively given over the long period of preparation.

When giving notice, especially in the case of unofficial industrial

Table 11.2 Some examples of notice required

Length of service	Notice required
Two weeks	Nil
One month	One week
Nine months	One week
21 months	One week
2 years, 1 month	Two weeks
5 years	Five weeks
7 years, 11 months	Seven weeks
12 years	12 weeks
15 years, 6 months	12 weeks
20 years	12 weeks

action, always state the date on which the notice period and thus the employment will end.

Mutual agreement   Beware of using 'mutual agreement' as a means of avoiding one's legal responsibilities under EP(C)A. If the agreement between employer and employee is genuine, that agreement shall be binding. But an Industrial Tribunal or court does not automatically accept mutual agreement as the cause of terminating the employment without strong evidence, especially when such a move is initiated by the employer. If the Industrial Tribunal or court considers that the move to obtain 'mutual agreement' was intended to deprive the employee of his or her legal rights and avoid the employer fulfilling his legal duty had the employee actually been dismissed, then the court may find in favour of a claim of unfair dismissal.

Ensuring fair dismissal

Whatever the reasons for dismissal, you must ensure that it is fair. In the event of an Industrial Tribunal hearing, it will be for the employer to prove that the dismissal was fair, not for the employee to prove that it was unfair (except for alleged dismissal on grounds of trade union membership, in which case the onus of proof is on the aggrieved employee—see Chapter 13). So follow the rules:

1 Check all the circumstances. Do they indicate fairness in the dismissal?
2 Was the person fairly selected for redundancy (see Chapter 9)?
3 In cases of disciplinary dismissal, especially 'summary' dismissal:
   (a) Have you kept written records of *all* events leading to the dismissal, including unofficial industrial action, with details of warnings (verbal and written), witness statements, etc.?
   (b) Have you exhausted the disciplinary procedure fully (see Chapter 8)? (If you short-cut the procedure, you may lose your case.)

In many cases in Industrial Tribunals, an employer who had every justification in dismissing an employee has been heavily criticized or lost the case because no proper records or copies of written warnings were kept. Often, the difference between successfully defending and losing against a complaint of unfair dismissal is the absence of adequate written records (see Chapter 13).

Written reasons

An employee who is dismissed may *require* the reasons for dismissal to be set out in writing in the following situations:

1 If notice is given by the employer that the employee's contract of employment is to be terminated.
2 If the contract is terminated by the employer without notice.
3 If a fixed-term contract expires and is not renewed under the same contract.

The employer is not required to issue written reasons automatically; but we suggest that it is always prudent to do so (unless it is felt such written reasons may contain substance of embarrassment to the employee). Employees may request written reasons for dismissal where notice has been given orally or in writing, as in (1), (2), (3) above, if they were employees for the purposes of PAYE and NIC on a contract of employment and fulfil either of the two following conditions:

- If their employment commenced before 26 February 1990, having completed the minimum six months' continuous service.
- If their employment commenced after 26 February 1990 and they have completed a minimum of two years' continuous employment; thus the earliest qualifying date in this situation would be 26 February 1992.

Freelance agents and contractors who are employed under contracts to provide services, share fishermen and those employed outside Britain cannot seek written reasons for dismissal.

The employee who requests written reasons may do so on any of the three following occasions:

1 If the employer gives notice, orally or in writing: on the day on which notice is given.
2 If no notice is given: the day on which the termination is effected.
3 If a fixed-term contract is not renewed: the date on which that fixed-term contract expired.

Compliance If a request for written reasons is made, orally or in writing, the employer *must* provide a written statement within 14 days of the request being made. The notice should include a simple statement of the reasons, and may refer to other documents such as warnings and the letter of dismissal.

Enforcement If the employer refuses or fails to provide written reasons, or the reasons given are untrue or insufficient, then the employee may complain to an Industrial Tribunal and seek enforcement. Such complaint must be made within three months of the date of termination of the employment. If the Industrial Tribunal finds in favour of the employee, he or she may:

- make a declaration of what the tribunal considers the true reasons for dismissal to be; and
- make an award equal to two weeks' pay, calculated as at the date of termination, which the employer must pay to the employee.

Constructive dismissal

Sometimes, an employee is not dismissed but feels compelled to leave employment because conditions make it untenable for the contract of employment to continue effectively. In such circumstances, it is usually the claim that the employer put pressure on the employee in order to force him or her to leave; so the employee gives notice of terminating the contract of employment but under quite adverse conditions. Examples of this might be:

1 The employer fails to fulfil certain conditions in the contract of employment and thus causes the employee to be unable to carry out his or her duty, thereby effectively terminating the contract without actually giving notice.
2 Demolishing the employee's office without providing alternative accommodation, leaving the employee nowhere to work (it has happened).
3 Disposing of the only lorry in the company and leaving the driver with no vehicle, though not actually dismissing him or her.
4 Making life so acrimonious and unpleasant with the objective that the employee will become fed-up and leave.
5 Saying words to the effect, 'if you don't like it you can always hand in your notice and leave'.

It would *not* be considered constructive dismissal if, say, the employee had committed a costly serious error or gross misconduct and the manager said words to the effect, 'either you hand in your notice or you will be dismissed'. It is always preferable for the employee to be able to say 'I left of my own accord' than to admit 'I was dismissed'. But do remember the necessity to maintain full records of events leading up to such a situation.

We trust that the foregoing will help you to keep on the right side of the law in cases of dismissal. But before proceeding to Chapter 12—Industrial relations, we have provided another health checklist for you to assure your correctness in actions.

Health checklist — dismissals

When you carry out a dismissal, before finalizing it check that the following criteria are fulfilled:

1. Do you know all the legal aspects of dismissal?
2. Have you considered the human-relations aspects?
3. Is the dismissal fair and equitable?
4. If the dismissal is because of redundancy, are you confident of showing that selection for redundancy was fair?
5. If the dismissal is because of a serious or continued disciplinary offence or because of continued poor performance, have you exhausted all available disciplinary procedures, including counselling (see Chapter 8).
6. Have you made and retained full written records of all events leading up to the dismissal?
7. Have you given the correct period of notice?
8. If no notice was given, have you given pay in lieu of notice? Is it taxable or non-taxable?
9. Remember that if the employee requests them, you *must* give written reasons for dismissal.
10. If the employee has terminated his or her employment, are you satisfied that no 'constructive dismissal' situation exists?
11. If a complaint of unfair dismissal was pursued at an industrial tribunal, would you be confident of a successful defence?

12 Industrial relations

Industrial relations laws affecting trade unions, employers and employees are numerous and complex, with literature on them no less so. We therefore summarize only the main points here.

In theory every employer is subject to all trade union law and activity, but in practice the effect upon you will depend on the size and nature of your organization.

However, even a small company which is 'non-union' is affected to some degree and will find certain important aspects which will have to be taken into account. We give the main points in this chapter. We shall deal with employees', employers' and trade unions' rights and responsibilities. You should also refer to Chapters 8—Discipline and grievance, 9—Redundancy, 11—Dismissals, and 13—Industrial Tribunals.

Employees' rights

Under the Employment Protection (Consolidation) Act 1978 (EP(C)A), as amended by the Employment Acts (EAs) of 1980 (s.15), 1982 (s.10) and 1988 (s.11), all employees in any organization of any size have certain inalienable rights which are not subject to negotiation by either employer or trade union. They are, the right:

1 To belong to any trade union of their own choosing.
2 Not to belong to any particular trade union or to any trade union at all, if that is their wish.
3 Not to be compelled to join a trade union or to be compelled to take part in the activities of a trade union.
4 Not to be required to make any payment as the alternative to joining or remaining as a member of any trade union.
5 Not to be prevented from joining a trade union or from joining in the activities of a trade union of their choice.
6 Not to be refused employment on the grounds of trade union membership (Employment Act 1990 (EA 90)).
7 Not to be unreasonably refused membership or expelled from membership of a trade union (EA 80). This relates mainly to a pre-existing closed-shop agreement (see opposite), where such would jeopardize a person's employment.
8 Not to have action of any kind whatever, whether disciplinary,

pecuniary or dismissal, taken against them for joining or refusing to join a trade union.

To frustrate these rights, even in a small business, renders the offending employer, trade union or fellow employee liable to prosecution.

Trade unions' rights
Trade unions can enjoy any (or all) of three statuses:

1 *Independent*: i.e. not controlled wholly or partially by any employer but acting independently of them.
2 *Affiliated*: i.e. registered with and affiliated to the Trades Union Congress (TUC) and able to take part in all TUC activities. Some unions prefer not to affiliate, some may be disaffiliated. Affiliation is *not* 'recognition'.
3 *Recognized*: i.e. recognition has been given by the *management* of a particular company, an agreement having been entered into with that employer for a single union, or group of unions, to negotiate on behalf of the employees of that company or a part of that company in respect of pay and conditions.

Notes:
1 Closed shops, which make either pre-entry or post-entry membership of a particular trade union, or group of trade unions, a condition of employment were permitted under the Trade Union and Labour Relations Act 1974 (commonly known as TULRA). Where they already exist, those closed shops continue under TULRA, though with some amendments under EA 80.
2 New 'closed shop' arrangements were outlawed by the Employment Act 1988 (EA 88) and employees cannot be dismissed for refusing to join an existing closed shop where it continues to exist. Also, the Industrial Relations Code of Practice (COP) and COP on Closed Shop Agreements were revoked on 1 June 1991.
3 The fact that employees in a company, perhaps 100 per cent of them, may be members of a particular trade union does not automatically bestow 'recognition' upon that union. Individiual membership of a trade union is an individual matter, no matter how many members there may be collectively.

Time off with pay If a trade union is 'recognized', an employee who is an elected representative is entitled to reasonable time off with full pay during working hours to undertake union duties and activities on behalf of members whom they represent—including the collection of union subscriptions. A new COP on Time off for Trade Union Acitivities came into effect on 13 May 1991.

The two exclusions to this clause are:

1 If the union is *not* recognized by the employer for the purposes of negotiation on pay and conditions.
2 If the activity is in connection with industrial action whether official or unofficial.

Consultation

Employers *must* consult with recognized trade unions when there are anticipated dismissals due to: (1) redundancy; (2) transfer of undertakings; (3) health and safety, and (4) pensions.

1 Redundancy When an employing company intends to dismiss employees because of redundancy and there is a recognized trade union, as above, existing in that company, they have a *duty* to consult with that trade union on all matters pertaining to those redundancies. Minimum periods of notice of the redundancies (i.e. 30 days or 90 days, as appropriate) must be given to the trade union, in addition to the notice given to the Secretary of State, and there must be full consultation with the elected representatives of the employees in that trade union. (Full details of consultation about redundancies are given in Chapter 9.)

Note: Remember the caution about delays in consultation in Chapter 9.

2 Transfer of undertakings A 'relevant transfer' in terms of the Transfer of Undertakings Regulations 1981 is one where a commercial undertaking is transferred from one owner to another as a going concern. This does not include sale of assets or shares.

When a transfer of undertakings is planned and there is a recognized trade union, as above, existing in the company from which the transfer is planned to be made, notice of that transfer *must* be given to that trade union in good time, early enough to enable consultations with the union to be fully undertaken. Notice should be given by the employer who is effecting the transfer (e.g. is selling the company), called the transferor; but where that is not possible it must then be given by the transferee (i.e. receiving employer). The notice must be given to the elected union representative or delivered to the union head/main office, and must include the following information:

(a) The facts of the intended transfer, including the reasons for the transfer and the date on which it is expected to be finalized.
(b) Any legal, social or economic implications for the employees.

(c) What action the transferring employer intends to take in relation to employees, or the fact that no action will be taken if that is the case.
(d) What action the transferee, i.e. the receiving employer, intends to take in relation to employees, or the fact that no action will be taken if that is the case.

In relation to (d), the transferee (receiving employer) must provide the transferor with all the necessary information that he will need.

The employer intending to transfer his undertakings to another employer must undertake consultations with the elected representatives of the employees in trade union membership, as follows:

(i) He must take account of the views and representations of members conveyed by their representatives.
(ii) He must give response to those views and representations, stating any reasons for rejection of any of those points raised.

3 Health and safety Where recognized trade unions exist, employers have a duty to consult and cooperate with their elected representatives for the purposes of health and safety. Those health and safety representatives may also be the same elected representatives for the purposes of pay and conditions or they may be elected separately. (Full details are given in Chapter 5—Health and safety, page 117.)

4 Pension In accordance with the Social Security Pensions Act 1975, and the Occupational Pension Schemes (Contracting-Out) Regulations 1985, where a recognized trade union exists, an employer must consult with that union on all matters relating to occupational pension schemes. This includes the establishing of a scheme and the issue, modification or surrendering of a 'contracting-out' certificate (see Chapter 4, page 99).

Trade disputes

In a commercial undertaking, a company manufactures and sells goods and services. To do this, it employs workers. In law, the company as a legal entity is regarded as a person, but the employees of that company are regarded as individuals, each with a contract of employment. There are many workers who have rare skills and can thus command high salaries and negotiate their terms and conditions to their satisfaction. However, where there are larger numbers of workers whose skills are less rare or are more interchangeable and who do not have the bargaining power of others more fortunate, there is usually an agreement with a trade union for 'collective bargaining'.

There would be no need for bargaining if there was complete and unchanging agreement on all things. Collective bargaining, therefore, invariably encounters some form of in-depth discussion and possibly disagreement. When the employees' trade union and employer representatives are unable to reach agreement, there is invariably recorded a 'failure to agree'. If the failure to reach agreement continues and it is a matter of great concern to either party, then 'industrial action' is often the only action open to trade union and employer. A trade union can take industrial action in a number of ways.

Official or unofficial Employees of a company may take official or unofficial action against their employer. The difference between these is simply that official action has the backing of the trade union officials concerned and may have been initiated or called by them, while unofficial action takes place without the backing or perhaps even the involvement of the trade union officials.

It is possible for a local trade union action to be 'unofficial' if the trade union head or main office does not support it.

Note: Employees who take unofficial strike action and are deemed to have broken the terms of their contract of employment, may be liable to dismissal by the employer and will not be able to claim 'unfair dismissal' at an industrial tribunal (EA 90).

Action short of a strike Workers may seek to avoid all-out strike action and take different forms of action short of a strike in order to achieve their objectives, e.g.:

- *Working to rule*: in which employees pedantically carry out their duties strictly according to all the rules laid down by the employer. This type of action is most disruptive where there is considerable regulation and detailed scheduling. One may reasonably say that if working to rule causes disruption, then the rules must be wrong; but most employers seek flexibility and do not lay down over-strict rules which will cause problems in the normal day-to-day running of the business.
- *Overtime bans*: in which all overtime working is banned. While normal hours are adhered to, the ban on overtime working can cause serious problems to companies with production schedules which are customer-led with delivery dates or times. Overtime working can be important to employers in overcoming peak demand periods or short-notice orders and may be part of an employment contract.

Strike As a means of applying pressure on employers, employees may withdraw their labour completely, *en bloc*, for stipulated periods of time, e.g. one day or one week, with a gradual effect upon the employer. If a series of one-day or one-week stoppages do not achieve the union's desired objectives, then withdrawal of labour may be indefinite. Sometimes, of course, employees may enter into an indefinite strike as the primary form of action, which may affect employees' rights to guarantee payments.

Strike notice Technically, taking strike action, i.e. withdrawing labour, is breaking a contract of employment; but as mentioned earlier, employees are individuals on individual contracts of employment. If a trade union intends to call upon its members to take industrial action in the form of a strike, then in theory all employees give legal notice of their intention to terminate their contracts of employment; though in practice, where there is a 'recognized' trade union, an elected representative may give notice on behalf of all its members.

Note: It is unlawful for a trade union to issue notice of its intention to call employees to strike as from a particular date and time in the future; but it is not unlawful for all the employees or their appointed representative to give notice of the termination of their contracts of employment. There are questions as to the legal interpretation and lawfulness of such notice of strike action depending upon the wording of the notice.

'Wildcat strikes' These are actions taken without notice by the employees and usually designed to have the maximum impact upon the employer, even where action is by a small group of employees as those on 'wildcat' strike may be key to the functioning of the business.

Unless proper notice of the termination of their contracts of employment has been given, as under Strike above, then this action is a breach of the contract of employment.

Blacking Another form of industrial action is one in which employees refuse to provide goods or services to another employer, or to receive goods or services from another employer. There are a variety of situations in which this may occur and they are usually associated with the main action being taken, e.g. a strike. It may be goods or services which are at the centre of a dispute in which work is carried out in another place which employees consider to be breaking a strike or using non-union labour.

Note: If an employee or group of employees in a 'blacking' situation refuse to carry out work which is clearly defined in their contract of employment, then that blacking is a breach of their contracts of employment and is unlawful.

Picketing The legal purpose of picketing is to enable the group of striking employees and/or their elected trade union representative to put their point of view across to other employees peacefully and, if appropriate, to encourage them peacefully to join in the industrial action. They may also seek to persuade non-employees from entering the premises, e.g. to deliver goods or services to the employer for production purposes. Many non-striking trade union members not on strike refuse to cross picket lines set by striking members and the Code of Practice on Striking gives employees the free-will choice as to whether to cross a picket line.

Notes:
1 It may seem a contradiction, but there is no legal right for employees to join a picket line. Unless the due notice to terminate their contract of employment has expired, to join in a picket line during normal working hours, or outside working hours with the object of damaging their employer's business, would be a breach of their contract of employment.
2 It is unlawful for picketing to be done in a way which is intimidating or threatening or to create a public nuisance.
3 The Code of Practice on Picketing points out that disciplinary action should not be taken *by a union* against one of its members who refuses to join or who crosses a picket line.

Secret ballots
Unless a secret ballot of all affected employees in membership and who are involved in the particular dispute has been taken by the trade union intending to call that action, inducement to take industrial action is deemed to be outside of the scope of TULRA and EA 90. In order for an action to be lawful, five conditions must be fulfilled:

1 The union must have held a ballot of its members in respect of the intended action.
2 The ballot must be called by a named, authorized person who represents the interests of the affected employees (s.7(2), EA 90).
3 The majority of those who voted in the ballot must have answered 'Yes' to the appropriate question.
4 The ballot must have been equally available to all those anticipated to be involved in the action, and no one not directly involved should have been able to vote (s.11 of EA 90).

5 Separate ballots must be held for separate workplaces, not one ballot covering multiple workplaces (s.11(1A) of EA 90).

A recognized trade union may request the employer to provide facilities on the employer's premises in which to give opportunity for its members to vote in the ballot. This request may not be refused unless it is not reasonably practicable for the employer to grant it and such refusal will give the trade union recourse to an industrial tribunal for compensation in an amount appropriate to the circumstances.

Statutory liability   Under s.15 of the EA 82, as amended by the EA 90, a trade union may, in certain circumstances, be liable to legal action for economic torts, i.e. those actions (torts) which were wrongful, damaging or economically injurious to the employer. To be liable, the trade union or its servants/officials must have clearly been responsible for the strike action during which the economic tort was committed. Thus, an unofficial strike by employees would not create liability for the trade union. Under the EA 90, there is no immunity from prosecution for economic tort in secondary action and trade union liability for industrial action has been considerably widened by EA 90.

Employer's rights and responsibilities

Whether a company (of whatever size) gives official recognition to a trade union as defined above is a matter for the directors of that company. Very small businesses probably do not need to recognize any trade union—but that is a matter for the directors or owner-managers. As an organization grows in size, advantages may be seen in dealing with one negotiating body rather than with each individual employee.

In some larger organizations, where there is no official trade union recognition, there is an elected 'works committee' or 'joint consultation committee' established which speaks for all employees.

Secondary action   An employer has the right *not* to have secondary action taken against the organization. Secondary action is where a trade union in dispute with one organization takes industrial action against another which, although an associated company, supplier or customer, is not a part of that organization. Under EP 90, secondary action is now unlawful and there is no immunity for trade unions involved in secondary action.

Blacking   You also have the right *not* to be 'blacked'. Examples of blacking are given under Trade disputes, above.

Lock-out A rare form of industrial action taken by an employer is 'lock-out', so called simply because employees who are on strike or in an unresolved dispute are literally locked out of the employer's premises and prevented from continuing with their contract of employment. Such lock-out is usually with the intention of compelling employees to accept certain terms and conditions of employment.

Notes:
1 Lock-out is lawful *only* if due notice of the termination of the contract of employment has been given, as it is not customary for lock-out clauses to be included in employment contracts.
2 Suspension without pay in a lock-out situation will similarly be unlawful.
3 For a lock-out to be lawful and in accordance with the contracts of employment, due notice as required by individual contracts and the EP (C) A 78 as amended would need to be given—which could be as much as 12 weeks for long-service employees.

Unfair dismissal You cannot dismiss someone from your employ simply because he or she is, or becomes, a trade union member. To do so would render you liable to a claim for 'unfair dismissal because of trade union activities' at an industrial tribunal—with extremely high compensation awards against employers found to have so unfairly dismissed their employee. In this situation, there is *no* minimum qualifying time for pursuing a claim for unfair dismissal because of trade union activities, unlike other unfair dismissal cases, and awards can be up to £26,800 (as at 1992/93) (see Chapter 13, page 229).

Advisory, Conciliation and Arbitration Service (ACAS)
In cases of difficulty, disagreement or official dispute, the Government's Advisory, Conciliation and Arbitration Service (ACAS) exists to give unbiased and impartial advice to either party involved in a dispute. The primary role of ACAS is to 'advise', as the name suggests, and not arbitration as perceived by many. ACAS involvement is entirely free and the address and telephone number of your local ACAS office will be in your local telephone directory.

Commissioner for the Rights of Trade Unions
Under the EA 88, the Secretary of State for Employment has appointed a Commissioner for the Rights of Trade Unions. The Commissioner's function is to give assistance to 'persons', i.e. trade union members, in any actual or intended proceedings which arise out of certain applications to a court under EA 90, EA 88 and the Trade Union Acts (TUA) of 1913 and 1984. Assistance may also be

provided in cases of proceedings against a trade union or its officials or trustees, such as the Secretary of State may specify in an Order.

These actions may include cases relating to the following rights of trade union members in respect of their particular trade union, including its branches and sections:

1 To be balloted before industrial action is authorized or members are induced to take part (EA 88).
2 To inspect their union's accounting records (EA 88).
3 Unlawful use of union property by trustees (EA 88).
4 Failure of the union to take a political fund ballot (EA 88).
5 Failure of the union to bring or continue with proceedings for the recovery of union funds which have been used to indemnify unlawful actions (EA 88).
6 Failure of the union to comply with the law in relation to union elections (TUA 84).
7 Breach by the union of restrictions on use of its funds for political purposes (TUA 13).
8 Breaches of union rules concerning:
   (a) appointment, election or removal of a person from office;
   (b) disciplinary proceedings, including expulsion;
   (c) authorizing or endorsing industrial action;
   (d) the balloting of union members;
   (e) the application of their union's funds or property;
   (f) the imposition, collection or distribution of any levy for the purposes of industrial action;
   (g) constitutional proceedings of any committee, conference or any other body;
   (h) other matters as the Secretary of State may order, subject to the approval of Parliament (EA 90).

European Commission Proposal (1991)

The European Commission (EC) has issued a proposal (1991) for a Directive to be passed concerning the establishment of a **Works Council** in Community-scale undertakings or groups of undertakings in the European Community.

The purpose of this proposed EC Work Council is the informing of and consulting with employees. The Directive lays down requirements for all undertakings or groups of undertakings which operate in more than one Member State and are above a certain size, i.e.:

- Undertakings with a minimum of 1000 employees in the Community and with at least two establishments in different Member States, each employing at least 100 employees in the Community (e.g. 900 in England and 100 in Germany).

- Groups of undertakings with a minimum of 1000 employees within the Community and at least two group-undertakings in different Member States, each employing at least 100 employees (e.g. one group with 900 employees in England and one group with 100 employees in Germany).

The EC Directive provides for the establishment of European Works Councils *where the employees request it*, with a special negotiating body drawn from employee representatives or (if none exists) from specially elected representatives for the purpose. There will be written agreements on the formation and constitution of the works councils. Where management and negotiating body agree *not* to establish a council, certain information and consultation requirements must be met.

Member states have until 31 December 1992 to comply with the provisions of the EC Directive.

The foregoing is only a brief summary of the main points of industrial relations law. Were we to enter into detail on every aspect, not only would the subject matter become very complex but it would take an entire volume. But we hope that this summary is of value at least at an appreciation level.

Health checklist — industrial relations

1 Are you aware of employees' rights with regard to trade unions?
2 Do you permit them to freely exercise their rights—remembering that you cannot dismiss anyone for trade union membership?
3 Do you, or do you need to, recognize a trade union or group of trade unions for the purposes of negotiation on pay and conditions? If so, do you have a policy on dealing with trade unions and industrial disputes? Are you aware of trade unions rights and responsibilities?
4 Are you aware of your duties to 'recognized' trade unions, i.e. to consult with them on matters of redundancy, transfer of undertakings, health and safety, pensions?
5 Do you understand the different forms of industrial action, i.e. action short of a strike (working to rule or overtime bans), strike, 'wildcat' strikes, blacking?
6 Do you understand the implications of unofficial industrial action?
7 Do you know the legal limitations on industrial action?
8 Do you understand the lawful and unlawful aspects of balloting, strike notice, strikes, picketing, unofficial action, blacking, secondary action?
9 Will you afford facilities for secret ballots to a 'recognized' trade union? If not, why not?
10 Do you know the recourse available in the event of economic tort?
11 Are you aware of the lawful and unlawful aspects of 'lock-outs'?
12 Do you have locations or companies in European Community countries? If so, how will the EC Directive on Works Councils affect you?

13 Industrial Tribunals

When all available means in attempting to resolve problems fail the final option open to employees and trade unions is to lodge a complaint against an employer at an Industrial Tribunal.

Certain conditions pertain to a complaint being brought to an Industrial Tribunal and set procedures apply when the case is heard. We trust that your company will not be in the position of having to defend a complaint at a tribunal but the following will be helpful should such occasion arise.

The situations in which a person can complain to an Industrial Tribunal for unfair dismissal or constructive dismissal are varied and depend very much on the circumstances of each case. We have already discussed, in Chapter 8—Discipline and grievance, the necessity to conduct the disciplinary (and unsatisfactory performance) procedure fully, retaining full written records and copies of all correspondence. We have also discussed consultation with trade unions in Chapter 12—Industrial relations.

Where procedures are not followed or particularly where employment contracts are not formally written, the result is often an application for redress at an Industrial Tribunal. The following are the general instances which qualify as unfair dismissal:

1 Summary dismissal, without a fair hearing being given to the employee (unless for gross misconduct).
2 Dismissal for a first offence which is not of a serious nature, even where the disciplinary procedure was followed. In other words, 'was the offence serious enough to warrant dismissal for a first occasion?'
3 Dismissal without the full disciplinary procedure being followed by the employer. (Note: In the event of a claim of unfair dismissal where the procedure had been followed, if no written records (or inadequate records) are kept, this may go against the defendant employer.)
4 Dismissal, or refusal to grant employment, because of *non*-membership or refusal to take membership of a trade union.
5 Dismissal for being a member of a trade union or for trade union activities.

6 Dismissal for taking part in, or intending to take part in, an official strike.
7 Dismissal because of discrimination against the dismissed employee on the grounds of sex or race.

Although not dismissals, the following occurrences will also qualify for a complaint at an Industrial Tribunal:

- Refusal to grant employment because of trade union membership.
- Refusal to grant employment because of the job applicant's sex or race.

Prerequisites to a complaint
There are certain prerequisites to bringing a complaint against an employer to an Industrial Tribunal.

Conditions Before an application to an Industrial Tribunal is originated, all the available processes must have been tried and, if possible, exhausted. These processes, i.e. all those that we have discussed in earlier chapters, are important to the successful application for, or response to, a complaint and include: disciplinary procedures, grievance procedures, consultation, negotiation and the use of the Advisory, Conciliation and Arbitration Service (ACAS).

Whenever an application is made to an Industrial Tribunal, ACAS will always seek to resolve the matter 'out of court' by advising both complainant and respondent and by seeking a resolution where possible.

If all available means to resolve a complaint have not been fully pursued, this will go against either complainant or respondent, as appropriate. For example:

1 Has an applicant who is claiming constructive dismissal exhausted the grievance procedure (unless denied opportunity)?
2 Has the respondent carried out the disciplinary procedure fully and kept written records of all events, including copies of letters?
3 Has the applicant in a complaint of unfair dismissal for trade union activities communicated fully with the defendant to attempt to assure understanding?

Qualification
A person who wishes to complain of either:

- unfair dismissal, or
- constructive dismissal, or
- failure by an employer to furnish written reasons for dismissal following a request for them.

must have completed at least two years' continuous employment up to and including the date of termination, i.e. the end of any notice period or the date of dismissal if no notice is given.

There is *no* qualifying period of employment for bringing a complaint to an Industrial Tribunal for a person who wishes to complain of any of the following:

1 Unfair dismissal for trade union membership or activities.
2 Unfair dismissal for joining or intending to join a strike.
3 Dismissal or refusal to grant employment because of the sex or race of the job applicant.
4 Discrimination against an employee in matters of equal pay and equal opportunity because of his or her sex, which now includes age.
5 Refusal to employ a person because of trade union membership (Employment Act 1990).
6 Failure by an employer to make necessary provision under the Health and Safety at Work Act 1974.

Time limits A person must lodge the originating application (see below) within the following periods of time in order for the application to be accepted:

- Within six months of termination, i.e. the date on which notice expired or the date of dismissal if no notice was given, for unfair dismissal because of industrial action (strikes).
- Within three months of termination, i.e. the date on which notice expired or the date of dismissal if no notice was given, for all other cases of dismissal.

Originating applications

A complainant must lodge an 'originating application' with the Secretary of the Tribunals at the Central Office. This application, to be on Form IT.1 where possible, but not essentially so. The following information must be provided:

- name and address of applicant;
- name(s) and address(es) of the person(s) against whom the complaint is lodged, and
- grounds on which the complaint is made.

The first task of the Secretary is to sift out hopeless cases which cannot succeed, so on receipt of the application, he or she will consider whether it seeks a 'relief' (i.e. an Order for reinstatement, re-engagement or compensation) which the Tribunal is now empowered to give for whatever reason. If the success of the application appears to be unlikely, the applicant will be informed. This is to avoid wasting valuable time of both Tribunal and employers.

If the applicant does not indicate that he or she wishes to proceed with the matter, the Secretary will not register the application. If, however, the applicant indicates that he or she nevertheless wishes to continue with the application, it will be registered in the usual manner.

Either upon initial receipt if the remedy applied for is within the power of the Industrial Tribunal; *or* if the applicant indicates the intention to proceed as above, the Secretary will give the application a registration number. The Secretary will inform the relevant parties of the registration number and forward copies of the originating application to the respondent(s).

The Secretary will also send to the respondent Information to Respondents (Form IT.2) and a Notification of Appearance (Form IT.3) (see below).

Responses

Within 14 days of receipt of the copy of the originating application, the respondent must make a response, called 'entering an appearance', on Form IT.3. The limit of 14 days is not rigid, and the Secretary of the Tribunals may grant an extension; but if an extension of time is needed, application for extension within 14 days must be made with reasons for the application being given.

If the respondent fails to respond within 14 days, except with an application for an extension of time, then he or she is automatically barred from taking part in any proceedings. He or she may only:

1 apply for an extension of time, as indicated;
2 ask to be called as a witness by another person;
3 ask to be sent a copy of the Tribunal decision and reasons;
4 make application for a review of the decision on the grounds that he or she did not receive a copy of the originating application.

Conciliation

Under certain laws, provision is made for conciliation to be attempted by ACAS. Where this is appropriate, this will be done. It will be the duty of the ACAS officer to attempt to bring about a settlement, while acting in an entirely unbiased and neutral manner. ACAS is not empowered to act for the Tribunal and does not attend any subsequent hearing.

Further particulars

Either the originating applicant or the respondent may make application to the Tribunal for an Order to be issued for the provision of further particulars of the grounds on which the complaint or defence are made. Similarly, an application for an Order for the discovery of documents relating to the case may also be made. The Secretary of the Tribunals may also issue such Orders of his or her own volition.

If either party fails to comply with the Order, the application may be dismissed or the respondent may be debarred from defending altogether.

Witnesses
The Tribunal has power to issue orders for the attendance of witnesses at the hearing of a complaint. This may often be necessary when, e.g. loyal employees and/or trade union members are reluctant to attend voluntarily and give evidence against either complainant or respondent.

Joinder of parties
The Tribunal may add other parties to the proceedings or dismiss parties, either on application of the applicant or respondent, or on the initiative of the Tribunal itself.

Striking out
The Tribunal may, at any stage in the proceedings, strike out any originating application (or any part of it) or any notice of appearance (or 'response') if it considers that it is scandalous, vexatious or frivolous.

Pre-hearing assessments
Sometimes, there may be difficulty in the two sides agreeing on matters pertaining to the application, or it may be that there are serious questions as to the validity of the application. In such situations, the Secretary to the Tribunals may order a pre-hearing assessment to determine the merits of the case.

Preliminary hearing
There may be some technical question as to the qualifications of the case to be brought and, therefore, whether the Tribunal should hear the case, e.g. as to whether the minimum continuous employment period has been fulfilled or whether the case has been brought within the laid-down time since termination of employment. So that time is not unnecessarily wasted in unqualified full hearings, a preliminary hearing can be ordered by the Secretary.

Attendance
Although personal attendance at a Tribunal hearing is customary, it is not mandatory (unless under a witnesses order). If, for example, a respondent knows with certainty that the applicant does not have any prospect of succeeding, a written representation may be sent.

Any such written response must be lodged with the Secretary of the Tribunal at least seven days before the date of the hearing.

Private hearing

Cases are normally heard in public and, as with any court, any member of the public is entitled to attend. However, the Secretary of the Industrial Tribunals may be requested to order a private hearing in cases where:

- evidence to be presented at the Industrial Tribunal contains information which would be against national security or the public interest;
- to present evidence in public would cause the witness to break a legal rule;
- the evidence contains evidence communicated in confidence or which the witness has obtained as a result of a confidence placed in him or her.
- the evidence, if given, would cause substantial damage to any undertaking belonging to the witness or in which the witness works (except matters covered under TULRA).

The burden of proof

Who 'begins', i.e. presents their case first, at a Tribunal hearing is dictated by the burden of proof. It is the party on whom this burden is laid who begins.

In most cases of unfair dismissal, it is accepted that the employee was dismissed. Therefore, the burden of proof is on the employer to prove that the dismissal was fair and so he or she begins. However, if the employer denies that the employee was dismissed as, e.g. in constructive dismissal cases, then the applicant begins.

In discrimination cases, the burden of proof is on the applicant and it is he or she who begins. This applies to discrimination on the grounds of sex and race.

However, in cases of discrimination for trade union membership and activities the burden of proof will differ between cases, depending on qualification, as follows:

1. Where the dismissed employee does not fulfil the qualifying continuous employment period of two years, the burden of proof is on the employee—so he or she goes first.
2. Where the dismissed employee has two years or more of continuous service, thus qualifying under normal rules, the burden of proof is on the employer—so the employer goes first.

Procedure

The Chairman of the Tribunal has complete control over the court and decides what happens, including the order of events, with some flexibility. However, while the conducting of a Tribunal will depend on what the Chairman thinks most suited to the case, the following will be the general pattern:

- Opening speech by the employer
    (or applicant on whom the burden of proof rests).
- Evidence of employer's witness
    (or witnesses of applicant).
- Cross-examination by applicant
    (or by employer if applicant goes first).
- Questions by Tribunal members.
- Re-examination of employer's witnesses
    (or of witnesses of applicant).
- Opening speech by applicant
    (or by employer, if applicant went first).
- Applicant's evidence
    (or evidence of employer, if applicant went first).
- Cross-examination, questions by Tribunal and re-examination.
- Evidence of applicant's witnesses
    (or of employer's witnesses, if applicant went first).
- Cross-examination, questioning by Tribunal, and re-examination.
- Closing address by employer.
- Closing address by applicant.

Whether all the above stages are included, or are in that order, is entirely a decision of the Tribunal Chairman who does not take kindly to 'suggestions'.

Evidence

Evidence presented at an Industrial Tribunal is usually given informally with the Chairman having a degree of flexibility and sometimes, in lengthy cases, permitting a certain amount of humour to relieve tension.

Unlike criminal courts, where a case must be proved 'beyond all reasonable doubt', an Industrial Tribunal can hear evidence of hearsay. The chairman and members of the court will weigh up all the evidence, written and verbal, and make their decision based on the balance of probabilities.

It must be remembered, however, that Industrial Tribunals have the full status of the courts and that evidence given in Tribunals has the same weight of seriousness. Serious consequences can follow for anyone who commits perjury when giving evidence.

Decisions

Judgments and Orders may be given by the Tribunal at the close of the hearing, after a short adjournment, or they may be reserved and given in writing at a later date.

If a judgment is in favour of the applicant, the Tribunal may make an Order against the employer. The types of Order which may be given are:

- Reinstatement or re-engagement (whether or not it is practicable).
- A basic award equal to the rates of redundancy pay (see Chapter 9) to a maximum of 20 years' service counting backwards from the date of dismissal. To quote the extreme, with a maximum of 20 years' service, multiplied by one-and-a-half, the maximum (as at 1992/93) of £205 per week, the maximum basic award could be as much as £6150.

  A compensatory award equal to the loss which the Tribunal considers that the applicant has suffered, including expenses reasonably incurred by the employee, loss of benefits which would have been due but for the dismissal. The maximum compensatory award is £10,000.
- A special award may be granted in cases of unfair dismissal for trade union membership activities as follows:

  – one week's pay multiplied by 104 (2 years' pay), or £13,400, whichever is the greater, but to a maximum of £26,8000.

  A special award may be granted in cases where an employer refuses to comply with an Order for reinstatement or re-engagement, unless the employer proves that it is not practicable to comply with the order, e.g. it would bankrupt the business, as follows:

  – one week's pay multiplied by 156 (3 years' pay), or £20,100 whichever is the greater. (There is *no maximum limit* on this special award.)

Note: All awards are likely to be increased from 1 April 1993.

Theoretical maximum
In extreme cases, e.g. of dismissal for trade union membership or activities in which the employer refuses to reinstate or re-engage, the theoretical maximum aggregate award which an Industrial Tribunal can make against an employer is **£42,950.00**—*or more* in the case of a highly paid person whom an employer refuses to reinstate or re-engage.

Interest on awards
Awards made by Industrial Tribunals are subject to the addition of interest if the award has not been paid within 42 days of the date the tribunal decision was sent to the parties.

However, interest is not due on expenses and is only payable on that amount remaining after the deduction of income tax.

Appeals

If either party disagrees with the decision of an Industrial Tribunal, there is a right of appeal to the Employment Appeal Tribunal (EAT). The EAT was the successor to the National Industrial Relations Court which was abolished in 1975.

That concludes our discussion on Industrial Tribunals. We stress that this is a summary only and reference should be made to detailed literature. Three useful sources of reference are:

- *Croner's Employment Law;*
- *Croner's Industrial Relations Law;*
- ACAS (local office).

To assist you, here is our final health checklist to guide you through the process.

Health checklist — Industrial Tribunals

Double check—it is so important:

1 Is your disciplinary (and unsatisfactory performance) procedure correct and followed to the letter, including full recording?
2 Is your grievance procedure correct and followed to the letter?
3 Do you permit your employees freedom in matters of trade union membership and activities?
4 Do you consult with your 'recognized' trade union (if one exists)?
5 Do you ensure there is *no* discrimination against anyone on the grounds of their sex, race or trade union membership or activities?

(If the answer to any of the above questions is 'No', you could well lose your case in a tribunal.)

6 Do you understand the prerequisites of qualification and conditions for bringing an application to an industrial tribunal?
7 Do you understand the applications procedure and your responsibilities as a respondent, should such occasion arise?
8 Will you use the facilities of ACAS to prevent a tribunal hearing, if possible?
9 Do you know that you must provide further particulars and discovery of documents, if ordered to do so by the tribunal?
10 Do you have an appreciation of the tribunal procedures?
11 Do you understand on whom the burden of proof rests in different cases and, based on that, who 'goes first'?
12 Do you know the types of award which an Industrial Tribunal may order against an employer? And how to avoid them in the first place?

We hope that this chapter and health checklist, if read in conjunction with Chapters 8 to 12 (inclusive), will be of help to you in Industrial Tribunals, or that, if a complaint or claim is made against your company, you will be able to respond with confidence and know what to expect.

That concludes our guided tour
through the 'minefield' of industrial legislation.

We do trust that, as a result of following the
guidance and signposts given in this book,
you will come through unscathed.

Appendix A Application form

Example (only) of an Application Form.
To be adapted to your particular situation, as relevant.

CONFIDENTIAL

                     THE ABC COMPANY LTD
                     Prosperity Street
                     Boomtown, Richshire

Please use BLOCK CAPITALS in black ink throughout.

PERSONAL INFORMATION

Surname: _____ Forenames: _____
Address: _____
Telephone numbers: _____ _____ Nationality: _____
                  (private) (business)
Date of Birth: _____ Age: ____ Marital status: _____
Do you own your own home? Yes/No. Do you own a car? Yes/No.
Do you have a current driving licence? Yes/No? Is it clean? Yes/No.
Give details of any endorsements: _____
National Insurance No.: _____ Height: _____ Weight: _____
What health problems do you have: _____
Are you registered disabled? Yes/No. Registration No.: _____

APPLICATION

Position applied for: _____ Salary: £_____ p.a/p.wk.
Would you work Part-time? Yes/No. If yes, what hours? _____
Have you previously worked for ABC Ltd? Yes/No.
If Yes, please give dates, from: _____ to: _____ Job Title: _____
Do you have any relatives who work at ABC Ltd? Yes/No.
If Yes, please give their names and relationships: _____
When will you be available to commence employment? _____
What qualifications, skills, knowledge or experience do you have
which you feel especially suited to the job applied for? _____

EDUCATION AND TRAINING RECORD

Establishment	From	To	Qualifications obtained
Schools:			
College:			
University or polytechnic:			
Further education:			
Formal industrial training:			

Membership of professional bodies:	Qualifications:

SERVICE IN HM ARMED FORCES

Have you served in HM Armed Forces?   Yes/No.
If Yes, branch: _____
Dates of Service, From: _____ To: _____
Final rank: _____
Special training and experience relevant to position applied for: _____

HOBBIES AND INTERESTS

Please give details of hobbies, interests, pastimes, sports or social activities:

EMPLOYMENT HISTORY

Present/last employer: _____ Type of industry: _____
Address: _____
Employed from: _____ to: _____ Job title: _____
Describe fully work and responsibilities: _____

Last pay: £_____ p.a./p.wk.   Reasons for leaving: _____

Please give details of previous employments, most recent first:
Employer: _____ Type of industry: _____
Address: _____
Employed from _____ to: _____ Job title: _____
Work and responsibilities: _____
Pay: Starting: £_____ Leaving: _____ Reason for leaving: _____

Employer: _____ Type of industry: _____
Address: _____
Employed from: _____ to: _____ Job title: _____
Work and responsibilities: _____
Pay: Starting: £_____ Leaving: _____ Reason for leaving: _____

May we approach the above employers for reference? Yes/No. If no: which employers do you *not* wish us to approach: _____, which do you wish to inform before we approach: _____.

CONVICTIONS

Do you have any convictions which affect this application?   Yes/No
If Yes, please give details: _____
Do you have any 'unspent' convictions? Yes/No. Details: _____

DECLARATION

The information given in this application form is true and complete.

Signature: _____   Date: _____

This page for Management use only:

REFERENCE CHECK

Company: _____   Comments: _____
_____
_____

Company: _____   Comments: _____
_____

INTERVIEW RECORD

Comments on first interview:

Interviewer: _____   Signature: _____   Date: _____

Comments on second interview:

Interviewer: _____   Signature: _____   Date: _____

Recommendations on Training and Development:

Comments of (Personnel) (Recruitment) Manager/Officer

Appendix B Interview checklist

Suggested Interview Checklist.
To be adapted to your situation, as relevant.

Interview Checklist

Name:
Position applied for:

Personal appearance::
Manner:
Speech/Conversation:
General enthusiasm:
Personality:
Ambition/Likely progression:

Experience relevant to job applied for:
Technical ability:
Knowledge of (1) Company
             (2) Products and/or service
             (3) Competitors
Enthusiasm for position:

Training needs for job:
Willingness to move/train/travel:
General impression:
How will he/she 'fit in' with the team?

Short-list rating:
Recommendation:

Appendix C Contracts of employment

Two examples (only) of simple Contracts of Employment to be adapted to your situation, as appropriate.

Example 1:

Contract of Employment
under the Employment Protection (Consolidation) Act 1978, as amended
between
(Name and Address of Company)
and
(Name and Address of Employee)
ABC Limited have pleasure in offering you the following Contract of Employment on the Terms and Conditions stated hereunder:

Position:
Department:
Date at Commencement:
Salary/Wages at Commencement: £ . p. per annum/week/hour, in arrears.
Salary/Wages Review: As reviewed periodically by the Company, or, As contained in the Wages register.
Hours of Work: 0830 to 1700, Monday to Friday; Less one/half hour lunch break.
Probationary Period: This offer is subject to satisfactory completion of a Trial period of three/six months from the date of commencement and subject to confirmation by management.
NB: At the discretion of management, this probationary period may be extended as appropriate, in order to allow for further training or other means necessary in order to achieve satisfactory performance standards.
Holidays: X days up to 31 March/December, then 20/25/30 days p.a. from 1 April/January each year; plus Public Holidays.
Sickness Benefit Scheme: As given in the Terms and Conditions of Employment.

(continued)

Terms and Conditions of Employment:	Attached. The company's Terms and Conditions of Employment form part of this Contract of Employment, and acceptance of this Contract confirms agreement to those conditions.
Additional Special Conditions:	(e.g.) A company car, 1600 cc, is provided for the job. You will be responsible for ensuring that it is maintained in a roadworthy and clean condition at all times. (e.g.) Contractual overtime will be worked at the rate of 5 hours per week, for which the Company guarantees payment at time-and-one-quarter.
Period of Notice:	As contained in the Terms and Conditions of Employment.
Pension Rights:	As contained in the Terms and Conditions of Employment.
Offer: We confirm this offer of Employment, subject to the Conditions stated above.	Acceptance: I hereby accept the above offer of a Contract of Employment under the Terms and Conditions stated above which are a contractual part of this Contract of Employment.

Signed: _____   Signed: _____
Name and Appointment: _____
Date: _____   Date: _____

Example 2:

Statement of
Contract of Employment
under the Employment Protection (Consolidation) Act 1978, as amended

---

This STATEMENT dated: _____ sets out certain particulars of the Terms and Conditions which: (*Name of Employer*) employs: (*Name and Address of Employee*).

Either: Your employment began on _____ and, for the purpose of your individual rights as an employee, your previous employment with: (*Name of Company in Transfer of Undertakings or change of name*) counts as part of your continuous period of employment which, therefore, began on: ___.
Or: Your employment with this Company began on: _____. Your employment with your previous employer does not count as part of your continuous period of employment.

You are employed as (Job Title):

Scale or Rate of Pay:, *or* Method of calculating Pay:

You are paid at   intervals. (monthly/weekly/hourly/annually)

Hours of work and overtime arrangements, including contractual overtime:

Holidays, Public Holidays, Holiday-Pay arrangements:

Sickness and Sick-Pay arrangements:
(e.g.) Your Sick-pay entitlement: 15 days @ full pay rates, plus 10 days @ half-pay, p.a.

Pension and Life Assurance:

A Contracting-out Certificate is/is not in force in respect of this employment.

(*continued*)

Notice Periods:
1. *By Employer*:
In first four weeks: two days.
After one month's service: one week.
After two years' service: one week for each completed year of continuous service, up to a maximum of 12 weeks.

   By Employee:
   Either: In first four weeks: two days; then
   After one month's service, and continuously thereafter: one week.
   Or: One calendar month, from the first day of the month.

Attached are the: Terms and Conditions of Employment,
    Disciplinary (and Unsatisfactory performance)
    Procedures, and Grievance Procedure.
Should you have any cause to be dissatisfied with any disciplinary matters under the foregoing procedures, or wish to redress any grievance, you may raise these matters with _____ (appointment) orally or in writing, as appropriate.

Special Conditions:
- (e.g.) You will be provided with a Company car, 1800 cc, for your job.
  You are responsible for ensuring that this vehicle is maintained in a roadworthy and clean condition at all times.
- (e.g.) Your work involves the handling and preparation of food for consumption.
  You are required to observe all the conditions of the Food Safety Act 1990 and relevant Food Hygiene Regulations at all times, for which the Company will provide all necessary training and information.

Employee Signature, acknowledging receipt and
agreement to the Terms and Conditions of this Statement: _____

Appendix D Terms and conditions of employment

Example (only) of Terms and Conditions of Employment to be adapted according to your situation:

**Terms and Conditions of Employment
for Employees of
ABC Limited
At this Address**

In accordance with the Employment Protection (Consolidation) Act 1978, as amended, the following are the Terms and Conditions of Employment relating to your employment with ABC Limited. These terms and Conditions are given in conjunction with your individual Contract of Employment and as such form an essential part of that Contract.

1. Personnel records
The following personal information is required in the Company's Personnel Records to assist in the administration of your employment . . . . Verification of certain details will be required and you will be requested to supply copies of birth/marriage certificates (etc.).

2. Reduced liability National Insurance Contributions
Certain married women and widows who elected to pay reduced-rate contributions prior to 6 April 1977, and who continue to do so, must hand their Certificate of Election (Form CF.383) together with their Form P.45 to the (Personnel/Accounts) Department.

3. Identification
All employees are issued with an identity card which is also an electronic check-in/out card. Great care must be taken to protect the safety of this card which contains the employee's personal details, registration number and photograph. The card *must* be surrendered upon termination of employment.

4. Probationary period
Employment is subject to a Probationary period of (3/6 months) from the date of commencement. Thereafter, permanent employment is

subject to satisfactory performance of your duties and to management confirmation.

5. **Hours of work**
Your hours of work are from: . . . . to: . . . ., less . . . . lunch break. Refreshment breaks (if any). Overtime . . . . Contractual overtime . . . . Flexitime arrangements . . . .

6. **Suspension of contractual overtime**
(For example) In the light of changing profiles of business conditions, where the Company cannot guarantee overtime to be worked, the cancellation or suspension of Guaranteed Contractual overtime will be at a minimum of two (2) weeks' notice.

7. **Continuity of employment**
Company rules on continuity for, e.g. pension rights:
   Part-time (16 hours or more) (8 hours or more after 5 years).
   Incapacity effects of periods of incapacity (e.g. 26 weeks or more).
   Unpaid absences (authorized and unauthorized).
   Pregnancy (the right to return—qualifications).

8. **Termination of employment**
Termination of employment will be in accordance with the requirements of the Contract of Employment and the Employment Protection (Consolidation) Act 1978, as amended, i.e.:

Notice by Hourly- or Weekly-paid Employees:	In the first four weeks: two days.* Thereafter: Minimum of one week.
Notice by Monthly-paid Employees:	One month's notice from the first day of the month, in accordance with the Contract of Employment.
Notice by the Company:	*To Hourly- or Weekly-paid Employees*: In the first four weeks: two days.* After four weeks and up to two years' completed service: minimum one week. Thereafter: minimum of one week for each completed year of continuous service, to a maximum of 12 weeks.
	To Monthly-paid Employees: During the first two-years' service: Minimum of one month's notice from the first day of the month. Thereafter: one calendar month, or a minimum of one week for each completed year of continuous service, to a maximum of 12 weeks.

* Not a statutory requirement.

9. **Pay periods**
Pay periods are: *Monthly Paid* . . . . . . *Weekly/Hourly Paid*: . . . . . .

10. **Holidays**
All employees shall be entitled to X days paid annual holidays per year, plus all statutory holidays. The holiday year for this Company is from 1 January/April to 31 December/March each year.

Employees joining will be entitled to *pro rata* holidays. Employees who leave the Company may be paid holiday pay in lieu of unused entitlement.

11. **Special compassionate leave**
Additional special compassionate leave may be granted at the discretion of management, according to the circumstances of the situation.

12. **Absence due to sickness or injury**
Notification of absence due to sickness or injury must be made to _____ by (time) to assure work schedules.

13. **Statutory sick pay (SSP)**
Self-Certification rules . . . .
SSP Rules . . . . . . Certification . . . . . . Qualifying Days . . . . . . etc. . . . .

14. **Sickness benefit**
Details of the Company's Sickness Benefit Scheme (including SSP above).

15. **Effect of extended periods of absence due to sickness or injury**
Details of possible decisions relating to employment in the event that absence due to sickness or injury extends beyond six months (e.g. invalidity pension).

16. **Maternity leave and benefits**
Details of Statutory Maternity Pay (SMP), rights during pregnancy and Right to Return to Work schemes, plus any conditions afforded by company above SMP rights.

17. **Pension**
Details of any occupational pension scheme in which the employee may participate.

18. **Health and safety**
Attention is drawn to the Company's Policy on Health and Safety. It is a condition of employment that all aspects of that Policy, of the Health and Safety at Work, etc., Act 1974 and of relevant Regulations must be complied with at all times.

19. **Disciplinary (and unsatisfactory performance) procedure**
Attention is drawn to the Procedures for dealing with matters of discipline and unsatisfactory performance which are set out in . . . .

20. Grievance procedure

It is hoped that good working relationships will prevent grievances from arising. However, every employee will have the right to air their grievances, should any arise, and to seek satisfactory redress, for which (either:) 'the Procedure is set out in . . . .', (or:) 'you should contact Mr/Mrs . . . ., . . . (appointment) . . ., who will hear your grievance'.

21. Training

Brief statement on Company Policy on Training and employees' commitment.

22. Time-keeping

Company policy and methods of time-keeping and recording.

23. Lateness and absenteeisms

Company rules on lateness and absenteeism, and action on infringements.

24. Care of personal property

Company disclaimer and need for personal care with regard to property.

25. General discipline

Specific rules in Company, of which some could be, e.g.:
- (a) use of company property
- (b) intoxicating liquor
- (c) smoking
- (d) health and safety
- (e) storage of vehicles
- (f) gambling
- (g) access to company premises
- (h) collections and clubs
- (i) pilfering
- (j) company purchases
- (k) right of search
- (l) drug abuse

26. Notice boards

Attention should be drawn to notice boards, to be taken notice of.

27. Trade Union membership

Statement about employees' individual rights. Company policy on the 'recognition' of trade unions (if any) and joint consultation (if any).

28. Medical examination

(For example) The Company reserves the right to seek an independent medical examination in certain circumstances.

29. Infectious diseases

Effect of employee contracting certain infectious diseases, e.g. smallpox, para-typhoid, diphtheria, food poisoning, impetigo, tuberculosis, erysipelas, ringworm, encephalitis, scabies, typhoid fever, dysentery.

30. Access to management

How employees may approach management/supervision to discuss problems and/or make suggestions.

31. Amendments

How the Company will amend these Terms and Conditions from time to time.

32. Breaches for these Terms and Conditions

(For example) Disregard for, or serious breach of, these Terms and Conditions of Employment may render an employee liable for action under the Disciplinary Procedures.

To the reader

In some sections suggestions only as to subjects are made with headings; in others, which are matters of law (e.g. Periods of Notice), full detail is given.

You will need to adapt, amend and extend the above Terms and Conditions of Employment according to your Company situation and business climate.

Notes:
1 Probationary or trial periods (Item 4) are very useful so that new employees know the tentative nature of the contract, i.e. that it is subject to satisfactory performance. However, they have no status in law affecting unfair dismissal rights and cannot be used as a means of contravening laws on, e.g. sex and race discrimination or on trade union rights. Trial periods have legal status only in redundancy cases.
2 Item 29, Infectious Diseases, is very important in food handling and preparation premises, e.g. kitchens, canteens, restaurants, dining rooms, cafés, abattoirs, food processing plants, mobile refreshments bars, food stalls in markets, buy-and-resell sections (see Food Safety Act 1990).

Appendix E 'Special' contract of employment

Example (only) of a 'Special' Contract of Employment. To be adapted according to your situation (see Note 1).

CONTRACT OF EMPLOYMENT

Made between: (Name of Employer), whose Registered Office is: (Address of Employer), and: (Name of Employee), of (Address of Employee).

1. *The Contract*: This Agreement sets out the terms and conditions on which employment is offered to the employee, whose signature below confirms acceptance of those terms and conditions. In addition to the specific terms and conditions set out in this Agreement, the Company's Terms and Conditions of Employment generally affecting all employees shall also form part of this Agreement (see Note 2).

2. *Variations to the Contract*: The employer may vary the terms and conditions of this Contract of Employment, in so far as changes become necessary in the light of changes in business conditions, by giving written notice to the employee. Such variations are subject to written consent by the employee, but such consent should not be unreasonably withheld.

3. *Date of Effect*: This employment shall commence (or is deemed to have commenced) from (Date of Commencement of Agreement). Previous continuous employment with this company from _____ to _____ shall count as a part of the continuous period of employment (Note 3).

4. *Place of Employment*: (either) The employment shall be at (Address of place of employment) (or) This employment shall require the employee to travel to other locations of the employer's business premises (or) This employment shall require the employee to travel to the premises of the employer's (customer's) (supplier's).

5. *Duration of Contract*
Either: This Contract of Employment shall be for an indeterminate

period until such time as terminated by either employer or employee. Such notice to terminate the employment must be in writing either in accordance with the Terms and Conditions, above, or, e.g. for three calendar months from the first day of the month, or the first day of the month following the month in which notice is given.

Or: Fixed-Term Contract: This Contract of Employment shall be for a fixed term of (one/three/five) years with effect from the date of this Agreement, i.e. (Date of Commencement of Agreement, as above). After the conclusion of this fixed term, the Agreement shall continue for an indeterminate period until such time as terminated by notice being given in writing by either employer or employee. Such notice to terminate the employment must be in writing for (one/three/six/ twelve) calendar months from either the date of tendering notice or the first day of the month, or the first day of the month following the month in which notice is given (see Note 4).

6. *Termination*: (Fixed-Term Contracts only) The employee agrees that, upon the expiry of this Agreement without its being renewed, any claim to this dismissal being unfair under the Employment Protection (Consolidation) Act 1978, as amended, shall be excluded.

7. *Redundancy Pay*: (Fixed-Term Contracts only) The employee agrees that, upon expiry of this Agreement without its being renewed, any rights to redundancy pay under the Employment Protection (Consolidation) Act 1978, as amended, shall be excluded.

8. *Salary*: The employee shall be paid a fixed salary of £n000 per annum. The salary shall be paid in 12 equal instalments, monthly in arrears at the end of each calendar month.

9. *Commission/Bonus*: In addition to the fixed salary, there shall be a commission of n per cent on all sales effected by the employee, payable or/and a bonus payment of n per cent of the company profits on sales, payable every three/six/twelve months in (months when paid).

10. *Covenants Following Termination*:

Example 1. The employee agrees that he/she will not be engaged, either directly or indirectly, in the business of (nature of your business) within a radius of n miles of the employer's premises (above) (at _____) for a period of n year(s) from the date of termination, whether on his/her own account or as an employee or partner in another commercial concern (see Note 5).

Example 2. The employee agrees that he/she will not be engaged, either directly or indirectly, in the canvassing, soliciting or acceptance of orders for business from any commercial concern which bought or agreed to buy the goods and services of the employer, whether for him/herself or any other person or commercial business, for a period of *n* years from the date of termination of this agreement.

11. *Financial Bonding*: You will be required to enter into a financial bond, effected through XYZ Insurance Co., as a condition of employment (see Note 6).

12. *Copyright and Patents*: Any original design, discovery or invention which the employee may make while in the employ of this Company shall be the sole property of the company. All papers, electronic data, models and any other representation of such design, discovery or invention shall remain the property of the Company and must be surrendered upon termination of this agreement.

13. This Agreement shall have effect and shall be binding upon both parties upon signature below.

We confirm the details of the terms and conditions of this offer of employment as given in this Contract of Employment:

(Signed): _____ on behalf of (**Name of Company**) Date: ___

I confirm acceptance of this Contract of Employment on the terms and conditions stated above:

(Signed): _____ (**Name of Employee**) Date: _____

Notes:
1 'Special' in the context of this Contract of Employment means simply that it is not of the routine type of contract issued to most employees. The word 'special' does not appear in the title.
2 In addition to the non-routine clauses above, you may either refer to the standard Terms and Conditions of Employment of the company, making this agreement an extension of, or amendment to, the original (paragraph 1), or include them in this 'special' contract.
3 Date of Effect (paragraph 3): Most special agreements are drawn up after a period of time has elapsed since the original contract of employment and when changes in conditions are necessary because of specific business interests. In such situations, the first date shown is the date of this new Agreement, while the 'previous

continuous employment' consists of the dates from the commencement of the original agreement up to the date of this new Agreement.
4 Duration of Contract (paragraph 4): this clause may be important in a number of situations, e.g.:
   (a) where you have a position which is 'key' to the function of the business (e.g. a director or senior manager);
   (b) where considerable costs of training are incurred, thus justifying a minimum term to recoup those costs;
   (c) a definite fixed-term may be appropriate, as in temporary employment for a specific project or for relief during a postholder's absence (e.g. on maternity leave). In this situation, the fixed-term may be months rather than years. With short-fixed-term contracts, no notice period would be appropriate.
5 Covenants following termination (paragraph 9): It should be noted that you cannot include such a covenant simply in order to claim protection from possible competition. This clause should be designed to protect your trade secrets or to reflect any direct, influential relationship which may have existed between the employee and your customers before such agreement is drawn up.
6 Financial Bonding (paragraph 10): Some form of financial bonding may be necessary to act as a security against possible loss arising from problems in the employee's acts or omissions.

Before finalizing 'special' Contracts of Employment as in this appendix, for key and sensitive positions, readers are advised to obtain professional or legal advice in order to assure the complete legality and satisfaction of the Agreement.

Appendix F Apprenticeship agreement

Example (only) of an Apprenticeship Agreement.
To be adapted according to your particular Company needs:

APPRENTICESHIP AGREEMENT

This Agreement made this _____ day of _____ 19__,
between   (Name and address of Employer)
hereinafter called 'the Company', and (Name and address of Employee)
herinafter called 'the Apprentice' and (Name and address of Guardian),
hereinafter called 'the Guardian', witnesseth as follows:

1 The Employer agrees with the Apprentice and the Guardian:
   (a) to employ the Apprentice with the effect from the
       .... day of .... 19 . .
   (b) to make available, as far as reasonably practicable, to the Apprentice the experience and facilities that are necessary for the Apprentice to achieve the standards required by the Company and by his/her skill and trade.
   (c) to observe the terms of this Agreement and other conditions set out in the Company's Terms and Conditions of Employment.
2 The Apprentice and Guardian severally agree with the Company that:
   (a) The Apprentice shall be employed by the Company and work for the Company from the date of this Agreement as in clause 1 above.
   (b) The Apprentice will observe the terms of this Agreement and other conditions set out in the Company's Terms and Conditions of Employment.
   (c) The Apprentice will pursue diligently and punctually his/her education and training, including taking such examinations and tests, and the maintenance of log books, manuals and records of his/her training as required by the Company or its representatives.

(d) The Apprentice shall at all times conduct him/herself in a responsible manner and promote the interests of the Company, to the best of his/her ability.
3 It is further agreed by and between the Company, the Apprentice and the Guardian that:
   (1) The first six months of this Agreement from the date at clause 1, above, shall be a Probationary Period during which time either the Company, the Apprentice or the Guardian may terminate this Agreement by tendering one week's notice in writing.
   (2) If, at any time, the Apprentice shall wilfully disobey the lawful instructions of the Company, its managers or its representatives, or shall persistently refuse to comply with the provisions of this Agreement or shall persistently commit gross misconduct or habitually absent him/herself from work, education or training without the Company's consent, then the Company may—without notice—terminate this Agreement.
   (3) If, in the opinion of the Company's managers or their representatives, the Apprentice fails to make satisfactory progress in his/her education, training and work-standards, the Company shall give notice in writing to the Apprentice and the Guardian to that effect. Such notice shall specify:
      (a) in what respects the Company considers that the progress of the Apprentice is unsatisfactory;
      (b) the improvement in standards of performance expected of the Apprentice; and
      (c) the time within which such improvement in standards must be achieved.
   (4) If the required improvements specified at (3) (b) above, are not achieved within the period of time notified in (3) (c) above, the Company may terminate this Agreement by giving the minimum statutory notice to the Apprentice and the Guardian, as required by the Employment Protection (Consolidation) Act 1978, as amended.
   (5) The Company may terminate this Agreement by reason of redundancy as defined in the Act by giving the Apprentice and the Guardian the minimum period of notice as required by the Act. In such circumstances, the Company shall take all possible action to seek employment for the Apprentice with another Employer.
4 This Agreement does not guarantee employment with the Company once the Apprentice has completed his/her period of Apprenticeship. This shall be a matter for discussion in the light of on-going business conditions and manpower requirements at the time, without prior commitment by either party.

Signed by the Company's representative, the Apprentice and the Guardian in the presence of two witnesses, as follows:

.... the Apprentice	.... First Witness
.... (Full Name)	Address: ....
.... the Guardian	....
.... (Full Name)	.... Second Witness
.... for the Company	Address: ....
.... (Full Name)	....
.... (Appointment)	Date: ....

TRAINING CERTIFICATE

This is to certify that the above-mentioned Apprentice served his/her Apprenticeship with this Company in accordance with the foregoing Agreement from (Date of Commencement) to (Date of Completion).

Signed on behalf of the Company:

_____ Name: _____

_____ (Appointment) Date: _____

Appendix G Health and safety policy

An Example (only) of a Health and Safety Policy.
You should follow the 'Statement of Policy' and the 'General Statement of Intent' fairly closely, according to your situation, ensuring that you include the signature of the chief executive; then adapt the remainder as appropriate to Company requirements. Sections in parenthesis should be worded to your Company structure.

ABC GROUP LIMITED
At this Address

HEALTH AND SAFETY POLICY

ABC Limited, in all its operations and locations, is hereinafter called 'the Company'. **Employees** of ABC Limited in all its operations and locations, are hereinafter called 'the Employees'. All **Contractors, sub-Contractors,** self-employed **Installers, Service Engineers, Advisers and Consultants**, are hereinafter called 'the Contractors'.

1. **STATEMENT OF POLICY**

CORPORATE RESPONSIBILITY
Overall control of the operations of ABC Limited is vested in the (Board of Directors). Responsibility for the executive control and implementation of this Health and Safety Policy (throughout the Company) rests with the (Managing Director).

RESPONSIBILITY FOR THE WORKPLACE AND WORKING ENVIRONMENT
The (Board of Directors) recognizes the importance of achieving a safe place of work and a healthy working environment. The Company accepts its responsiblities to all its employees and (contractors, customers) others who are affected by the Company's operations, for ensuring that safe and healthy working conditions and practices exist.

PLANT AND EQUIPMENT

The Company Policy includes health and safety considerations in the purchase, maintenance and updating of plant and equipment, with the requirement of health and safety legislation taken as the minimum requirements for the Company's own practices.

UNIT SAFETY PRACTICES

It is the personal responsibility of managers of the separate (units) (factories) (shops) (offices) (business centres) and (branches) to study and publish that part of this Policy Document relevant to their individual locations and operating circumstances. It is also their personal responsibility to train their subordinates (and contractors) in that Policy, and to ensure that relevant Policy is carried out in their respective locations.

March 1992

A.B. Ceedee
Managing Director

(continued)

2. GENERAL STATEMENT OF INTENT

It is the Policy of this Company that the Company will ensure, so far as is reasonably practicable:

(a) the health, safety and welfare of all its employees while they are at work (in whatever operation or location, whether on-site or in transit on authorized business), of visitors to company premises and operations, and of others who may be affected by its actions.

(b) the provision of systems of work which are safe and without risks to health, with necessary supervision and control mechanisms to ensure health and safety.

(c) the maintenance of a working environment that is safe and without risks to health, and the provision of adequate facilities and arrangements for welfare at work.

(d) the provision of plant, machinery, equipment and vehicles (whether owned or hired) in conditions which are safe and without risks to health; and to provide systems for inspections and preventive maintenance to ensure safe conditions.

(e) that arrangements are in place for ensuring safety and absence of risks to health in connection with the use, handling, storage and transportation of articles and substances.

(f) the provision of such information, instruction, training and supervision necessary to ensure the health and safety at work of employees, and information to contractors and others who may be affected by the Company's operations or products.

(g) the provision of a safe means of access to, movement and egress from places of work.

(h) cooperation with, and involvement of employees in meeting health and safety objectives.

The necessary resources and input will be afforded to the achievement of the foregoing Policy, and to this end the Company will:

1. ensure that all requirements of the Health and Safety at Work, etc., Act 1974, Regulations and Approved Codes of Practice (ACOPs) issued under the Act, and other relevant Acts which apply to the Company's operations, are complied with.

2. provide the necessary management information and involvement, financial resources and safety engineering input, so far as it is reasonable and practical to do so, to achieve the standards laid down in this Policy.

3. maintain necessary up-to-date knowledge; maintain contact with relevant outside bodies including health and safety advisory and specialist services; and keep up-to-date with developments in health

and safety legislation, Codes of Practice and other technical or guidance material relating to the Company's operations.

4. disseminate such information within the Company to employees, contractors and visitors, as such information affects them.

5. ensure that all health and safety factors are taken into account when new and revised systems of manufacture, operation, storage, materials handling, etc., are planned and effected. Further, the Company will, when considering the reorganization of its operations or new premises from which to conduct its operations, take account of the necessary health, safety and welfare requirements for that new organization or location.

6. provide all new employees, and those redeployed to different jobs and/or departments, information on health and safety, welfare, fire precautions, first aid and medical, as appropriate to their occupations and locations.

7. ensure that all the requirements of the parent Group Health and Safety Policy as they affect the Company's operations, are complied with.

3. ARRANGEMENTS FOR THE OPERATION OF THIS HEALTH AND SAFETY POLICY

MANAGEMENT OF HEALTH AND SAFETY

Responsibility   The (**Managing Director**) may delegate authority for specific health and safety matters to (**senior location/department managers**). They will be personally responsible for health, safety, welfare, and fire precautions within their sphere of operation, as a part of their normal management duties, as follows:

- ensuring that this policy is complied with;
- ensuring job-safety; reviewing the systems of work in their (locations or departments);
- ensuring (on-site) safety in (installations); ensuring health and safety in new and changing situations;
- ensuring the use and wearing of safety protective equipment and clothing by employees, contractors and visitors, as appropriate.

Health and Safety Committee   A statement on Company policy concerning health and safety committees. **'HEALTH AND SAFETY WORKING PARTY'** is an alternative in very small businesses.

Safety representatives   A statement on Company policy concerning health and safety representatives (trade union or non-trade union members).

Health and safety monitoring   For example, standards of health, safety and welfare and the compliance with this Policy Statement will be monitored by the (**Managing Director**), assisted by any necessary specialist health and safety adviser.

Suggestions   The Company welcomes suggestions . . .

Safety management structure   Figure G.1 is the management structure. The positions shown have accountability to the (**Managing Director**) for health, safety and welfare, through existing lines of authority as follows:

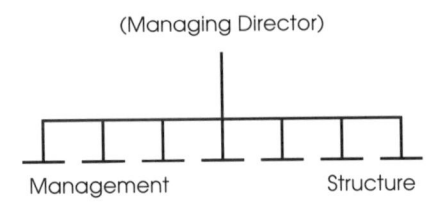

Figure G.1   Management structure.

RESPONSIBILITY AND ACCOUNTABILITIES

List the duties and responsibilities of each (type of) management and supervisory and other positions in the company, e.g.:

Executive responsibilities   The (**Managing Director**) is responsible for . . . .

Senior Managers   Senior Managers have responsibility for . . . .

Personnel Manager/Safety Officer   The Personnel . . . .

Line managers and supervisors   Line managers and supervisors are responsible for, e.g.:
  (a) induction training, including health and safety law, job safety, fire precautions, emergency procedures, location of fire exits, correct use of fire-fighting equipment, first aid and accident reporting;
  (b) ensuring subordinates and contractors are aware of health and safety policy and that they obey the rules;
  (c) keeping up-to-date with health and safety matters;
  (d) ensuring good housekeeping standards;
  (e) ensuring all access and egress routes are clearly marked and kept clear; access to all fire doors and fire-fighting equipment clear;
  (f) reviewing all existing plant and equipment periodically and all new plant and equipment as it is ordered and installed;
  (g) carrying out regular health and safety checks;
  (h) ensuring accident reporting carried out according to RIDDOR;
  (i) ensuring appropriate disciplinary action taken in cases of clear breach of health and safety rules;
  (j) monitoring welfare arrangements under guidance of (**Personnel Manager**).

Employees   What you expect of your employees. They are to, e.g.:
  (a) obey health and safety legislation and company rules;
  (b) cooperate with managers and supervisors;
  (c) receive and act upon health and safety training, instruction and information;
  (d) report faults, hazards, non-injurious incidents and injuries to management;
  (e) raise with immediate manager/supervisor any situation of conflict between health and safety requirements and the demands of the job;
  (f) wear and/or use safety protective equipment and clothing;
  (g) not interfere with, abuse or remove anything provided in the interests of health and safety;

(h) keep all access and egress routes and access to all fire doors and fire-fighting equipment clear at all times.

Fork-lift/power truck drivers Duties of drivers, include, e.g.:
  (a) safe operation, transportation, depositing, storage;
  (b) keeping access and egress routes clear; also access to fire doors and fire-fighting equipment;
  (c) speed limits;
  (d) maintenance and records.

Health and safety representatives Statement of their duties and privileges.

Health and Safety Committee/Working Party Statement of their functions.

HEALTH AND SAFETY TRAINING
Policy on health and safety training.

ACCIDENT PREVENTION
Policy on accident prevention, methods and involvement.

CONTROL OF SUBSTANCES HAZARDOUS TO HEALTH (COSHH)
Statement of commitment to COSHH, e.g.:

- Initial and periodic assessments
- Exposure, prevention and control
- Recording
- Monitoring
- Control
- Health surveillance

DUTIES TO NON-EMPLOYEES
Outline duties towards visitors, contractors, public under s.3 of HASWA.

DUTIES AS A (manufacturer) (supplier) (installer) (seller)

PERSONAL PROTECTIVE CLOTHING AND EQUIPMENT
Policy on what is issued to whom (including contractors and visitors) under what conditions, e.g. helmets (hard hats), face masks/visors, goggles/glasses, ear defenders, overalls, gloves, boots/shoes, ventilators, harnesses, etc.

MACHINE GUARDING AND FENCING
Policy on guards and fences, including warnings about interference and unauthorized removal.

ACCIDENT/INCIDENT REPORTING
Details of Company's accident, incident and injury reporting and recording procedures.

FIRST AID
Policy on first aid, e.g.: First-Aid Boxes; First-Aid Attendants; *Obtaining First Aid*—First-Aid/Medical Room; Company Doctor.

HOUSEKEEPING
Importance of good housekeeping standards to health, safety and welfare.

HYGIENE
Importance of hygiene in workplace and personal standards of hygiene in relation to food, working with lead, wood and metal dust, oils and chemicals, etc.

- *Canteens and restaurants*: importance of hygiene and of adherence to standards of Food Safety Act 1990 and associated Regulations.

HEALTH AND SAFETY SIGNS
Importance of obeying, and note as to types, i.e.:
    Red—prohibition   Yellow/black—warning
    Green—safe condition   Blue—mandatory—**MUST DO**.

STORAGE AND HANDLING
Policy on safe storage and handling of articles and substances, including temporary storage.

PETROL
Policy if petrol is used and/or stored.

LEAD
Policy if any lead is used in manufacture of products, stating method and frequency of assessments, MELs (0.10 mg or 0.15 mg pm^{-3} in 8-hour TWA), protection, medical surveillance, and rules in areas where lead is worked, i.e.: food and drink not consumed at work benches. No smoking in the workplace (by anyone). Protective gloves, impervious aprons, masks/visors (if appropriate). Wash hands before eating, avoid contact of gloved-hands, or ungloved lead-contaminated hands, with mouth and eyes.

NICKEL
Policy if any nickel is used in manufacture of products, stating frequency of assessments, MELs (e.g. 0.10 mg or 1.00 mg pm^{-3} in 8-hour TWA); face-masks to be worn, ventilation/extraction to be provided.

ASBESTOS
Procedures if types of asbestos are discovered in process of installations, demolitions, etc., in compliance with Asbestos at Work Regulations.

OTHER HAZARDOUS SUBSTANCES
Policy in similar manner as for lead, nickel, asbestos, etc.

FIRE EQUIPMENT
Policy on types and use of fire-fighting equipment, including who is authorized to take what action.

FIRE AND EMERGENCY DRILLS
Outline the fire drill to be followed; from raising/hearing alarm, through calling fire brigade, first-aid fire fighting, to hand-over to fire brigade, etc.

SMOKING
State the policy on smoking, if one exists.

OFFICE SAFETY
Reminder that offices can also be dangerous places, with policy on handling, storage, paper, smoking, fire-preventions, etc.

ABRASIVE WHEELS
Policy on compliance with Abrasive Wheels Regulations.

GENERAL SAFETY RULES
Those health and safety rules which apply to every employee.

HEALTH AND SAFETY AUDITS AND INSPECTIONS
What audits and inspections will be carried out, by whom, with what frequency. Who will act upon the findings of audit reports.

WELFARE
Detail what welfare facilities are provided, e.g. sanitary conveniences, washrooms, rest rooms. The necessity for cleanliness and hygiene in them to protect the interests of employees.

CHECKING IN AND OUT
Importance of checking in and out for fire safety.

ELECTRICAL SAFETY
Rules, including 'no unauthorized person to carry out electrical work'.

ISOLATION AND LOCKING-OUT
Rules on isolating and locking-out plant and equipment when under maintenance, especially electrical and large mechanical plant.

COMMUNICATION AND COOPERATION
Statement on importance of good communication and cooperation in having effective health and safety policy implementation.

APPENDICES
Statement that any appendices are an integral part of main policy document.

REVIEW AND UPDATE
Statement as to how frequently this Policy will be reviewed and updated, and how amendments promulgated.

Date of this Policy: (31 March 1992)

REVISIONS: *Serial Number*:   *Date*:

APPENDICES: the Appendices to this Policy follow:

Description: *Date*:

A—Policy for On-Site Health and Safety.
B—Policy for Dealing with . . .
C—Policy for Installations.

Note: In addition to the Statement of Policy and General Statement in the above example of a Health and Safety Policy, we have given headings of the types of subject-matter which could be included. It is impossible in this appendix to go into full detail on every subject to cover every eventuality. Thus, under certain headings some detail has been given, but in most subjects you will need to delete or expand the content according to your particular situation.

Appendix H Induction training checklist

An example (only) of an Induction Checklist.
To be adapted to your particular situation and training needs.

INDUCTION TRAINING CHECKLIST

Department: _____   Name of Trainee: _____
Job Title: _____   Date(s) of Induction: _____

1. WORKPLACE SAFETY

Facilities	Breaks	Organization Structure	Procedures, Pay, etc.	Hygiene Requirements

Health and Saftey Law	Employees' Duties	HSE Poster: H and S Law . . .	COSHH Arrangements	Workplace Hazards

Fire Ext'shers	Personal Protection	Fire Drills	First Aid	Accident Reporting

(continued)

Emergency Shut-down	Safety Rep'tive	Safe Working Practices	Safety Signs (Types)	Signature of Employee

2. JOB KNOWLEDGE

Tools	Materials	Procedures	Quality Standards	Hazards of Job

Personal Protection	Machine Guarding	Shut-down and Isolation		Signature of Employee

Notes
1 Record dates on which each module of induction training is given and/or signature of instructor in each block.
2 Ensure that employee signs to confirm training given.

Appendix I Job description

An example (only) of a Job Description,
Including knowledge and skills, objectives and key results areas.

JOB DESCRIPTION
JOB TITLE:
DEPARTMENT:
SUMMARY OF MAIN PURPOSE OF JOB:
POSITION IN ORGANIZATION: Responsible to: Subordinates directly supervised: Works in collaboration with:
MAIN DUTIES AND RESPONSIBILITIES: 1. 2. 3. 4. 5. 6. 7. 8.

– 2 –

Knowledge and Skills Required

Responsibility	Knowledge and Skills Required
1. 2. 3. 4. 5. 6. 7. 8.	

(continued)

Appendix I

– 3 –

Agreed Objectives

Name: Job Title:	Department:
Responsibility Reference No. 1. 2. 3. 4. 5. 6. (preferred maximum)	Agreed Objectives to be Achieved

– 4 –

Key Results Areas

Name: Job Title:	Department:
Responsibility Reference No. 1. 2. 3. 4. 5. 6.	Agreed Key Results Area

Notes

1 The four pages of this Job Description are condensed into two pages.
2 Note that the person's name is not on pages 1 and 2. The Job Description relates to the Job, *per se*, while Objectives and (particularly) Key Results Areas are agreed with the individual job-holder.

List of abbreviations

ACAS	Advisory, Conciliation and Arbitration Service
ACOP	Approved Code of Practice
AEOs	Attachment of Earnings Orders
ATN	Analysis/Analyses of Training Needs
AVCs	Additional Voluntary Contributions
BET	Business Enterprise Training (formerly BGT)
BGT	Business Growth Training
CSA	Child Support Agency (DSS)
CC-AEO	Community Charge Attachment of Earnings Order
COP	Code of Practice
COSHH	Control of Substances Hazardous to Health
CS Act	Child Support Act 1991
DEOs	Deduction from Earnings Orders
DP	Data Protection
DSS	Department of Social Security
DWA	Disability Working Allowance
EA	Employment Act
EAs	Enterprise Agencies
EAT	Employment Appeals Tribunal
EC	European Commission/Community
ECJ	European Court of Justice
EHO	Environmental Health Officer
EPA	Employment Protection Act 1975
EP(C)A	Employment Protection (Consolidation) Act 1978
EWC	Expected Week of Confinement
FA	Factories Act 1961
FSAVCs	Free-Standing Additional Voluntary Contributions
FSB	Federation of Small Businesses (formerly NFSE)
GOQ	Genuine Occupational Qualification
GNC	Graphical Numerical Control
GCHQ	General Command Headquarters
HASWA	Health and Safety at Work, etc., Act 1974
HMSO	Her Majesty's Stationery Office
HSC	Health and Safety Commission

List of abbreviations

HSE	Health and Safety Executive
IIM	Institute of Industrial Management
IIP	Investment In People Initiative
IQ	Intelligence Quotient
IPM	Institute of Personnel Management
IR	Inland Revenue
IR	Industrial Relations
ISBN	International Standard Book Number
ITOs	Industry Training Organizations
ITBs	Industry Training Boards
IVB	Invalidity Benefit
JCITB	Joint Council of Industry Training Boards
KRAs	Key Results Areas
KITA	Kick in the (Pants)
LECs	Local Enterprise Companies
LMS	Local Management of Schools
Ltd	Private Limited-Liability Company
LEL	Lower Earnings Level
MA	Maternity Allowance
MB	Maternity Benefit
MPP	Maternity Pay Period
MSC	Manpower Services Commission (now superseded)
NFSE	See FSB
NIC	National Insurance Contributions
NJICs	National Joint Industrial Councils
NTTF	National Training Task Force
NVQs	National Vocational Qualifications
OMO	Open Market Option (Pensions)
PAYE	Pay As You Earn (Tax)
PE	Period of Entitlement
PEP	Private Enterprise Programme
PIW	Period of Incapacity for Work
PLC/plc	Public Limited Company
QDs	Qualifying Days
QW	Qualifying Week
RR(Act)	Race Relations (Act 1976)
RIDDOR	Reporting of Injuries, Diseases and Dangerous Occurrences Regulations 1985
RMS	Regional Medical Service

ROC	Return on Capital
ROI	Return on Investment
RTITB	Road Transport Industry Training Board
s.	Section (of an Act)
SAYE	Save As You Earn
SB	Sickness Benefit
SC	Self-Certification
SCOPs	Statutory Code(s) of Practice
SD(Act)	Sex Discrimination (Act 1975)
SDA	Severe Disablement Allowance
SERPS	State Earnings Related Pension Scheme
SMP	Statutory Maternity Pay
SSALE	Social Security Advice Line for Employers (DSS, Glasgow) (known as the 'Sally Line')
SSP	Statutory Sick Pay
SOS	Sick Office Syndrome
TA	Training Agent
TECs	Training and Enterprise Councils
TEED	Training, Enterprise and Education Directorate
TM	Training Manager
TUA	Trade Union Act 1984
TUC	Trades Union Congress
TULRA	Trade Union and Labour Relations Act 1974
UEL	Upper Earnings Level
VAT	Value Added Tax
VDUs	Visual Display Units
YT	Youth Training
YTS	Youth Training Scheme (replaced by YT)

Bibliography and recommended reading

Advisory Booklets and Handbooks—Series. ACAS.
Angel, J.—*Industrial Tribunals*. Tolley and IPM (1984).
Annual Report 1988/89; Health and Safety Commission (1990).

Brimson, T. J. *Research into Attitudes and Morale among Managers.* University of Salford (1979).
Code of Professional Conduct. Institute of Personnel Management.
Corfield, A. *Safety Management*. Institute of Supervisory Management (1987).

Data Protection Act 1984—Guidelines 1–9. Data Protection Registrar.
Dewis, M. and Stranks, J. *Health and Safety at Work Handbook*. Tolley and RoSPA (1988).

Employer's Manual on NIC, NI.269 plus supplement. DSS.
Employment Law (subscription). Croner.
Employment Legislation Booklets—Series. Department of Employment.
Environmental Protection Act 1990. HMSO.
Essentials of Health and Safety, by HSE; HMSO. (1988).

Factories Act 1961. HMSO.
Farmer, D. *Classic Accidents*. Croner (1989).
Farmer, D. *So Far as is Reasonably Practicable*. Croner (1989).
First Aid at Work—Approved Code of Practice. HMSO (1990).

Guide to Discipline. Croner (1982).

Health and Safety Executive 1986. *Essentials of Health and Safety*. HMSO.
Health and Safety at Work (subscription). Croner.
Health and Safety at Work Act 1974. HMSO.
Health and Safety (First Aid) Regulations 1981. HMSO (1990).
Health and Safety Monitor (subscription). Monitor Press.
Herzberg et al. *The Motivation to Work*. New York. Wiley (1959).
Hillier, A. *Employment Act 1982*. Tolley (1983).

Industrial Relations Law (subscription). Croner.

IR.53—*Thinking of Taking Someone One?—PAYE for Employers*. IR.
IR.56/NI.39—*Employed or Self-Employed—Guide for Tax and NIC*. IR/DSS.

Lichtenstein, E. *Model Employment Contracts*. Hutchinson (1989).
Lickert, R. *The Human Organisation—its Management and Values*. (1967). Explained in Glen, F. *The Social Psychology of Organisations*. (1975).

Maslow, A. H. *Motivation and Personality*. New York. Harper (1965).
McClelland, D. C. *The Achieving Society*. New York. Van Nostrand (1961).
McGregor, D. *The Human Side of Enterprise*. New York. McGraw-Hill (1961).

NI.35—*NI for Company Directors*. DSS.
NI.268—*Quick Guide for Employers*. DSS.
NI.269—*Guidelines on Gross Pay for NIC*. DSS.
NI.270—*Employer's Manual on SSP*. DSS.
NI.271—*SSP Flow Chart*. DSS.
NI.274—*Fact Card—Company Directors*. DSS.
NI.275—*Information for Employers*. DSS.
NI.278(1991)—*SSP—Small Employers' Relief*. DSS.

Offices, Shops and Railway Premises Act 1963. HMSO.

Race Discrimination Act 1976.
Recruitment Code, IPM. Institute of Personnel Management.
Reference Book for Employers (subscription). Croner.

Sex Discrimination Act 1975
Slade, *Employment Handbook*. Tolley (1987).
SSP.55—*SSP Tables*. DSS.
SSP—Employers. Do You Know the Costs? NFSE (1991).

Index

Abbreviations, list of, 268–270
Absenteeism, 133
Accident, 120, 133
Action short of strike, 214
Additional Voluntary Contributions (AVCs), 102
Advertising, 18–23
Advisory, Conciliation and Arbitration Service (ACAS), 174, 175, 183, 218, 223, 225
Agency worker, 6, 7, 48
Analysis of Training Needs (ATN), 134
Annual Reports of Health and Safety Commission, 109
Application form, 23, 24, 232–236
Appraisal, 2, 155–157
Apprenticeship agreement, 39, 41, 62, 251–253
Attachable earnings, 64
Attachment of Earnings Orders (AEO), 64
Average earnings, 87, 92

Barber Judgment, the, 101
Benefits, 12–15, 132–134, 198
Blacking, 215, 217
Blocking orders, 64
Breach of Contract, 42
Business Enterprise Training (BET) (formerly BGT), 53, 147, 148, 154
Business owner, 1
Business plan, 1, 3

Cash-flow, 1, 2, 58
Cash-plus pension mix, 100
Casual worker, 52
Check-lists, 2, 17, 34, 56, 107, 125, 161, 172, 184, 195, 202, 209, 221, 231
Check-list, recruitment, 24, 237
Child Support Act 1991 (CS Act), 63
Child Support Agency (DSS)—(CSA), 63
Coaching, 145
Code of Professional Conduct,

Institute of Personnel Management, 33
Collective agreement, 39, 40
Commissioner for Trade Union Rights, 218–219
Communications, 30, 143
Community Charge Attachment of Earnings Order (CC–AEO), 64, 66, 67
Company cars, NIC on, 72
Conciliation, 225
Conditions of Employment, 41
Constructive dismissal, 223
Consultation with trade unions, 212, 213
Consultants, 52, 53
Contract of Employment, 35–43, 58, 62, 173, 181, 186, 213, 214, 215, 216, 238–241, 247–250
Contracting out, 99, 103
Contributions Agency (DSS), 78
Control of Substances Hazardous to Health (COSHH), 36, 136, 141
Costs, 11, 22, 58
Council tax, 66
Covenants, 248, 250

Data Protection (DP), 53–55
  Act (DP Act) 1984, 53
  Registrar, 54
Deduction from Earnings Orders (DEOs), 63
Deductions, 62
Delegation, 145
Directors, 1, 8
Disability, 5, 15
  Pension, 100
  Working Allowance (DWA), 62
  Living Allowance (DLA), 62
Disabled Persons (Employment) Act 1944 and 1958, 5
Disciplinary interview, 179–181
  procedures, 174–181, 222, 244
Discrimination, 5, 19–21, 31
Dismissal, 15, 177, 178, 203–209
  constructive, 208
  discrimination, 223, 224

Dismissal (*Cont.*)
  fair, 205, 206
  trade union activities, 223, 224, 229
  trade union (non-)membership, 222, 224, 229
  taking part in strikes, 223, 224
  unfair, 218
  written reasons for, 206, 207
Drug abuse, 115
Duty:
  of employees, 122, 123, 125
  of employers, 113, 114, 125

Earnings, 57
  cap, 100, 104
  limits, 87
Employer information, 64
Employer's Manual:
  on NIC (DSS), 78
  on SMP (DSS), 97
  on SSP (DSS), 92
'Employers—Do You Know the Costs (of SSP)' (FSB), 92
Employees' rights, trade union, 210
Employers' rights, 217, 218
Employment Act (EA) 1980, 1982 and 1990, 186, 210, 211, 214, 216, 217, 218, 224
Enterprise Agencies (EAs), 148
Employment Appeals Tribunal (EAT), 230
Employment agencies, 23
Employment:
  refusal of, 222, 224
  Terms and Conditions of, 242, 246
  Training (ET), 51, 116, 147, 148
'Employed or Self-Employed—Guide for Tax and NIC' (IR.56/NI.53), 52
Employer's Liability Insurance (ELI), 11, 36
Employment Protection (Consolidation) Act 1978 (EP(C)A), 37, 40, 41, 173, 186, 204, 206, 210, 218
Environment, 115
Environmental Health Officer (EHO), 121
European Commission/Community (EC), 13, 219
European Court of Justice (ECJ), 101
Evaluation, 131, 159, 160
Expected Week of Confinement (EWC), 44, 45, 92, 93, 94, 96
Experience, 5, 6, 147

5-Ms, the, 126, 129, 163
Fact Card—Company Directors (DSS), 74
Factories Act 1961 (FA), 116
Federation of Small Businesses (FSB) (formerly NFSE), 55
Fees (for DEOs), 65
FIMBRA, 98
Fire Certificate, 36
Fre Precautions Act 1971, 36
First Aid, 119, 120
First Aid at Work—Approved Code of Practice (ACOP), 119
First impressions, 27, 30
Fixed-term contracts, 42, 80, 248, 250
Free-lance, 51
Free-Standing Additional Voluntary Contributions (FSAVCs), 102, 103
Fringe benefits, 12–15
Full-time employee, 6, 60
Further particulars, 225

Gender, 4
Genuine Occupational Qualification (COQ), 4, 19
Grievance, 181–183, 245
Group development, 153, 154
Guarantee pay, 59
Guidelines on Gross Pay for NIC (DSS), 78, 92
Guides on:
  PAYE/NIC, 78
  SSP/SMP, 92, 97

Health, 112
Health and Safety at Work, etc, Act 1974 (HASWA), 46, 50, 112–113, 224
Health and Safety:
  Commission (HSC), 109
  Committee, 118
  Executive (HSE), 35, 36, 56, 109, 117, 121, 124
  (First Aid) Regulations 1981, 119
  Law—What You Should Know (poster), 36, 56, 116
  Policy, 116, 117, 254–263
  Representatives, 117, 213
  Training, 114, 140, 141, 170
Help lines, 78, 97
Herzerg, F., 164–166, 169
Hierarchy of needs, Maslow's, 163–164
Holidays, 12, 13, 244

HSE Annual Reports, 109
Hygiene factors, 164, 165, 169

IR.53 and IR.56, 52, 78
Income Tax, 67, 68
Induction training, 139, 141, 264–265
Industrial action, 214–218, 223
Industrial Relations Code of Practice, 187
Industrial Relations (IR), 210–221
Industrial Tribunal, 4, 45, 47, 174, 177, 186, 187, 203, 222–231
Industrial Tribunal:
  appeals, 230
  application for, 224
  burden of proof, 227
  decisions and awards of, 228–229
  evidence, 228
  hearings, 226, 227
  procedures, 228
Industry Training Boards (ITBs), 148
Industry Training Organizations (ITOs), 149
Information for Employers (DSS)—NI.275(1991), 92
Inland Revenue (IR), 8, 36, 59, 70, 105
Inspectors, DSS, 67
Institute of Industrial Management (IIM), 10
Institute of Personnel Management (IPM), 8, 10, 33
Instructional Techniques/Instructors, 143, 144, 197
Intelligence Quotient (IQ), 30
Interview, 19, 25–32, 237
Invalidity Benefit (IVB), 96
Investment in People Initiative (IIP), 146
Itemized Pay Statement, 60

Job:
  analysis, 139, 140
  breakdown, 138, 139
  description, 2, 3, 137, 266–267
  evaluation, 10
  offer, 18, 33
  sharing, 7
  title, 3
Job, the, 32
Joinder of parties, 226
Joint Council of Industry Training Boards (JCITB), 136

Key points, 138, 139
Key Results Areas (KRAs), 3, 155, 156, 267
Kick in the (Pants) (KITA), 166

Labour turn-over, 132, 133
Lateness, 132, 133
LAUTRO, 98
Learning styles, 30, 150, 151
Legal requirements, 36
Legally enforceable agreement, 36, 37
Lickert, R., 167, 169
Life assurance, 14, 100, 106, 198
Linking (SSP), 79, 83
Linking letters (DSS), 86
Local Enterprise Companies (LECs), 49
Local Management of Schools (LMS), 7
Lock-out, 218
Lower Earnings Level (LEL), 74, 75, 79, 80, 91, 93

Maslow, A. H., 163, 164, 168
Machine utilization, 131, 132, 133
Management by Walking Around (MBWA), 169
Management development, 128, 152–157
Market value, 10
Maternity Allowance (MA), 80
Maternity Benefit (MB), 93
Maternity certificate (Mat.B.1), 93, 94, 97
Maternity leave, 44–46, 56
Maternity Pay Period (MPP), 80, 92, 94
Manpower Services Commission (MSC) (now superseded), 146
McLelland, D.C., 167, 168, 169
McGregor, D., 167, 168, 169
Medical certification, 82
Misconduct, 178
Misrepresentation, 21
Most valued asset, 108, 126, 162, 169
Motivation, 30, 132, 155, 162–171
Multiple orders, 64

National Insurance Contributions (NIC), 6, 7, 8, 12, 48, 60, 61, 67–78, 87–90, 103, 107
National Joint Industrial Councils (NJICs), 10, 13
National Training Task Force (NTTF), 146

Index

National Vocational Qualifications (NVQs), 5, 49, 147, 160
National Wage Rates, 10
Net pay arrangements, 99
Net relevant earnings, 104
NIC on company cars, 72
NI for company directors, 73
NIC tables, 73
NFSE (*see* FSB),
Non-employees, 121
Non-permanent employees/staff, 7, 46–53
Notice periods:
 dismissal, 204–205
 redundancy, 188–190

Objectives, 3, 152, 153, 154, 155, 156, 157, 267
Occupation, 58
Occupational Pensions, 98–102
Offences and Penalties, 78, 91, 123
Offices, Shops and Railway Premises Act 1963 (OSRP), 116
Open Market Option (Pensions) (OMO), 105
Organizational Development, 157–159
Out-workers, 8
Overhead, 7
Overtime bans, 214
Owners (of businesses), 1
Owner-manager, 8, 14

P.8, 70
P.11, 89
P.14, 70
P.15, P.38(S), P.45, P.46, 61, 67, 70
Panel interviews, 32
Pay As You Earn (Tax) (PAYE), 7, 8, 48, 60, 61, 63, 64, 67–71, 78
Pay in lieu of notice, 59, 204
Pay day, 61
Pay periods, 60
Part-time employee, 6, 99
Partnership, 1
Penalties, 78, 91, 123
Pension, 6, 13, 98–106, 197, 212, 213
Pension fund, 59, 98
Pension scheme, appropriate, 101
Pensioners, 6, 7
Performance appraisal, 155–157
Performance, poor, 174
Period of Entitlement (PE), 85
Period of Incapacity for Work (PIW), 79, 80, 81, 83, 84, 85, 86, 107
Permanent employees, 7

Personal pensions, 14, 103–106
Personnel specification, 4, 5, 6, 21, 24
Picketing, 216
Policy, health and safety, 36, 116, 117
Portable pension, 14
Presentation, 21
Private Enterprise Programme (PEP), 148
Private limited-liability company (Ltd), 1
Private retirement pensions, 102–106
Protected earnings, 64
Protective clothing/equipment, 11, 121
Public Liability Insurance, 36
Public limited company (PLC/plc), 1

Qualifications, 5, 6, 24
Qualifying Days (QDs), 79, 82, 86
Qualifying Week (QW), 92, 93, 94, 95
Quality, 132
Questions (open-ended), 28, 180
Quick Quide for Employers (DSS), 92, 97

Race, 4, 20
Race Relations (Act 1976) (RR Act), 20, 31
Reasonably practicable, 113
Recognized trade union, 117, 211, 212
Recruiting, 18
Recruitment Code, IPM, 33
Redundancy, 15, 186–194, 195, 212
 consultation, 189–190, 212
 counselling, 188
 definition of, 186
 disqualification, 192, 193
 effect of resignation, 192, 193
 mitigation of, 186, 187
 notification, 187, 188, 189
 pay, 59, 190–192
 selection for, 186–187
Relationships, 31
Relevant earnings, 104
Reportable accidents, 109, 121
Reporting of Injuries, Diseases and Dangerous Occurrences Regulations 1985 (RIDDOR), 121
Representatives, safety, 117
Response to advertising, 22
Restrictive clauses, 42
Restrictive practices, 43
Retirement, 195–202
 age, 195–196
 pension, 99
 training, 199

Index

Return on Capital (ROC), 130
Return on Investment (ROI), 131
Re-work, 131, 132, 133
Right to return, 44, 45, 46
Road Transport Industry Training Board (RTITB), 136

SMP.1, 96, 97
SMP.2 and SMP.3, 97
SSP.1, 81, 87, 88, 96
SSP.1(L), 84, 85, 88, 91
SSP.2, 89
Safety:
  awareness, 110, 111
  committees, 118
  consciousness, 110, 111
  representatives, 117
  supervisor, 118
Salary, 58
Save as you earn (SAYE), 106
Savings and investments, 106, 198
Scrap, 132
Screening, 18, 23, 24
Secret ballots, 216
Selecting, 18, 30
Self Certification (SC), 79, 81
Self-employed, 8, 51, 52, 55, 104
Seminars, 137–138
Sex differences, 100–102
Sex Discrimination, 4, 31, 32, 45
Sex Discrimination Act 1975 (SD Act), 19, 20, 31
Severe Disablement Allowance (SDA), 62
Short-listing, 25
Sickness Benefit (SB), 79, 80, 86, 244
Sick pay, 14, 244
Sitting by Nellie, 130, 143
Small businesses/firms, 6, 7, 55, 70, 97
Small employers relief (SSP), 88
Social Security Advice Line for Employers (DSS, Glasgow) (SSALE) (known as the 'Sally Line'), 67, 73, 78, 97
Social Security, Department of (DSS), 59, 62, 65, 66, 68, 71
Sole proprietor/trader, 1, 2, 8, 14
Special Contract of Employment, 39, 140
SSP Flow Chart (DSS), 92
SSP—Small Employers' Relief (NI.278(1991)) (DSS), 92
SSP Tables (SSP.55) (DSS), 92
Staff development, 157
Standing statement, 62

Starting employment, 61
Starting Certificate (P.46), 61
State Earnings Related Pension Scheme (SERPS), 98, 99, 105
Status, 41, 58
Statutory Maternity Pay (SMP), 14, 44, 48, 59, 63, 69, 70, 78, 80, 92–97, 107, 244
Statutory Sick Pay (SSP), 14, 48, 59, 63, 69, 70, 78–92, 95, 96, 97, 107, 244
Stock, 12
Strike notice, 215
Striking-out, application for Tribunal, 226
Students, 7, 61
Styles of management, 167–169
Succession planning/training, 196, 197
Summary dismissal, 223
Supervision (safety), 115, 118, 161
Suspension, 177, 178
Systems of work, 114

Tax Code, 67, 70
Taxpayers Charter, 71
Temporary worker, 2, 7
Temporary contracts, 47, 48
Termination of employment, 243
Terms and Conditions:
  of Business, 1
  of Employment, 1, 35, 36–42, 58, 62, 88, 174, 175, 239, 242–246
Thinking of Taking Some-one On?—PAYE for Employers (IR.53), 78
Time-off, 41
Top-up (pension) schemes, 101
Trade disputes, 213
Training, 12, 114, 127, 128, 170
  agent (TA), 49, 50, 51
  allowance, 49
  credits, 50, 148
  health and safety, 114, 115, 136, 140, 141, 170
  job, 141–144
  manager (TM), 50, 51
  needs, 134–137
  off-the-job, 138, 142
  on-the-job, 137, 142
  programme, 137
  structured, 137–140
Training and Enterprise Councils (TECs), 49, 53, 147, 148
Trades Union Congress (TUC), 211
Trade Union Act 1984 (TUA), 218

Trade Union and Labour Relations Act 1974 (TULRA), 211, 216, 227
Trade Union Rights, 211–213
Transfer of Undertakings, 15, 212
Tribunal:
    Chairman of the, 227, 228
    Secretary of the, 224, 225, 226, 227
Truck Acts 1831–1940 (repealed), 59

Unfair dismissal, 45, 47, 218, 223
Upper Earnings Level (UEL), 71, 74, 75, 79, 91, 93

Validation, 131

Wage, 58, 59
Wages Act 1986, 59
Waiting Days, 79, 83, 84
Warnings (verbal, written), 175, 178
Welfare, 11, 116
Widows Pension, 100
Wildcat strikes, 215
Witnesses in an Industrial Tribunal, 226
Work-place, 109, 115
Working to rule, 214
Works councils, 219–220
Written Particulars, 37, 38, 39, 40

Youth Training (YT), 48, 49, 50, 51, 76, 116, 147, 148
Youth Training Scheme (YTS) (replaced by YT), 48